*The Fisheries of
Raritan Bay*

1. *View from space of Raritan Bay, rivers leading into it, surrounding land, and Atlantic Ocean. Illustration from display at Monmouth Museum, Lincroft, New Jersey. Photograph by author.*

The Fisheries of Raritan Bay

Clyde L. MacKenzie, Jr.

Rutgers University Press
New Brunswick, New Jersey

Library of Congress Cataloging-in-Publication Data

MacKenzie, Clyde L., 1931–
    The fisheries of Raritan Bay / Clyde L. MacKenzie, Jr.
      p.   cm.
    Includes bibliographical references and index.
    ISBN 0-8135-1839-3 (cloth)—ISBN 0-8135-1840-7 (pbk.)
    1. Fisheries—Raritan Bay (N.J. and N.Y.)—History. 2. Raritan
Bay (N.J. and N.Y.)—History. 3. Delaware Indians—Fishing.
I. Title.
SH221.5.R37M23   1992
639.2'09163'46—dc20   91-43031
                                                                 CIP

British Cataloging-in-Publication information available.

Manufactured in the United States of America

"There'd be days when 2,500 boxes of porgies were landed in Belford and we never put a dent in the supply in the bay."

Louie Egnatovich, Keansburg fisherman

"We ate claws as fritters, pies, and sandwiches, and steamed."

Marion Thompson, Belford fisherman's wife

"They called it hard clamming because it was such hard work, not because clams have hard shells."

Jigs Apel, Belford fisherman

"Fishing is feast or famine. Today we caught twice what we could sell; some days we don't get any."

Cris Anthropolis, bunker-seining captain

"If a man is good, he wants to go into the business for himself; if he is no good, he will remain with you."

Ed Raposa, eel potter

"There's no pencil-and-paper work in fishing; you take it as it comes. . . . You can come up with all the management plans you want, . . . and when you get done, the Man upstairs decides how many lobsters there'll be!"

Norman Sickles, lobster boat captain

Contents

Preface

This book is about the formation and characteristics of Raritan Bay, and, most of all, about the gear, methods, and working lives of the people who have fished its waters, both commercially and for sport, for over three hundred years. Raritan Bay, although only about one-thirtieth the size of Chesapeake Bay, the largest and most famous fishing estuary in the United States, has had nearly as large a variety of fisheries. Its fishing activities have ranged from the catching of various fishes in commercial pots, seines, nets, trawls, and with hooks and lines by sport fishermen, to the digging of soft clams and worms on intertidal flats, to the dredging of oysters, hard clams, and blue crabs. Although I know of no scientific comparisons with other Atlantic coast bays regarding fish and shellfish abundances, certainly Raritan Bay has been one of the most productive per unit area. The bay is unique for having had its main market for shellfish and fish—New York City—only twenty miles from its principal port of Belford. Fish arrived in the city on the day they were caught and thus were the freshest the city received. New York City was important to bayshore residents in other ways, too, because its manufactured products and its vacationers helped to support them in their preferred rural way of life for 150 years. Ironically, however, the city became so large that its waste products have polluted the bay and nearly eliminated the shellfisheries.

Having been raised on Martha's Vineyard, Massachusetts, where I was a part-time shell fishermen, I gained an early appreciation of the cultural lives of commercial fishermen and their gear, methods, and skills. I learned, too, of their hard times when shellfish and fish were scarce and market demand and prices were poor, and their joys when times were good. I became aware, as well, of the enjoyment that sport fishermen experience. The appreciation grew when I worked for several years at improving the economic lives of oyster fishermen as a provincial government employee in Prince Edward Island, and as a United States government employee in Long Island Sound, Delaware Bay, and Mississippi Sound. When I came to New Jersey in the early 1970s to work for the Sandy Hook Laboratory, National Marine Fisheries Service, on the eastern shore of Raritan Bay, I began to talk with local fishermen. They expressed a great warmth both for Raritan Bay, its oysters, clams, lobsters, blue crabs, bluefish, bunkers, porgies, and other fish, and for their boats, gear, fishing methods, and way of life. They also had a wealth of information in their heads about the history of their fisheries. I soon began to record their remembrances. Because I have long felt that the history of inshore commercial fishing has been neglected, I wrote this book. It is a product of my interviews with eighty-two fishermen, their wives, and people knowledgeable about local history, ranging in age from 55 to 104, and of the few published accounts of Lenape, colonial, and postcolonial fishing in the bay.

I have used the development of new technology and gear as the basis for separating the various periods of the bay's history. But no one period in the bay's fishing history, which has lasted at least three centuries, has been completely independent of those that preceded or followed it. For that reason, I have sometimes interwoven interviews of fishermen from the present into chapters that deal with the fisheries of the past. Thus, the quotations and the references provide a modern context for some of the historical discussions, a context that I hope will enrich an understanding and appreciation of the diverse fisheries of Raritan Bay.

I obtained documents and photographs from a number of museums and libraries, whose personnel gave courteous cooperation. I would like to thank especially Steven Bartow of Richmondtown Restoration (Staten Island Historical Society, Richmondtown, Staten Island); Jack Jeandron of the Steamboat Dock Museum (Keyport, New Jersey); Gary Parks of the Monmouth County Historical Association (Freehold, New Jersey); and Hugh Powell of the Staten Island Museum (Staten Island Institute of Arts and Sciences, St. George). I also obtained information from newspaper articles about Monmouth County from the *Red Bank Register,* compiled by Kenneth A. Norton of Port Monmouth, New Jersey; the *Red Bank Register* microfilm collection in the public library in Red Bank, New Jersey; and papers by Bonnie J. McCay of Rutgers University. The trips I made on pound net, purse seine, eel, sport fish, hard clam, blue crab, and lobster boats enabled me to describe current methods and catches.

Anthony L. Pacheco, Robert N. Reid, and Frank W. Steimle, Jr., of the Sandy Hook Laboratory, National Marine Fisheries Service, Dexter S. Haven of the Virginia Institute of Marine Science, Gloucester Point, Virginia, and Len Speigel of the New Jersey Marine Sciences Consortium commented extensively on earlier drafts of the manuscript.

My warm thanks to everyone I interviewed for their generous help in describing the history of their working lives and recollections of other fisheries. They all made contributions to this book. I telephoned or visited many of them several times to verify the accuracy of information, and I appreciate their patience. My gratitude goes to the following: Bea Adubato, Joe Adubato, Cris Anthropolis, Jigs Apel, Jack Baker, Jack Boyce, Bill Braun, Hank Brink, Lloyd Cottrell, Stanley Cottrell, Leona Crosby, Mary Cubbage, Elvira Cunningham, William Decker, Lou Defonzo, Walter DeGrote, Louie Egnatovich, Jr., Ed Fisler, Jr., John Fisler, Euretta Glass, Pete Glismann, Marty Haines, Stockton Hopkins, Wilbur Huylar, Joseph Irwin, Angel Jeandron, Jack Jeandron, Bill Jenks, Fred Johnson, Jim Kaplinger, Margaret Kendrick, William Kendrick, Ted Kenzia, Cris Kohlenbusch, George Kaveleski, Elmer Layton, Gene LoVerde, Betty Martin, Mrs. Chester Matthews, Harold Moody, Bill Morrell, Anna Morris, John Mount, Clara Myers, J. Richards Nelson, Lester Nelson, Kenneth A. Norton, Irving Parker, Arnold Pedersen, William Pedro, Mrs. Rudolf Peseux, Albert Poling, George Porter, Henry Pulsch, Ed Raposa, Alfred Richardson, Bill Richardson, Ray Richardson, Lester Rogers, Pete Rosenberg, Harry Sage, Otto Schnoor, Ron Schnoor, William Schnoor, John Seminski, Norman Sickles, Al Sonic, Walter Thompsen, Albert Thompson, Charles Thompson, Dave Thompson, Marion Thompson, Arthur Thorstensen, Dave Timadowski, Emil Usinger, Helen Volk, John Volk, John Wallace, Everett Walle, James Walling, Mrs. Frank Weigand, Elsie Werner, Jimmy White, Bob Wilson, and Margaret Wittich.

PART
ONE

The Bay:
An Introduction

1

The Bay and Its Fauna

Bay Origins and Its Fish, Shellfish, and Crustaceans

Some fourteen to eighteen thousand years ago, much of the earth's water was locked up in two polar icecaps, and the oceans were four hundred feet below their present level (Edwards and Merrill 1977). The ice cap in the north, now known as the Wisconsin Ice Sheet, extended over Canada to what is now the northern United States; part of it terminated at Staten Island. The coastline then was located more than sixty miles southeast of the present-day Verrazano Narrows. Extending just south of Staten Island was a shallow valley covered with mosses and lichens, characteristic of arctic tundra. A river knifed through that valley and continued eastward, where it joined the primordial Hudson River many miles out on the future continental shelf; finally they emptied into the ocean.

About thirteen thousand years ago the period of global warming had begun, the coastline was about thirty miles seaward of its present boundary, and the river valley was dominated by spruce and pine (*An Atlas . . .* 1977). At this time, the coastline was indented with large brackish and saltwater lagoons. Many fishes used them as nursery areas for their young and for feeding during summer. The ancestors of river herring, shad, and striped bass used the valley's river for their spawning and as the nursery of their young; for eels the valley provided an adult habitat. The lagoons also harbored oysters, hard clams, soft clams, lobsters, and blue crabs along with a myriad of other invertebrates. As the sea level rose, lowland areas were flooded progressively and became young estuaries and bays. The community of estuarine-adapted animal and plant life

3

moved westward with them and populated the new areas. Most estuarine fauna, such as oysters and soft clams, cannot survive in ocean waters.

About twenty-five hundred years ago, the sea began to fill the valley beyond Staten Island; eventually the valley was filled with ocean water to form Raritan Bay. Oysters, clams, and mussels populated it by means of their larvae, which swim in the water for about two weeks while feeding and developing. Then they attach to substrates to begin their sedentary lives. Oyster larvae cannot attach to objects as small as sand grains; when invading new territory, they attach to stones and empty shells of the short-lived blue mussel. Once established in an area, they also attach to shells of live and dead oysters. Curiously, nearly all oysters are males when they first attain maturity at a length of about one and a half inches in their second year of life, and by the time they are four to five inches long in their fourth and fifth years, most have changed their sex to female. The sex change serves oysters well because their eggs are about forty-five times larger than their sperm (Galtsoff 1964); thus a small oyster cannot produce many eggs, but can produce many sperm. The clam larvae settle among sand grains to which they attach.

The level of the Atlantic Ocean and the bay has been rising at a rate of about one foot per century. By 1620, when the Pilgrims arrived at Plymouth Rock, the sea had risen to within almost four feet of its present level and Raritan Bay was slightly smaller than it is now. Currently, the bay is triangular, thirteen miles long, eleven miles wide, and has an area of about eighty square miles. Its northern shore was formed by the glacial moraine reaching down along the Staten Island coast. The character of its southern coastline changes markedly from west to east. The lowlands and marshes of its western south shore give way to the high bluffs of the Highlands of Navesink to the east. The southeastern end of the bay terminates with the youngest stretch of shoreline in this region—the sand spit of Sandy Hook, which formed over the last thousand or so years by sand carried northward along New Jersey's Atlantic coast (Bokuneiwicz 1988).

The bay has three major sedimentary regions. The Lower Bay sands cover 50 percent of its area to the north; the muddy bottom runs east-west in midbay and covers about 35 percent of its overall area; and the Keansburg sands off the south shore cover 15 percent of its area (Bokuneiwicz 1988). The accumulation of mud probably began when the bay first began to fill, its main sources being the Raritan River in the west and the ocean; it accelerated after the European colonists arrived and cut down forests and plowed the land, leaving it susceptible to erosion. Currently, the rate of sediment deposition in the main channel of the bay is three-fourths of an inch a year. The river flowing eastward across Raritan Bay out onto the exposed shelf had a narrow channel whose depth reached about 150 feet in the bay; it is now buried under the mud (Bokuneiwicz 1988).

The main sources of fresh water for the bay are the Raritan River in the west and Hudson River in the northeast; the Arthur Kill in the west is a minor source. The earth's rotational forces induce these effluents to flow to their respective right sides, with creation of a large counterclockwise gyre of slowly mixing water masses in the bay. The mean tidal range is five and a half feet (Jeffries 1962). About sixty tides are required to flush Raritan River water through the entire bay (Ketchum 1951). At the end of the ebb current, water salinity at the bottom ranges from about twelve parts per thousand in the Raritan River mouth to about thirty-two parts per thousand off Sandy Hook; during the flood current, however, salinity rises to above twenty parts per thousand at the river mouth. Water temperatures range from about 33°F in late January to 78°F in late August (MacKenzie 1984).

In winter, the prevailing wind direction across the bay is from the northwest, whereas during summer it is from the south and southwest. When the wind blows strongly from the northwest and the moon is full, the tide drops extremely low; in the late 1800s and early 1900s, coastal flats up to a mile wide were exposed along the south shore. When the wind blows from the east or northeast, the tide does not fall as far.

The physical aspects and location of Raritan Bay make it an exceptionally good habitat for fish. The land surrounding the bay, along with the bay's depth, keep its waters from being severely roiled during storms. Its edges consist of wide shallows, which were covered until the mid-1930s with eelgrass (so named because eels were abundant in it) beds, an excellent feeding and growing environment for both juvenile fish and adult residents, such as killifish and silversides. Its depth slopes gradually from the intertidal zone to about twenty-five feet in its broad central area, where the water remains sufficiently cool for most fish to remain in midsummer. In addition, the bay is at the apex of the ninety-mile coasts of Long Island and New Jersey. Large numbers of bluefish, bunkers, fluke, porgies, and weakfish migrate northward and westward in the spring from wintering grounds on the continental shelf, funnel into the bay, and remain there for spawning and feeding in the summer. Finally, the bay is the passageway of fish to five rivers—the Hudson, Hackensack, Passaic, Raritan, and Navesink—each of which have been the spawning runs for river herrings, shad, and striped bass, while their freshwater sections are habitats for eels.

The river herrings are the first fish to enter Raritan Bay each year. They spend most of the year on the continental shelf from Newfoundland to North Carolina, but they aggregate between Block Island, Rhode Island, and Cape May, New Jersey, before their annual spawning migration shoreward into coastal rivers, streams, and ponds to spawn in fresh water. After spawning, they return immediately to the ocean (Mayo 1982).

The peak run of shad in Raritan Bay occurs in April, as they head toward the Hudson and Raritan rivers to spawn. The shad live most of the year on the continental shelf from Nova Scotia to Cape Hatteras, remaining there until maturity at an age of three to five years. During early spring, different spawning stocks of mature fish segregate out and move inshore to ascend the river in which they had hatched and spent their larval life. They use all the principal watersheds along the Atlantic Coast from the St. Johns River, Florida, to the St. Lawrence River, Canada, to spawn in the freshwater sections. Repeat spawners comprise half of the Hudson River fish population, and some spawn as many as five consecutive years. The shad is a plankton feeder, as are the other herrings. Its foods consist of small crustaceans, including barnacle larvae, and fish eggs (Bigelow and Schroeder 1953). The life span of the shad is usually eight years (Pacheco and Despres-Patanjo 1982; Talbot 1954).

The young of Atlantic sturgeon hatch in fresh water and spend up to five years there. Then they leave and range into Raritan Bay and the ocean. When mature, from age eight to twelve, females return to rivers to spawn. Sturgeon feed on mollusks and worms that they root out of the sand or mud with their snouts. After about 1900 sturgeon became scarce in the bay for two reasons: fishermen caught large numbers of them before they were old enough to spawn, and dams cut them off from some of their spawning grounds (Murawski and Pacheco 1977).

Bluefish inhabit Raritan Bay from early May into October. They range from Nova Scotia to Texas. Off the east coast of the United States bluefish, usually grouped in schools of similar-size fish, are concentrated in the north in the spring and summer and then travel southward in the fall. Bluefish feed on silversides, young bunkers, spot, weakfish, shrimp, crabs, and worms. At a typical size of five pounds, bluefish are four years old. Few live beyond nine years (Wilk 1977).

Weakfish inhabit Raritan Bay from July into October. They range from Massachusetts Bay to southern Florida. In the spring and summer young fish, less than four years old, move into near-shore areas and bays, where they spend the summer. In the fall, the northern population migrates south and spends the winter offshore of North Carolina. Weakfish feed on killifish, silversides, young herring and porgies, shrimp, small crabs, worms, and clams (Bigelow and Schroeder 1953). They usually live about nine years (Wilk 1979). Weakfish acquired their name because they have small, easily broken bones in their jaws, and many are lost when fishermen try to retrieve them after hooking them with cast or trolled lures.

The American eel ranges from Newfoundland to the north coast of South America. All water areas in the interiors and along the coasts, from warm, saline estuaries to cold, freshwater trout streams in mountainous areas, are fit habitats for eels. Females live almost exclusively in fresh water, while males also live in brackish and salt water. Eels remain in fresh and brackish water for fifteen to twenty years. As they approach sexual maturity, they leave, pass slowly through estuaries such as Raritan Bay, and travel to the ocean toward the Sargasso Sea, located about midway between Cape Hatteras and Spain, to spawn. Their eggs hatch there in February. Juveniles then drift north and west toward land and enter estuaries as elvers, two to two and a half inches long, about a year after hatching (Fahey 1978). Curiously, the Sargasso Sea is also the spawning area for European eels. In estuaries, such as Raritan Bay, eels feed on worms, small crustaceans, and small clams (Bigelow and Schroeder 1953). The catadromous habitat cycle of eels is reversed from that of the anadromous cycle of river herring, shad, striped bass, and other fishes, which inhabit the ocean and migrate to fresh water for spawning.

Bunkers are the most abundant fish in Raritan Bay, at least in weight. The nomenclature of this species is interesting. Biologists call them menhaden, a corruption of the Lenape word *munnawhatteaug*, meaning "manures the soil"; the Lenapes had used bunkers and herrings for fertilizing their corn. But fishermen in Raritan Bay have termed them bunkers, short for mossbunkers. *Mossbunker* is a relic from the Dutch colony of New Amsterdam and was used as early as 1661. The name is derived from the scad, or horse mackerel, which occurred off Europe in dense schools, swimming at the surface, like the bunker. The Dutch called the scad the Marsanker. The name was variously spelled "mossbunker," "mossbonker," "massbanker," "mousebunker," "marshbunker," "marshbanker," and "morsebonker" (Goode 1880).

Schools of bunkers appear in coastal New Jersey and Raritan Bay in late May and early June and remain through the summer. In September, with the first autumnal cooling, a southward movement along the Atlantic Coast begins and is completed by late November. The food of bunkers is planktonic algae and small crustaceans they sift from the water with a straining apparatus in the shape of successive comb layers (Bigelow and Schroeder 1953).

Bunkers mature at about two years of age and spawn annually in the ocean, Raritan Bay, and other large saline bays and sounds along the Atlantic coast. Larvae are carried by currents or swim into estuaries, where they metamorphose into juveniles. In five years, they are eleven inches long (Reintjes 1982).

Porgies inhabit Raritan Bay in large numbers from about the first of

July until late October. Termed *scup* in other areas, porgies usually weigh as much as one and a half to two pounds; some range to three pounds. Normally, they dwell on the bottom, feeding on worms, small crustaceans, and mollusks. From May to August, they spawn in the near-shore ocean and various bays and their juveniles develop there. After October, they migrate to offshore winter grounds, located off southern New Jersey to Cape Hatteras on the outer continental shelf in 120 to 480 feet of water. Porgies weigh a pound when five years old, and one and a half pounds when about seven years old (Morse 1978).

Fluke, or summer flounder, begin to enter Raritan Bay in April, and they reach their peak abundances in July and August. They range mainly from Cape Cod to Cape Hatteras. In the fall, they begin to emigrate to the continental shelf, where they spend the remainder of the year. They spawn on the shelf in the fall (Azarovitz 1982). In contrast, winter flounder spend the winter in Raritan Bay, the Navesink River, and other estuaries, and spawn there in the spring. While most emigrate in April and spend the warmer months on the continental shelf, some remain in the deep middle area of the bay in summer.

Some other fish that have inhabited the bay, but usually in smaller numbers than those just described, are croaker, cunner, kingfish, mullet, sculpin, Spanish mackerel, spot (lafayette), tomcod, and silver hake (whiting or frostfish). Other visitors have included the loggerhead turtle and harbor seal.

The bay also became an excellent habitat for shellfish, in part because surrounding land protected it from storms. In the 1600s, oysters grew in two beds of substantial size in its western end. The larger one measured about a mile across and was located just beyond the mouth of the Raritan River continuous with an oyster bed that extended five miles into the mouth of the Raritan River (Hall 1894). The smaller one, several acres in area and known to the Lenapes as the Chingarora Bed, was located in what became Keyport Harbor (Ingersoll 1881). Oysters also grew abundantly along other tributary rivers of Raritan Bay, namely the East, Hudson, Navesink, and Shrewsbury, as well as along most of the Arthur Kill and in the southern portion of Newark Bay.

The oyster beds were located where salinities ranged from about five to fifteen parts per thousand at the end of the ebb current. The primary enemies on the beds were bay anemones, which snatch oyster larvae along with other tiny drifting animals from the water for food if they touch one of their tentacles (Lockwood 1883), mud crabs, which prey on oysters up to a quarter inch long, and blue crabs, which prey on larger oysters. Oysters grow relatively slowly—a little over half an inch a year—in salinities from five to ten parts per thousand, prevalent in the tributary rivers and the Arthur Kill, but more rapidly, about an inch a year, in salinities from twelve to twenty parts per thousand, prevalent in the bay.

In salinities above fifteen parts per thousand, natural enemies of oysters were too prevalent for any beds to develop. Enemies included fouling organisms (algae, barnacles, bryozoans, slipper shells, and other animals), growing too profusely on shells for many oyster larvae to attach, and rock crabs, blue crabs, and oyster drills (boring snails), which killed nearly all those that did attach. Starfish, a destructive predator of oysters, especially in Connecticut, are sparse in most of Raritan Bay, because temperatures above 73°F, common in the bay in midsummer, adversely affect them (MacKenzie 1970).

Hard clams have been distributed over most of the bay and grow in sand and mud. The only places they have not occurred are intertidal zones and the southwestern end of the bay, where salinities range below fifteen parts per thousand. Soft clams have been distributed along all intertidal flats and in waters beyond them out to a depth of several feet, except in the northeastern part of the bay. They were most abundant on the broad intertidal flats in Great Kills Harbor and those from Keyport to Atlantic Highlands, as well as in shallow zones around Highlands and in the Navesink and Shrewsbury rivers.

The hard clam, also termed the hard-shell clam and the quahog, has the scientific name *Mercenaria mercenaria,* so named because the North American Indians used its shells for money. *Quahog* was the North American Indian's term for the hard clam and was adopted by Europeans colonizing the area from eastern Connecticut through New England and eastern Canada. The pronunciation varies from "kohog" (Martha's Vineyard, Massachusetts) to "kwahog" (Prince Edward Island, Canada), the "wa" sound being more pronounced in some areas than others. From central Connecticut southward, colonists brought the term *clam* with them from England and termed it the hard clam or clam.

The names for the three sizes of hard clams are not entirely logical. The small littleneck was so named because it has a short neck, about one-third of an inch, in contrast to the large neck of a soft clam, which can extend at least six inches, but hard clams of all sizes have short necks. The medium-size cherrystone is shaped like the pit (stone) of a cherry, but so are all hard clams. The large chowder clam is perhaps most logically named, because nearly all of them were made into Manhattan or New England clam chowder; it is too large and tough to be eaten comfortably on the half shell. The demand for chowder clams was strongest in the winter when people made clam chowder, which was so popular in the northeastern United States that it was often referred to as "the great American dish." Hard clams smaller than little necks and about an inch-and-a-quarter long were sometimes referred to as tea clams.

The soft clam, or soft-shell clam, has the scientific name *Mya arenaria;* the species name means "sandy." Soft clams' shells, while hard, are much thinner and more brittle than those of hard clams. A person can easily break the shell of a large soft clam, but not that of a hard clam, by hand. "Steamers" are soft clams, so called because they were commonly cooked by steam in a pot having little water. Their bodies contain a relatively large quantity of blood, which is almost clear, and whitish-gray in color. People drained the water-blood mixture after the clams were steamed and drank this broth while eating the meats from the shells. Usually steamers were soft clams of a small size, from one and one half to two and a half inches long. The larger soft clams, two and a half to three and a half inches long, were shucked and their meats eaten fried or in various dishes.

The neck of both species of clam is actually a siphon divided into two parts, one larger than the other. The larger siphon draws in water rich in their food—microscopic algae—and oxygen, while the smaller siphon ejects water carrying wastes—feces and carbon dioxide. The hard clam, living subtidally and usually positioned just below the sediment surface, needs only a short neck to reach water. The soft clam, however, living in intertidal as well as subtidal zones, is usually positioned about three inches below the sediment surface for protection from extremes of temperature and thus requires a long neck to reach water.

Raritan Bay has been the southernmost bay in North America where the American lobster can live. Lobsters range from Labrador to Cape Hatteras, but south of the bay warm inshore waters force it to live only offshore on the cooler continental shelf (Burns 1982).

Conversely, Raritan Bay has been the northernmost area where the blue crab occurs in large numbers almost every winter. Raritan Bay blue crabs spend their summers in tributaries, such as the Hudson River, Arthur Kill, Raritan River, various tributary creeks of the bay, and the Navesink and Shrewsbury rivers. In late fall, the crabs, mostly females, migrate to the eastern part of the bay and bed in mud there through the winter in a dormant state. The following spring, the eggs that females had been carrying during the winter hatch, larvae emerge and drift in the water, and after metamorphosis settle to the bottom as young crabs.

Horseshoe crabs (actually not crabs but arachnoids related to spiders) spend most of their life on the continental shelf but migrate into bays such as Raritan Bay to spawn each spring. At high tide, mating pairs walk to the upper edges of intertidal zones. The female digs a hole a few inches deep, deposits most of her eggs in it, and the male fertilizes them. After spawning repeatedly on several successive high tides, each horseshoe crab returns to the continental shelf. These crabs live fourteen to nineteen years, and adults spawn every year (Botton and Ropes 1987).

All the bay inhabitants have fluctuated in abundance through time. Environmental conditions such as temperature and weather varied each season, favoring the spawning and survival of some species and adversely affecting others. Food availability and predation on their young have also had a large effect on the abundance of various species.

2

Early Days: The Lenapes, the Colonists, and the Beginnings of the Fisheries

Archaeologists believe that the North American Indians arrived at the East Coast from western parts of the continent between ten and seven thousand years ago (Kraft 1977; Squires 1981). If so, the sea level was perhaps fifty feet lower than it is now and the coastline of eastern North America was from sixty to ninety miles farther east (Kraft 1987). Presumably these humans gathered shellfish and caught fish in the estuaries penetrating the coastline, and, as the sea level slowly rose, they gathered from the prevailing shoals. Archaeologists have not found artifacts and other evidence on the present continental shelf, however, to prove that people ever dwelled there (Edwards and Merrill 1977). If people once lived along the shores of the river when it ran through the wooded valley now claimed by Raritan Bay, remnants of their encampments would now lie under the many feet of mud deposits that cover its former banks.

During the years before the arrival of the Europeans, the North American Indians around Raritan Bay, who called themselves Lenapes, hunted deer, bear, turkeys, geese, and ducks using bows and arrows and spears. They used traps to catch rabbits, raccoon, otter, and weasel, and bolas to catch ducks, geese, and other marsh birds (Kraft 1987).

13

The Lenapes caught fish with seines and weirs made from reeds. The haul seines were as long as 475 feet and had stones tied along the bottom and sticks along the top to keep them spread. In the spring, river herrings were the first fish caught, followed by shad and sturgeon (Pearson 1972). The Lenapes usually boiled their fish and meat. To preserve shad and striped bass for eating in winter, they sun-dried them on tree bark and stored them in deerskin bags (Pearson 1972).

The Lenapes also gathered oysters from the shallow edges of the Arthur Kill, the Great Beds, and the Chingarora Bed. They gathered hard clams, probably by treading with their feet through the sand, and soft clams by scooping through the sand with shell tools and sticks. These mollusks were eaten fresh or preserved by drying or smoking and then stored in pits in the earth (Kraft 1987). Broken hard clam shells have been found in the Lenape middens (refuse heaps), and thus it is known that the Lenapes must have removed the meat by first breaking the clam shells. The Lenapes used the larger fragments of hard clam shells as scrapers, knives, and projectile points (Stanzeski 1981). They used large mussel shells attached to sticks as spoons, and they ground up shells as temper to harden pottery. The Lenapes also used the shells as money ("wampum") and ornaments ("rundee"). Later, cash-short colonists adopted clam-shell wampum as currency and used it into the late 1700s, until postcolonial factory production by non-Lenapes deflated their value.

The Lenapes began to practice agriculture—growing beans, corn, pumpkins, and squash—around 900 A.D. (Squires 1981; Kraft 1987; Ritchie 1969). They used bunkers, mussels, and sea lettuce to fertilize these crops (Pearson 1972). Despite the addition of cultivated crops, the Lenapes did not abandon their dependence on hunting, fishing, and gathering until considerably after the arrival of European colonists (Kraft 1987). When the Europeans first arrived, there were about two thousand Lenapes on Staten Island (Powell to MacKenzie, 3 December 1990) and eight to twelve thousand in what is now New Jersey (Kraft 1987). Peter Kalm, the Swedish naturalist who traveled through the Middle Atlantic colonies in the 1740s, made the following observations of North American Indians around the outskirts of New York City; they probably apply also to the western shores of Raritan Bay:

> The Indians, who inhabited the coast before the arrival of the Europeans, have made oysters and other shellfish their chief food; and at present, whenever they come to salt water, where oysters are to be got, they are very active in catching them, and selling them in great quantities to other Indians, who live higher up the country: for this reason you see immense numbers of

oyster and mussel shells piled up near such places, where you
are certain that the Indians formerly built their huts. (Kalm
1937)

Colonists found Lenape middens of oyster shells at Tottenville, Perth
Amboy, and Union Beach on the shores of western Raritan Bay. By 1883
the Union Beach midden had nearly disappeared; local residents used the
shells for making roads and for ballast in Keyport schooners sailing to
Chesapeake Bay for oysters. Crews threw the shells overboard into
Chesapeake Bay (Lockwood 1883).

When the Dutch and English colonists arrived in the 1600s in the
area around what was to become New York City and western Raritan
Bay, they were impressed by the large quantities of shellfish available,
especially oysters, compared with what they had observed in Europe.
They ate oysters raw, broiled on coals, boiled in fat, and preserved in
vinegar (Pearson 1972).

Colonial settlements developed in western Raritan Bay, and by the
late 1600s the towns of Tottenville, Perth Amboy, and Keyport were
incorporated. While most residents were farmers, many were fishermen,
and some were craftsmen and merchants.

Thomas Rudyard, recently emigrated from England, wrote in 1683
about fish and shellfish in the area near Perth Amboy:

We are supplied with salt fish at our doors or within half a
tide's passage and fresh fish in abundance in every little brook,
as perch, trout, eels, which we catch at our doors.

Round the point [Amboy] are oysters of two kinds: [one]
small as English and others two or three mouthfuls, exceedingly
good for roasting and stewing. The people say our oysters are
good and in season all summer. The first of the third month I ate
them at Amboy . . . very good.

We have store of clams, esteemed much better than oysters.
On festivals the Indians feast on them. There are scallops but in
no great plenty. Fish we have great store . . . but they are very
good when catched. . . . I brought a sea net over with me,
which may turn to good account; sea nets are good merchandise
here, mine cost me about four or five pounds and can have
twenty pounds for it, if I would sell it now.

Oyster shells upon the point, to make lime withal, will
wonderfully accommodate us in building good houses [of
stone] cheap, warm for winter and cool for summer. (Pearson
1972)

The colonists also spread the lime on their farmland to increase crop production and besides used it as flux in primitive iron furnaces, for example, in nearby Tinton Falls, as early as the 1680s.

The colonists were impressed by the large numbers of fish they saw in the bay. They described vast schools of herring, shad, and bunkers, which they caught, along with striped bass and sturgeon (Pearson 1972).

The colonists developed gear and procedures to catch fish. The first fin fishermen and shell fishermen were farmers. Fishing provided extra food for their families. When they caught more fish than their families could eat, they shipped the fish to New York for sale, and they were in the fishing business. Many found that fishing was more lucrative than farming and went at it full-time. Such recruitment into fishing continued in the 1800s and into the mid-1900s.

In the 1600s and 1700s, the most efficient gears available for catching fish were the haul seine and fyke net, which caught only those occurring close to shore. During the 1600s and the 1700s, the netting for fyke nets and haul seines was made of hemp. At first all the hemp netting was probably imported from England. Then, net makers came from England and continued their trade in the colonies. They supplied fishermen with nets or hemp twine to make their own seines and fyke nets (Pearson 1972).

Haul Seines

The only limitation to the length of a haul seine was how much net a crew could stack in its boat. The seines used were about two thousand feet long, ten feet deep, and had a mesh size of two and a half inches. The seine boats were twenty-five to twenty-eight feet long and had a wooden roller across their sterns. A crew of seven or eight men who spent most of their time farming handled each seine. Each crew set out its seine once a day, at high tide when the current was nearly slack. The water depth at the offshore side was six to eight feet. Since the tide advanced about an hour each day, the crews had to seine an hour later each day. Whenever the high tide advanced toward evening, they had to switch the next day and seine early in the morning.

Each crew piled its seine carefully in the stern of its boat. As the boat was rowed by two or three crewmen in the bow, two at the stern guided the net over the boat's roller and overboard; one handled its cork, or upper side, while the other handled its lead, or lower side. The three or four remaining men of the crew remained on shore with one end of the net. After the boat crew had rowed the net out in a semicircle and back to shore, landing perhaps one hundred feet from where they left, it pulled in

2. *Crew loading a haul seine onto a skiff west of Keyport, New Jersey, circa 1900. Courtesy of Louis Booz.*

one side of the net while the others pulled in the other side. When the net was close to shore, some fish could escape. To catch them, some crewmen waded into the water and pulled the ends of the net several feet behind the rest of the net, tied them together, and then pulled in this backup net after the main part of the net was ashore. By doing this, they recaptured those that had escaped.

Fishing crews used haul seines in various places in the bay. For example, each spring, some seined for shad in the Narrows in the northeast corner of the bay. There, in one exceptional haul in 1770, a crew caught 11,500 shad; in 1774 another crew caught 9,000 shad in one morning (Pearson 1972). Along the other coasts of the bay, haul seine crews caught mainly bunkers, river herring, striped bass, and weakfish. The seines caught some bluefish, flounders, shad, blue crabs, and horse-shoe crabs as well. A typical catch was eight to ten bushels of fish. Haul seining was most profitable in June, when the bunkers were abundant.

Fyke Nets

Colonists began installing fyke nets along the bay's shores in the late 1600s (Pearson 1972). The name probably came from the Dutch word *fuik,* and was doubtless introduced by colonists from the Netherlands, where a similar net was used in the form of hoops or bowed twigs (Smith 1894). The fyke nets used in the bay measured about thirty feet in length

3. *Fisherman emptying a fyke net, circa 1910. Note the fish he is holding.*
Courtesy of Kenneth A. Norton.

and four to six feet in diameter. They were cylindrical, held open by
wooden hoops spaced about eight feet apart. Net funnels, aiming to the
head (back) of the fyke, were tied to each hoop. Fishermen positioned
two heart-shaped nets in front of each fyke, one on each side of its
mouth, and a leader about forty feet long and five and a half feet high
directly in front of its mouth. The leader extended inshore to fifteen or
twenty feet from the shore at high tide, enough distance for a small boat
to pass through. At low tide, this inshore area usually became dry and the
body of the fyke was in about two feet of water. Ropes tied to oak stakes
held the fykes in position.

When fish swimming along the shore encountered the leader, they
turned instinctively offshore, and most went into the mouth of the fyke.
Those that went to either side swam into a heart that directed them back
to the mouth. Fish swam through the funnels. The fisherman in his
rowboat arrived at his fyke each day at low tide and removed the fish
from the head with a sturdy dip net. Following a schedule similar to that
of the haul seiners, fyke fishermen emptied their nets an hour later each
day as low tide advanced.

Fishermen made the hoops for fyke nets from oak strips about an
inch thick. They steamed them, rolled them around a wagon wheel, and
nailed their ends together. Individual fykes may not have lasted more
than a month or two, because the netting probably rotted. New nets had

to be knitted, but the wooden parts could be reused. In later years, fishermen dipped the nets and hoops in hot tar before use every spring and fall to help preserve the netting; such fykes lasted several years.

Every Staten Island farmer whose land bordered the shores had one or more fykes installed in the water off his property, and they were installed along the New Jersey shore as well as the Arthur Kill (Akerly 1843). Fishermen who had four fykes, a typical number, got fifty to one hundred pounds of fish a day. The species included blackfish, bluefish, croakers, flounders, herring, kingfish, mullet, sculpins, shad, striped bass, tomcod, and weakfish. In the spring, horseshoe crabs were also part of the catch but were a nuisance to remove. Fishermen installed fykes only in the spring, beginning in March, and the fall, because the fish were away from the shores and congregated in deeper, cooler water of the bay in the summer.

Hooks, Lines, and Eel Pots

The only early gear available for catching the abundant fish in the main part of the bay were the hook and line and the pot for eels. In the 1700s, metal hooks, lines made of hemp and flaxen, and lead weights were available for hand-lining fish; colonists had imported them from England (Pearson 1972). On a small scale, fishermen rowed boats out on the bay and caught fish with baited hooks for market and sport.

Fishermen used baited pots to catch eels. The eel pot was a cylinder made of oak splints, about thirty-six inches long and nine inches in diameter (Sim 1975). A funnel at one end led the eels into the "kitchen," where the bait was placed. An interior funnel in its middle, also made of oak splints, led the eels into the "parlor." The end of the "parlor" had a hinged wooden door for emptying out the eels. It was important to construct the pots to specific dimensions. If the kitchen was much longer than eighteen inches, the eels could turn around and escape. Fishermen put a piece of iron or a stone in each pot to hold it on the bottom.

Fishermen used parts of horseshoe crabs or broken soft clams as eel bait. For many years, they collected horseshoe crabs from beaches caught them in fyke nets in the spring, holding them in floating wooden cars for later use. If they ran out of horseshoe crabs, fishermen obtained broken soft clams from clammers and put several in each pot. They set out the pots singly, each with a buoy, and tended them using rowboats and catboats.

The prime eeling areas were the southwestern side of Staten Island and the area from Keyport to Highlands. Eels began entering pots when the water temperature rose to about 50°F in April, and they continued to do so until the temperature fell below about 60°F in early November. In April, fishermen placed pots close to shore in water only twelve to eighteen inches deep at low tide, the eels in the shallows becoming active earliest as the water warmed there first. With the seasonal rise in temperatures, eels moved to deeper water; by midsummer, most had moved to the deep central areas of the bay. Fishermen moved the pots there accordingly. The fishermen in Highlands, however, quit during summer and resumed when the eels returned in the fall. Fishermen caught more eels during windy weather and on muddy rather than sandy bottoms. Probably the wind stirred the bottom and stimulated eels to move. Fishermen lifted their pots every day, except in the fall when they usually lifted every other day because catches had declined.

Spears

As winter approached, the eels sought muddy areas and lay in them to spend the winter. Fishermen found that the dormant eels could be caught with spears. The most effective spear had a head with three or four prongs on each side of a broad prong in the center and a handle twelve to eighteen feet long. Most fishermen and farmers living near the bayshore obtained an eel spear or two and used them every winter. The fishermen's gear also included an axe to cut holes in the ice and a bag to carry the eels.

Fishermen speared eels at several sites around Raritan Bay—in Fresh Kills on Staten Island, along the harbor front in Keyport, in a muddy area about two miles east of Belford, in Spermaceti Cove, near Plum Island on Sandy Hook, and most of all in the Navesink and Shrewsbury rivers. Fishermen could spear eels in these two rivers before doing it in the bay because the rivers' water, being fresher, iced over earlier. The best catches were along the banks of channels. A local saying ran:

> In pine, tar is;
> In mud, eel is;
> In clay, none is.

The saying was true: eels avoided hard clay and buried only in mud (*Red Bank Register,* 7 January 1925). Usually, the eels were covered by one to two inches of "stiff" rather than "soupy" mud.

When the ice became at least three inches thick, enough to carry the weight of a man, fishermen walked to areas where they had caught eels in the past. The usual water depth was eight to twelve feet. They chopped holes about fifteen inches in diameter and inserted a spear at an angle to

4. *Fisherman spearing eels in the Navesink River, circa 1955. Courtesy of Louie Egnatovich.*

the ice. Then they moved the spear slowly up and down about two feet at a time, jabbing the bottom in the same spot two or three times while they rotated it to cover its area. When they struck an eel, they felt it quivering on the downward stroke. They pulled the impaled eel from the mud slowly, then pulled it quickly through the water to the surface, and shook it off. If they pulled quickly when the eel was in the mud, the barb on the spear could be pulled through it. Most jabs did not get any eels; rarely, as many as three were caught at once. Fishermen jabbed around the same circle as much as five times when it yielded many eels. Afterward, they shortened up a little and speared around another circle just inside the first, and then continued spearing around ever smaller circles until the spear was aimed directly below their hole. The diameter of the speared area was twelve to fifteen feet. Fishermen had to chase away gulls, which tried to pirate their eels lying on the ice (Interview, Bill Richardson, 5 October 1985).

It usually took about an hour to fish out a hole having many eels, a good catch being ten to fifteen pounds of eels (three eels to a pound) and perhaps a winter flounder. An exceptional catch totaled seventy pounds. After a fisherman had finished spearing the eels from a hole, he chopped another about fifteen feet away and continued.

Fatigue of the fishermen's arms was an important factor in the day's catch. Fishermen caught the most eels during the first couple of hours and fewer afterward as they tired. After five or six hours of spearing, they had to quit from fatigue. Fishermen put the eels in a bag and carried them ashore on children's sleds or over their backs. The area fishermen caught the eels from remained barren for the winter unless eels moved back into it during an extended thaw.

Early Boats

Early fishing boats included skiffs used for tonging oysters, catboats, cabin sloops, and schooners. It is unclear when they first became available.

Oyster-tonging skiffs were eighteen to twenty-two feet long at the waterline; their overall length was three to four feet longer. Their beams were five to six feet, their depth twenty to twenty-two inches. Their bottoms were floored over for shoveling oysters. Many skiffs had a mast and a small sail placed just forward of amidships and a centerboard; others were rowed (Guthorn 1982; Hall 1894).

Catboats were used for oystering and in later years for hard clamming, lobstering, gill netting, and eel potting. There were two sizes. The larger one had a keel as long as twenty-five feet, a four-foot overhang, and a cabin for sleeping two persons. The smaller one was about eighteen feet long and had an open cockpit with no cabin (*Red Bank Register,* 23 March 1898). Catboats were wide, shallow-draft, easy to handle, and could be operated by one man. They were gaff-rigged, with the mast set "well up in the eyes." Their broad beam provided a stable platform for hauling nets and pots (Leavens 1986).

Cabin sloops had a thirty-five- to forty-foot keel and a four- to five-foot overhang. Their hulls were lined with bricks for ballast (*Red Bank Register,* 23 March 1898). Most schooners were sixty to seventy feet long and had raked masts so crews could use their booms to load and off-load freight (Interview, Wilbur Huylar, 12 October 1986).

A sail-making factory was constructed in Perth Amboy to supply the fleet of vessels in Raritan Bay and Newark Bay. Vessels' crews could not allow their sails to remain wet, so they had to raise wet sails during clear days to dry them. If the sails were not dried after rains, they rotted in a month. Any holes and tears in sails had to be patched.

Vessel owners were plagued by several local invertebrates. Teredo shipworms were a great problem because they ate away the wood in boat hulls, causing them to leak and shortening their lives. Boat builders learned to construct hulls of cypress or longleaf yellow pine, which repelled shipworms much better than locally available white pine. These two woods grew only in the southern United States and had to be imported by schooner. To kill the shipworms, oystermen anchored their boats in fresh water, such as Fresh Kills on Staten Island, for three or four weeks during slack working periods, especially in summer. The settlement of fouling organisms—sea squirts, barnacles, bryozoans, and algae—on hulls was another problem. The organisms substantially slowed the sailing speed of boats because they grew profusely in roughly textured layers. To rid the hulls of fouling, crews had to float their catboats and sloops onto beaches at high tide, let them lie on one side as the tide fell, and then remove the fouling from the opposite side with metal scrapers. On another high tide, they tipped the vessels the other way and after the tide fell scraped the other side. Crews also caulked any leaking seams while they had this opportunity.

Schooners had to be hauled into boatyards located on gradually sloping shores to rid their hulls of fouling and caulk leaks. The yards used horses pulling blocks and tackles to haul the vessels in and out of the water. Planks were laid down first and rollers placed beneath them to ease their passage.

Boat owners found they could repel shipworms and fouling with copper sheeting and paint. In the early 1800s, crews of schooners carrying freight along the Atlantic Coast nailed a continuous layer of copper plates to the hulls of these vessels for this purpose (Ronnberg 1980). In the 1830s and 1840s, bottom treatment for boats became available; the first was verdigris mixed into paint. It was only partially effective in repelling shipworms and fouling organisms and lasted only about two months. In the late 1850s and 1860s, the C. A. Woolsey Paint and Color Company of Jersey City developed copper-based paint that kept hulls free of shipworms and fouling for over a year. Another great feature of the paint was that it did not have to be dry to remain intact on boat hulls after the boats were put into the water. Thus, during a single low tide, half the bottom of a boat could be scraped and painted, and the wet paint remained intact on the hull when the boat refloated. This copper paint was used everywhere after its introduction (Marine paints 1925).

Boat owners were also plagued by dry rot in their boats, especially in the hulls. Dry rot is caused by a fungus living on the wood fibers. Owners found they could substantially slow the fungus growth by spreading salt grains over the insides of the hulls (Rabl 1925).

Oystering

In the late 1600s and early 1700s, many residents of Staten Island, Perth Amboy, and Keyport gathered oysters from the Great Beds and

Chingarora Bed, and also from the nearby Arthur Kill and the Raritan River. They gathered them by hand at low tide, in skiffs (rowboats) using tongs, and in catboats and sloops by towing dredges. Oysters from the Arthur Kill and Raritan River, being small, were less desirable than the larger ones growing in Raritan Bay. The oysters were one of the main sources of protein for local residents. They consumed most immediately, shucked some and pickled them in vinegar, and stored the remainder live in their cellars for eating during winter. For storage, they placed the oysters with the bottom, deeper shell down to retain liquid; if positioned otherwise, the liquid would drain out, and the oysters would die in two or three weeks.

Around 1700, New York and New Jersey agreed that an east-west boundary line should be drawn through the bay, dividing it in half. About half of the Great Beds lay in New York and half in New Jersey (Ingersoll 1881).

About this time, fishermen from New York City, Long Island, and Connecticut began to sail into the bay in catboats and sloops to dredge oysters from Great Beds on a regular basis, and the oysters' abundance slowly declined. Consequently, local residents became alarmed, and in 1715 New York authorities passed the first colonial law in relation to oysters on its half of the Great Beds. According to Ingersoll, the provisions were that "no one except the Lenapes could gather oysters between May first and September first and that no Lenape, Negro, or Mulatto could sell oysters in New York City at any time." In 1719, New Jersey passed a conservation law stating that "no gathering of oysters from its half of the Great Beds should take place between May tenth and September first and none of its oysters should be taken by any vessel not owned within New Jersey." New York and New Jersey made successive laws, somewhat in a spirit of mischief and retaliation against one another. Authorities named special officers to enforce these acts and arranged legal provisions for seizure and punishment. In 1730 and 1737, New York had to make additional laws to protect the beds because boats from New England and New Jersey continued to take away loads of New York oysters. The acts restricted boats from outside the state from taking any of the oysters, under penalty of having the boat and all its contents seized. In 1775, New Jersey changed its closing date to 1 May to match that of New York, and it forbade the taking of oysters for the purposes of making lime only (Ingersoll 1881).

Most of the Lenapes left the area. By the Treaty of 1670, the Lenapes were supposed to leave Staten Island. A few stayed, however, and lived in the western part of the island (Powell to MacKenzie, 3 December 1990). The Lenapes of the New Jersey bayshore and other areas ceded their lands to the state, and most were moved to the Oneida reservation in New York State by 1802 (Ingersoll 1881).

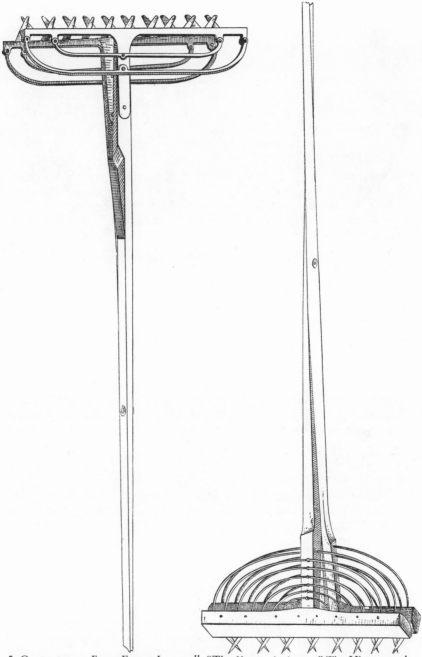

5. *Oyster tongs. From Ernest Ingersoll, "The Oyster-Industry,"* The History and Present Condition of the Fishery Industries, *G. B. Goode, ed. (Washington, D.C.: U.S. Government Printing Office, 1881).*

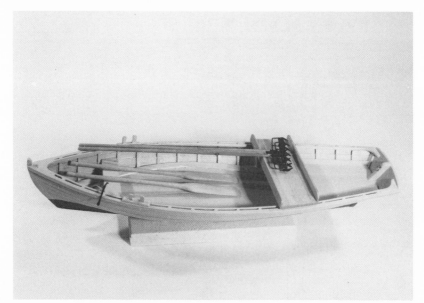

6. *Model of oyster-tonging skiff with tongs, culling board, and oars made by Cris Kohlenbusch, a retired fisherman. Photograph by author.*

Bitter feelings existed between Staten Island and New Jersey oystermen over rights to the oysters in the bay. There were frequent arrests. During the Revolutionary War oyster fishermen from Staten Island and New Jersey carried their disputes over oyster territories into battles between Loyalists and Rebels (McCay 1984). The disputes continued into the 1800s, when small planters in their sloops sailed into the other state and stole oysters from leases granted to planters. Despite the protective laws, the two natural oyster beds in the bay were nearly depleted by the early 1800s.

Heavy fishing was not the only cause of depletion of the Great Beds. Undoubtedly, loads of suspended silt from the Raritan River settled as a layer of thin mud on its oysters and contributed to the decline by inhibiting the settlement of oyster larvae and smothering seed. The silt resulted from the colonists' clearing of forests and plowing of fields, leaving the land bare and subject to erosion.

By the early 1800s, the Great Beds and Chingarora Bed were nearly barren of oysters, and production of oysters from the bay had been relatively small for a number of years. The demand for protein foods, such as oysters, was high, however, because the human population, especially in New York City, was growing. To meet this demand, local fishermen founded a different type of oyster industry. It consisted of importing partially grown oysters, termed "seed," from other areas,

7. *Raritan Bay sloop with full sail raised, circa 1870. Sloops such as this one dredged oysters off the Great Beds. They were used for dredging oysters off leased beds and hauling them to New York City for sale, dredging hard clams, and dredging blue crabs, between about 1870 and 1880. Courtesy of Staten Island Historical Society, Richmondtown Restoration, Staten Island, New York.*

planting them on bottoms in the bay, growing them to three to four inches long (which took only one growing season if they were from Chesapeake Bay), and then marketing them.

The first crew to import seed brought them from Chesapeake Bay in a schooner in the spring of 1825 and planted them on Round Shoal, a many-acre bed with firm sand bottom, off Prince's Bay, Staten Island. The oysters grew well, and the crew recovered and sold them the next fall. In the ensuing years, this crew and others from Prince's Bay, Perth Amboy, and Keyport joined in this endeavor. Within about twenty years, various crews were importing as many as 300,000 bushels of seed oysters each year from late February to May from the James, York, Rappahannock, and Choptank rivers and Tangier Sound in Chesapeake Bay (Ingersoll 1881). By then, the oyster industry had become the main industry in the towns of Tottenville, Perth Amboy (Gordon 1973), and probably Keyport. Raritan Bay was not the only bay where Chesapeake seed was being imported, grown, and marketed: oystermen from Wellfleet Harbor in Massachusetts, Narragansett Bay in Rhode Island, Long Island Sound (Connecticut), and Delaware Bay were also doing it (Ingersoll 1881).

Planters in Raritan Bay employed about fifty schooners, as well as some sloops for transporting the seed oysters from Chesapeake Bay. Most schooners had two masts; the largest had three or four. A captain and a crew of four manned each schooner. The sailing time from Raritan Bay to the oyster-producing rivers of lower Chesapeake Bay was thirty-five to forty hours. It took about two days to load a vessel with 2,500 to 3,500 bushels of seed, and another thirty-five to forty hours to return. Crews sailed day and night; light breezes made the trip longer, while a storm with moderate winds made it shorter. When the Chesapeake tongers could not work due to bad weather, the schooners had to remain longer in the rivers. During such delays, the crews splashed buckets of water on the seed to keep it alive.

In the Virginia rivers, crews of two or three men per boat tonged the seed. Each man gathered 8 to 10 bushels of rough culled seed (mixed with small quantities of shells) an hour; on good days, the crew gathered as many as 125 bushels of seed in six to seven hours.

When an oyster schooner sailed into a river to purchase oysters, it headed up the channel, and its crew dropped anchor opposite the oyster beds. If tongers did not know the vessel, the crew hoisted an empty basket up the mast to signal that it wanted to purchase seed. Schooners had four loading sites, which the tongers called *falls*. Often a few tonging boats at a time sailed over and tied opposite each one to sell seed. The schooner crew lowered a bushel container from each fall to the boat closest to it. Using shovels, the tongers filled the containers with seed level to their brims. To minimize the quantity needed to fill the containers and thus increase the quantity to sell, the tongers carefully emptied the seed off their shovels to produce a short measure, a procedure known as *stacking*. If, by accident, a container happened to hit the side of the schooner, the seed would settle at least four inches and more oysters

8. Boats used for tonging seed oysters in the James River, in port of Deep Creek, Virginia, circa 1910. Courtesy of the Mariners' Museum, Newport News, Virginia.

would be needed, but tongers took care to prevent that. They had learned how to stack oysters and handle the containers in boyhood. Despite the "short" bushels, Raritan Bay oystermen were getting a good deal, because the Virginia bushel was about a third larger than the New York and New Jersey bushel used when planters sold the oysters in the fall (Interview, J. Richards Nelson, 10 March 1985). A Virginia bushel contained four to five hundred seed, each measuring about two inches long, besides some smaller oysters.

The schooner captain penciled the number of bushels being loaded from each tonging boat on a cedar shingle and then paid the tongers. Planters called the Chesapeake oysters "Virginia seed," "Chesapeakes," "soft," or "fresh," and the oyster seed native to the vicinity of Raritan Bay "hard" (Ingersoll 1881). When a crew had loaded its schooner, it raised its anchor, set its sails, and headed out of Chesapeake Bay and up the coast to Raritan Bay. Storms occasionally wrecked a schooner during these passages. A Staten Island newspaper, the *Richmond County Gazette,* published on 15 February 1868, described one such incident:

> The schooner *Edward M. Thorn* of Mariners' Harbor, Captain John Burbank, bound to the York River for oysters, was wrecked the beginning of the present month on the Middle Ground, near Cape Charles, during a severe snow storm. All hands were saved, after being thirty hours on the vessel, and becoming badly frost-bitten. A physician in Norfolk attended them without charge. Having lost everything, the captain applied for a passage on board a steamer coming north, after stating the condition of his crew and himself, but was refused unless he should pay for it. A friend in Norfolk, learning this, kindly paid the expenses of the whole party by another conveyance.

9. *Northern schooner in the James River, Virginia, purchasing seed oysters from tongers, circa 1910. Such schooners purchased seed oysters from Chesapeake Bay for Raritan Bay beds from about 1825 to the early 1920s. Courtesy of the Mariners' Museum, Newport News, Virginia.*

When a loaded schooner arrived in Raritan Bay, the captain headed for Keyport or another port and took on about twelve more men, probably idle farmers needing some money. About sixteen, including the original crew of four, were required for the oyster planting operation (Ingersoll 1887). On a designated bed, the captain maneuvered the schooner back and forth while the crew, using shovel-shaped forks, broadcast the seed overboard. After some trial and error, planters found that the most efficient density to spread seed was about 750 bushels per acre. Thus a schooner load of about 3,000 bushels of seed was spread over four acres. If the seed was spread much more densely, the oysters grew too slowly and their meats were too thin. The Chesapeake Bay oysters remained plump during the summer because they did not spawn in the colder waters of Raritan Bay.

Young oysters set sparsely on the imported oysters (Ingersoll 1881). Oystermen termed the young oysters *spat*. If an oyster "spits" out spawn, why should not the result be "spat"? Setting of spat may have been denser than the oystermen were aware, however; most were probably killed by predators.

When the planting, or bedding, of oysters began, no system of leasing bottoms existed. During the first few years, a planter staked the boundaries of a plot with freshly cut saplings (only their bushy tops showed) and claimed that the oysters he had planted on it were his. Penniless oystermen frequently disputed such claims, however, and asked the courts to decide on them. These oystermen said that the planters were staking off natural beds containing oysters and using them privately to the detriment of the community. They disputed the right of anyone to claim bay bottoms for their private use. The courts ruled that if a man staked a plot and planted oysters on it, his claim would be upheld. Gradually, the claim system evolved into a formal leasing system under which individuals had a legal right to hold oysters on designated sections of bottom and retain ownership. Authorities in the states of New York and New Jersey issued the leases, which ranged from a fraction of an acre to about one hundred acres each. Although they did not charge fees for most leases, authorities charged one dollar a year for leases at Ward Point on the southwest side of Staten Island, since they produced especially high-quality oysters bringing the highest prices (Ingersoll 1881).

By the 1850s, there were two extensive leased bottom areas in Raritan Bay. One, off the Staten Island coast, covered about 5,000 acres; the other, about a third as large at 1,600 acres, was off Keyport. Water depths ranged mostly from eight to twenty-four feet.

Planters harvested the entire crop of Chesapeake Bay oysters in the fall and early winter, leaving the beds empty for a new crop of seed the following spring. The oysters on beds less than about sixteen feet deep were harvested by tongers. Those growing at depths from sixteen to twenty-four feet were harvested by crews on the sloops using hand dredges.

Planters also purchased some seed from tongers in the Arthur Kill and the Raritan River. These oysters measured only about three-fourths of an inch long, however, and had to be left in Raritan Bay for two or three years of growth. Crews had to transplant them each year, using tongs to gather them. The larger planters hired crews to do the transplanting, but the smaller planters did the work themselves (Hall 1894).

Rock crabs, blue crabs, and oyster drills preyed on most of the spat attached to the imported oysters, but oysters longer than two inches were pretty safe from them (Ingersoll 1881; Lockwood 1883). The growing oysters faced other hazards, however. For example, in some years, mussels set on them, grew, and suffocated many with their abundant feces. To reduce this type of loss, oystermen were forced to tong up as many oysters as they could, pick off the mussels by hand, and replant the oysters (Ingersoll 1881). Every few years the drumfish occurred in the bay in substantial numbers and ate oysters. Drumfish crushed the oysters with their powerful teeth, swallowed the meats, and dropped the shell fragments to the bottom. The planters tried to frighten them away by anchoring wooden shingles, tied to ropes held in place by bricks or stones and small buoys, over the beds. They believed that the shingles waved in the water currents and scared the drumfish. The method was called *shingling the beds* (Ingersoll 1881).

The oyster pea crab occurred in many of the oysters. The pea crab, less than an inch wide, lives within shell cavities of oysters and mussels and grazes on phytoplankton the mollusk collects on its gills for food. An oyster having one of these has relatively thin meat. Oyster shuckers in ports along the Atlantic coast often saved the pea crabs and sold them separately from the oyster meats, because they were eaten in soups; George Washington was one notable who particularly enjoyed pea crab soup (*New York Times,* 17 March 1882).

Severe easterly storms buried some oysters with sediment, causing additional losses. The easternmost beds in the bay were exposed to these storms and were the least safe for oysters. Planters with oysters there tried to harvest them in September before the autumn storms.

The almost continuous beds of oysters across the western and northern portions of Raritan Bay probably changed the composition of other life in the bay substantially. Since oyster clusters projected as much as five inches above bottom, plantings resulted in a huge increase in the surface area over the unsculptured bottom. The shell substrate provided both a setting environment for encrusting species such as filamentous diatoms, sponges, bay anemones, bryozoans, slipper shells, mussels, barnacles, and polychaete worms, and surfaces for oyster drills to deposit their egg cases. The oysters also provided cover for mud crabs, hard clams, and small fish. Hard clams are sometimes abundant under oysters, which serve to protect the seed from crab predation. All associated species could occur in higher abundances after the large-scale oyster industry developed. Conversely, any invertebrates, such as hermit crabs, that required open, sandy bottoms most likely declined in abundance where the oysters were planted. Planters removed most biota when they harvested the oysters for market, but new generations settled on the new crop of seed oysters during the following spring and summer and proliferated.

In addition, the feeding by oysters and encrusting animals had a large effect on the phytoplankton of the bay. An extra-large oyster, four to five inches long, can filter about twenty-five quarts of water hourly while feeding and respiring (Galtsoff 1964). Moreover, the quantities of feces and pseudofeces (defined as mostly silt and detritus that has not passed through oyster's digestive system) they produced would have provided a rich environment for bacteria, protozoans, and deposit-feeding invertebrates. The many oyster stakes marking the boundaries of the oyster beds provided a macrohabitat of their own. Encrusting organisms attached to these stakes, and fish, such as the cunner, remained around them.

Oysters were a popular food item. During the 1700s and 1800s, oysters were a common part of the diet of many Americans living near the East Coast. They were an inexpensive, wholesome food; peddlers sold shucked oysters from horse-drawn carts on the streets of eastern U.S. cities, and sections of some cities, such as New York City, boasted an oyster and clam stall on almost every block, much as small restaurants and coffee shops exist now, and saloons commonly served oysters. Before 1860, the regular produce markets in New York City, especially Catherine Market, handled oysters. New York City was the principal market for Raritan Bay oysters.

During the first several years that oysters from Raritan Bay were marketed in New York City, many had mud in them, bringing loud complaints from customers. The planters discovered that oysters would pump out the mud if they spread them for a day or so in shallow water at the mouth of Luppatatong Creek in Keyport and other creeks along the Arthur Kill. Afterward, planters brought all their oysters to the creeks at high tide in tonging skiffs and scows and shoveled them overboard. The following day at low tide, they shoveled them into baskets and brought them back to the sloops for transport to New York City. Besides being clean of mud, the oyster meats also absorbed brackish water, increasing their volume by about a third while they became whiter and had a milder flavor. Crews tried to gather the oysters at the very end of the ebb tide when the water was freshest and would thus be absorbed in largest quantity by the oysters. Workers who retrieved the oysters suffered, since they had to wade into ankle-deep water with only leather shoes for protection and gather the oysters in fall and winter temperatures (Ingersoll 1881).

Commercial production of oysters constituted the largest fishery in the bay; it also involved more ancillary work than the others. Oystering involved building skiffs, catboats, sloops, schooners, tongs, rakes, dredges, anchors, baskets, and oars; cutting and hauling stakes out of woods and then setting them in the bottom to mark the leased-area boundaries; making sails; and waterproofing oilskins with linseed oil. Hand operations included rowing tonging skiffs to the beds, operating tongs, and hauling dredgefuls of oysters aboard catboats and sloops.

Crews shoveled oysters overboard to plant them on growing beds; after harvesting, they shoveled oysters onto the bottoms of shallow brackish creeks, where they remained for about eighteen hours, then shoveled them into baskets, and hand-carried the baskets to scows and then to sloops. Workers hand-shucked every oyster, packed their meats in barrels, and covered them with ice, whose procurement and storage also involved much labor. Finally, they carried shucked shells in wheelbarrows and dumped them in shell piles. The following year, the crews shoveled the shells into wheelbarrows, loaded them onto sloops, and then sailed them to a nearby dock where they shoveled them onto dump wagons and took them to a lime kiln, where processing required additional labor.

As was true in every fishery, the activities in oyster production involved interpersonal competition. Which schooner captain made the fastest round trip to obtain oysters in Chesapeake Bay? Which deckhand shoveled seed overboard fastest? Which tonger harvested the most oysters daily from the beds? Which sloop captain made the fastest trip from Prince's Bay and Keyport to New York City with a load of market oysters? Who was the fastest at opening oysters? Men's reputations were based on their strength and skill, and the work they performed.

Crews were most active on the oyster beds during the planting season in the spring and the marketing season from 1 September to early January. There was little activity during the summer and none from late January to late February. Planters employed workers about six months each year.

The schooner trips to Chesapeake Bay created problems for crew families. Mary Demlin of Keyport recalled that her grandmother did not like to be left alone at night when her husband, a schooner captain, went on one of those trips. She asked Mary, then a girl about eight years old, to stay with her, and enticed her by offering to cook anything she wanted to eat while visiting (Interview, 18 November 1985).

Hard Clamming and Soft Clamming

Besides oysters, the colonists gathered hard clams and soft clams from the bay. They had copied the Lenapes' practice of treading hard clams (that is, gathering clams after feeling for them with their feet at wading depths) for food, and blacksmiths made metal rakes for gathering them. The rakes were shaped like a bird's claw, measured about ten inches wide, and were attached to wood handles about six feet long. On most shores of the bay, fishermen treaded and raked hard clams in depths from about their knees to just above their waists at low tide. The clams were used mainly as supplements to vegetable soups.

10. *Fishermen digging soft clams with four-tine drags at low tide, Leonardo, New Jersey, circa early 1950s. Courtesy of John Seminski.*

In the 1700s and early 1800s, colonists referred to soft clams as "pissers" or "pisser clams" (Pearson 1972) because their necks resembled the penes of small boys and when picked up they squirted water in a manner that resembled the boys pissing. Their siphon holes peppered the wide, intertidal flats along the New Jersey shore when they fell bare. Seed clams were usually abundant among the adults. Colonists probably dug the clams with four-tine potato diggers after first cutting the handles down to about eight inches. At times, digging soft clams was impossible. If, as the consequence of a strong easterly wind, the tide did not recede, fishermen could not work. And during unusually cold winters, ice on the flats prevented any clamming.

At least as early as the 1850s, most soft-clam shucking in Highlands was done in shanties constructed for this purpose along the shore (Ingersoll 1887). Managers of the shanties bought the clams from diggers and hired women to do the shucking, paying them on a piece-rate basis. The clam meats were packed in barrels over a piece of ice and shipped on schooners to New York City. Some shucking was done in the homes of the clammers, who cooked them for their own tables or sold the remainder to neighbors.

Lobstering and Horseshoe Crabbing

Lobster fishing in the bay began in the 1700s (Pearson 1972). The first description of lobster pots and the fishery, however, was provided by a U.S. government fishery agent in the 1850s. The fishermen made the lobster pots about forty inches long and semicircular in shape, using wood lathes. The shape was formed by nailing the lathes over half a barrel hoop. The pot had a funnel on each end and was open in between. Using catboats to tend their pots, fishermen caught lobsters in Raritan Bay and in the ocean off the coast of New Jersey. The lobster season began about 1 May and continued until the end of September, but some lobstering began in March and finished later in the fall. The lobster catch in one pot averaged about four pounds; individual lobsters ranged in weight from one and a quarter to one and three quarters pounds. Nearly all the lobsters were shipped to New York City (Rathbun 1887).

Another crustacean gathered from the bay was the horseshoe crab. Every year in May and June, farmers gathered thousands as horseshoe crabs came into intertidal zones to spawn. They drove their horse-drawn wagons down to the shore and tossed the crabs into them, then brought them back to their farms. They fed them to chickens and hogs and used some as fertilizer.

PART
TWO

Expansion of the Fisheries: 1855–1910

3

Fin Fishing

The year 1855 is significant because the pound net was introduced to Raritan Bay then. A pound net consisted of six sections: a pocket, or pound, measuring about 40 feet by 50 feet and commonly 25 feet deep; a leader 540 feet long; and two hearts, a little one consisting of two sections each 100 feet long and installed opposite one another, and a big one consisting of two sections each 200 feet long and also installed opposite one another. The two hearts were curved and placed near the mouth of the pocket. The mouth was 15 feet wide and went from the bottom of the pocket to the top. It opened into the funnel leading into the pocket and was 20 feet long; its small end had an opening 5 feet by 10 feet. The mesh size in the pound-net pocket was small—2 1/4 inches—to prevent the trapped fish from gilling themselves. With this gear, fishermen could catch in large quantities the food fish and bunkers available beyond the immediate shorelines of the bay.

Around this time, other gear introduced to catch these fish were the less-efficient gill net for food fish and the purse seine for schools of bunkers. The gill net was usually rather long and extended from the water surface to the bottom. It had meshes large enough for the heads of fish but not their bodies to pass through, and they got stuck when they swam into it. Fish could not see the thin, pale cotton twine; sometimes linen thread, also thin and strong, was used instead of cotton twine. The purse seine was also a long net. Fishermen circled it around a school of bunkers and then drew its bottom together like a lady's purse to trap the fish.

Nearly all nets were made of cotton. After the invention of the cotton gin by Eli Whitney in 1793, cotton was produced in large

11. Model of pound net used in Raritan Bay showing, left to right, the leader (most of which is not shown), big heart, little heart, and pocket. Photograph by author.

quantities and was available for making nets. The twine netting of cotton was thinner and smoother than hemp and thus much easier to handle, yet it was as strong but more durable than hemp. Hemp, though bulky, could have been used for pound nets, but it was too bulky for gill nets and purse seines.

During the second half of the nineteenth century, haul seining continued but with longer seines, eel pots were improved, and the design and construction of fyke nets were improved. The transporting of food fish to New York City markets grew in importance, as did sport fishing and worm digging.

Pound Nets

In the mid-1850s, George Snediker, a fishermen from Gravesend Bay, introduced the pound net to Raritan Bay and other New Jersey sites and to Chesapeake Bay (Smith 1892; True 1887). These nets did not come into regular use in Raritan Bay, however, until 1873, and in 1880 the bay had only a few of them (True 1887), including one off the coast of Staten Island (*New York Times,* 15 June 1947). More were installed later. Pound nets caught far more fish than haul seines, fyke nets, and hooks and lines, because each pound net could trap up to one thousand bushels of fish, mostly bunkers, a day.

Almost as soon as commercial fishermen installed the first pound nets in the bay, sport fishermen tried to encourage politicians to have the nets banned. Besides those in the bay, fishermen had installed them in the ocean off Long Island and along the coast of New Jersey from Sea Bright south to Cape May. Sport fishermen believed that the pound nets in the ocean and bay were catching most of the fish and threatening their fishing. On Staten Island, they founded a Protective League of Salt Water Fishermen to obtain the passage and enforcement of laws to protect saltwater fish from commercial fishing by nets, including pound nets, and from chemical pollution (*New York Times,* 18 July 1899). In the spring of 1877, members of the Excelsior Club, one of two fishing clubs then in existence on Staten Island (the other was the Walton Club), complained about pound nets to the justice of the peace of Staten Island. He ordered the local sheriff to round up a posse of men, who forcibly removed some of the nets from the south shore of the island. Finally, in 1878 the two fishing clubs convinced New York State authorities to abolish pound nets permanently in Staten Island waters, citing them as "an evil" (*New York Times,* 4 March 1878).

The New Jersey pound-net fishermen successfully countered the sport fishermen's attacks, saying that the numbers of fish had not declined in the years that the nets were in use and that the principal fish caught were bunkers, porgies, and weakfish, all present in abundance. The netters also said that they were taxpayers, that the livelihoods of many people in their communities depended on pound-net fishing, and that "laws should not be made at the instigation of a few sporting gentlemen who for the sole purpose of gratifying their desires for pleasure would take the bread off the table of the poor man. Moreover, thousands of people depend on cheap fish for part of their diet." They asked where the fish would come from if pound nets were banned (*New York Times,* 29 March 1875).

In the early 1890s, Eugene Blackford, the United States fish commissioner, was called upon to testify at various hearings about this issue. He stated that the harmful effect of pound nets was greatly exaggerated: "Of course, anglers claim that pound netting depletes the fish supply, but in my opinion, there are no grounds for the claim" (*New York Times,* 11 September 1892). Nevertheless, for decades sport fishermen kept up the pressure to have the nets banned. Pound nets have remained in use in New Jersey into the 1990s; in New York they were reinstalled in the 1940s and 1950s.

Pound-Netting Gear and Facilities

The gear and facilities a pound-net crew needed included a sloop; two sets of nets for each pound net; stones, tied every three paces or nine feet along the bottoms of the leader and hearts to hold their bottoms against the substrate; poles; a furnace and tank for tarring the nets; a field at least two acres in size in which to spread out and work on the nets; a storage building for the nets during winter; and a mooring site in Compton's Creek, Belford, for the sloop. (Compton's Creek was named after the Compton family, which once owned most of the land in Belford. The family had been granted the property by the king of England in 1664.) In the late 1800s and early 1900s, each crew had a small icehouse also.

The first netting for the pound nets was knitted by local fishermen and women during the winter, but this method became too slow after the turn of the century, when fishermen installed motors in their boats and were able to install more pound nets. Thereafter, local people made some netting, but fishermen obtained most of it from a New York company that made it by machine. Around 1900 a net cost five hundred to six hundred dollars, and the remaining items—the poles, ropes, and stones—brought the cost to about one thousand dollars for a complete pound net, not including the boat (*Red Bank Register*, 23 March 1898).

To prevent the cotton twine from rotting, fishermen had to remove the nets from the water, dry and clean them, and dip them in tar about every two weeks in spring and fall and every week in summer; the nets would last only about a month otherwise. The tar had the consistency of water even when cold.

One of the two sets of nets for each pound was installed in the bay while the alternate set was being dried, cleaned, repaired, and tarred in a local field. After it was dried, the fishermen had to shake it vigorously to clean off the mud, as well as the animals and plants that had grown on it. They tarred their nets only on days when the wind blew from the south, carrying the tar fumes toward the bay and away from human settlements. Fishermen heated the tarring tank, which was five to six feet wide, with a little brick furnace fired with driftwood. They brought the tar to a high temperature and then pulled the nets through it and over a slanted platform carrying the tar drippings back into the tank. Fishermen believed that the hotter the tar was, the more it penetrated the net, but once in a while, the tar caught fire and burned some of the net. After the nets were tarred, fishermen spread them in the field to dry.

Each pound net had seventy hickory or oak poles, each of which was thirty to forty feet long. During the winter, fishermen cut the poles in the local woods and hauled them to their docks by horse and wagon; in the early spring they coated them with copper paint. During the off-seasons, the poles were left on the docks. When fishermen were ready to install their pound nets, they slid the poles into the water, tied them in bundles, and towed them to the site. The pocket had sixteen poles plus four extra poles to brace its corners; the leader had nineteen to twenty poles spaced about twenty-one feet apart; the little heart had four poles on each side for a total of eight; and the big heart had ten poles on each side for a total of twenty. The pocket poles each had a block at their bottom. Ropes went through them from the top of the pole to the bottom of the pound. When fishermen emptied the pound, they untied the ropes, pulled up the net to concentrate the fish into a tight mass, transferred them into the pound boat, pulled the ropes through the pulleys to pull the bottom of the pound down again, and then tied them. The transfers were made with hand scoops holding about a peck (Interview, John Fisler, 3 November 1987).

It took three or four days to install a single pound net: two or three days to set in the poles and a day to tie on the sections of net. The bottom substrate, where fishermen installed most pound nets, consisted of mud. Crews "jumped" in the poles; that is, they tied two-foot wooden boards horizontally on them and then two men got on them and jumped up and down. Each pole went about twelve feet into the mud; if less, the poles would lean over under the strain of a strong current on the net when it became dirty. In the 1890s, fishermen drove the poles into sand bottoms with a light pile driver rigged on their sloop (*New York Times,* 11 September 1892). They also could drive in the poles by putting a heavy iron sleeve over each one and raising it up and down with the boom of their boat. By the early 1900s, hand-operated pumps became available to jet in the poles.

When the fishing season ended in the fall, the crews removed the net. Then they attached a chain to the poles in mud and sailed the boat ahead to pull them out. The poles in sand had to be pulled straight up, or else they would break. Under federal law since the early 1900s, pound poles have had to be removed by 1 December.

In the late 1800s, most crews had only one pound net; some had two. In 1898 the bay had thirty-seven pound nets tended by twenty-eight pound-boat crews (Stevenson 1898). As boats became motorized, each crew increased its number of pound nets to two or three, and by 1910 about fifty pound nets were installed in the bay (*Red Bank Register,* 8 March 1911).

Before 1900 the pound boats were gaff-rigged sloops, which could carry 250 to 300 bushels of fish in their holds (Stevenson 1898). Crews poled the sloops out of Compton's Creek to the pound nets, most of which were installed less than a mile and a half from the creek (Frye 1978). Since a channel beyond the mouth of Compton's Creek was not dug until around 1900 by the federal government and the flats were shallow at low tide, sloops had to go to and from the pound nets at high tide. At times, the tide was high before dawn, and crews had to leave then. To lift the pound nets installed at Sandy Hook, crews had to sail four miles; on calm days they had to row there using a pair of sixteen-foot oars. It took about three hours to row a sloop to Sandy Hook.

The first engines made for boats had only one cylinder and four horsepower: "They were big hunks of iron—some heavy!" Charlie Schnoor of Belford, who started pound-net fishing with his father at age ten in 1894 because his mother had died, described an experience when he was about seventeen with the first engine in his father's pound boat:

> The damn things would run and they wouldn't. Men got blisters on their hands trying to start them. One day, my dad and his crew wanted to take a load of fish to New York from Belford and the doggone engine wouldn't start. The crew worked two or three hours on it and it still wouldn't go. My dad says: 'Well, we'll sail. We'll take a chance that there'll be a little breeze.' We were poling down the creek and I said: 'I'll help you.' I turned the engine by hand once and, by God, she says plunk and she ran all day. (Interview by Ken Norton, 10 July 1977)

The engines could also fail when the boats were fishing. Once, in the early 1900s, two men were dredging crabs in a boat without a cabin or a sail. It was extremely cold. Their engine stopped late in the afternoon, no one saw them, and they could not return to Belford. When another crew found them drifting on the bay the next day, both had frozen to death.

Pound-Netting Methods and Catch

Pound nets caught fish much as to fyke nets did. Fishermen installed pound nets perpendicular to shore, with the pockets offshore of the leaders. When fish encountered the leader, they turned offshore toward deeper water and swam along it. They went either into the mouth of the pocket and through its funnel into the pocket, or veered to one side and followed the little heart around. This directed most back toward the mouth. Those that went around the little heart swam into the big heart and were also redirected back toward the mouth.

The type of fish caught varied seasonally. The first fish in March and April were alewives and shad. In April and May pound nets caught some sturgeon, from which fishermen took the roe to be sold as caviar after processing; a 350-pound female sturgeon, the largest ever caught in the bay, had about 45 pounds of roe. From mid-April through May, pound nets caught huge quantities of bunkers. Beginning in June, bunkers form tight schools and go into pound nets in smaller quantities through

October, when they leave the bay. Nevertheless, catches of bunkers always exceeded those of food fish throughout the season. From about July fourth on, the food fish ("good" fish in the fishermen's parlance) came into the bay. Pound nets caught bluefish, weakfish, porgies, and some less important species from then into October, though in some years bluefish appeared in May. The shad that did not die after spawning came back down the rivers, through the bay, and out into the ocean in June. Some of these "back-runners" were caught in pound nets, but they were much thinner than they had been in March and April.

Pound nets caught more fish after a strong wind, but a violent storm could drive fish out of the bay temporarily. Sometimes a storm killed the bunkers trapped in pound nets, and if too many bunkers were in the nets during hot weather, they died from a lack of oxygen. Crews had difficulty removing these from a net because they did not rise to the surface when they lifted the pocket.

Pound-net crews have always consisted of three or four men, one being the owner of the boat and gear. A day's work involved sailing to the pound nets, lifting the pocket from the bottom to concentrate the fish, transferring fish from the pocket to the sloop, removing two sections of the pound net bearing heavy growths of organisms and mud and replacing them with clean sections (done only three days a week), selling some bunkers to lobstermen and hand liners as bait, returning to Compton's Creek and unloading the by-catch of bunkers at a fish factory and boxing and putting the food fish on a freight boat for New York City or selling them to peddlers or fish markets, hauling the dirty sections of net to a field in a horse-drawn wagon, and finally working on the nets in the fields. The work could be unpleasant: the growth on the nets attracted many flies, and mosquitos were usually numerous in the low-lying fields when the wind did not blow.

A crew with two nets brought in one of the two nets every week. They could bring in only two of a net's six sections at a time because more, along with the fish, would be too heavy for the boat. Three days a week, they carried out two cleaned sections, removed two dirty sections, and installed the cleaned sections in their place. If they left a dirty net in the water, the leader and hearts would lift off the bottom, many fish would go under them, and the catch would be much smaller. During the first month a pound net was installed—March or April—a crew could get by without shifting it because the water was cold and did not get as dirty.

Some pound-net crews had their own horse and wagon team for hauling their nets to and from their fields, but at least two men did this hauling for a living. They each had a team and charged twenty-five cents for each trip they made (Interview, Ken Norton, 17 December 1987).

Gill Netting for Shad

Gill netting for shad in Raritan Bay was first described in the late 1800s (First Annual Report of the Commissioners of Fisheries, Game and Forests, New York, 1896). The concurrent arrival of shad and ospreys (fish hawks), which nested around the bayshore and fed on fish until late September, heralded the onset of the fishing year, bringing excitement to fishermen and local consumers. The main shad run began about 17 March and ended about ten weeks later on what was to become Decoration Day, 30 May. Fishermen often tied the arrival and departure of fish to religious or national holidays and even sporting events, such as the baseball World Series, as a way of remembering them. July Fourth, when the main body of food fish came into Raritan Bay, was perhaps the most important date.

From February to early May, gill nets set for shad were hung between stakes set about twenty-five feet apart. Some fishing crews installed as many as twenty-five nets and used catboats for tending them.

The shad were caught mostly at night. Fishermen lifted the nets early the next day, removed the shad, and brought them and the nets ashore. They stretched the nets out on racks for drying and for picking out the plant debris that had collected on them. If the nets were not dried, they rotted within a month; if they were not picked clean, fish could see the debris and fewer would be caught. In the late afternoon, crews put in an alternate set of nets, which had been drying and then cleaned.

Shad were by far the most common fish caught. Others caught included striped bass, alewives, blue crabs, and the occasional sturgeon. A census of the number of shad nets and the number of shad caught in Raritan Bay in 1895 produced the following data:

Location	Number of staked gill nets	Number of shad caught
Keansburg	83	34,986
Port Monmouth	17	8,143
Belford	103	40,900
Highlands	11	22,130

Source: First Annual Report of the Commissioners of Fisheries, Game and Forests, New York, 1896.

In 1896, fishermen caught 61 percent of the shad they landed in pound nets, 36 percent in staked gill nets, 2.3 percent in haul seines, and only 0.7 percent in fyke nets (Stevenson 1898). The fishermen pulled out the gill nets for the season when bunkers came into the bay, because bunkers sold for too low a price to be worth catching with gill nets.

Each spring about thirty fishermen from Newburg and Catskill,

12. *Crew at shad fishing station, Stapleton, Staten Island; cotton gill nets are spread out and drying, circa 1894. Photograph by Alice Austen. Courtesy Staten Island Historical Society, Richmondtown Restoration, Staten Island, New York.*

New York, came to Staten Island to catch shad with drift gill nets in the Narrows at the northeast corner of the bay. Their nets were 1,200 feet long and 8 feet deep with meshes were 2 1/2 inches square (*New York Times,* 25 April 1974).

Gill Netting for Bluefish and Weakfish

Drift gill netting for bluefish and weakfish was first described in the 1890s (Smith 1894). Drift gill nets were made of cotton or linen and were about 2,250 feet long and 20 feet deep. They had corks along their topline and leads along their bottomline to keep them spread. Fishermen used these nets from catboats; each crew consisted of two men. They stretched out the nets in the water as they sailed along slowly, let them drift for about ten minutes, and then retrieved them.

A problem for fishermen was that two general sizes of bluefish inhabited the bay, and nets with different mesh sizes were needed to catch them: three-and-a-half-inch mesh netting for fish weighing from one to

13. *Drying drift gill nets on a rack in Keyport, circa 1915. Gill nets were used for catching bluefish and weakfish. Courtesy of Steamboat Dock Museum, Keyport, New Jersey.*

three pounds, and heavier five-and-a-half-inch mesh netting for large bluefish, termed "slammers." If fishermen used the wrong mesh size, few fish would be caught. Some slammers were caught in three-and-a-half-inch mesh netting, but they cut up the net.

Drift gill netters also had to have two sets of nets to prevent them from rotting. Each day they used one set to fish with and had the other set drying on a pier or net rack. They switched the sets every day. The steamboat company in Keyport allowed fishermen to dry gill nets along the rails of its dock, and some fishermen in the town had racks on the shore. Belford had two racks, both about forty-five feet long, made of discarded pound-net poles for gill nets. New nets lasted only one season and had to be purchased each year; the corks and leads were recycled to the new nets.

Each May fishermen began setting their gill nets in New Jersey waters, starting in eight to twelve feet of water, for bluefish. Roughly half of the net lay on the bottom, but later in the season, when set in the deeper parts of the bay, the net was just deep enough to touch bottom.

Fishermen arrived at fishing sites at dawn each day, because at that time the water surface was usually calm and feeding bluefish could be spotted by breaks on the surface or by birds diving for the minnows that the bluefish drove to the surface. Although New York authorities did not

14. *Fishing boats tied up in Compton's Creek, Belford; most are catboats used in several fisheries including drift gill netting, eeling, hard clamming, and lobstering, circa 1900. Courtesy of Moe Coucci.*

permit gill netting in their waters, New Jersey fishermen sometimes sneaked over the state jurisdictional line early in the morning if they saw a school of bluefish breaking water there. If the water was too choppy to spot bluefish, fishermen tried to locate them by towing a metal lure painted yellow and feeling for strikes. If they felt any, they put out their net. Fishermen tried to go gill netting every day to keep track of the location of fish. If they missed two or three days, it might take a whole day to find them again.

Weakfish did not break water or attract birds, and the netters had to make blind sets for them. Bluefish and weakfish gilled themselves within about a yard of the bottom.

Fishermen retrieved the net by hand. The soaked net with the added weight of fish was heavy. One fisherman brought in the lead line at the stern of the boat while his partner took in the cork line nearer the bow; both removed the fish as they came to them and tossed them into a bin. The catch included some croakers and spot. If a large number of fish were gilled, the two brought in the entire net and removed the fish afterward. A crew could make a set in one to one and a half hours and make five or six sets a day (Interview, Johnny Wallace, 20 October 1985).

Typically, fishermen caught 200 to 400 pounds of fish a day; a catch of 1,000 to 1,500 pounds was possible but unusual. If a net had more fish than the boat could safely hold, the crew called over another crew from their port, let them take the net and extra fish, and asked them to lay out the net on their rack when they returned to port.

Once, when a crew had caught a large quantity of bluefish in their net, instead of taking out only the fish their boat could carry and then giving the remainder to another crew or anchoring out the net holding the remainder, they tried to take aboard the entire netful. Their boat swamped. The captain swam to a nearby bell buoy and remained there for about twelve hours until being rescued, but his mate drowned.

Drift gill netting ended for the season in October, when the fish left the bay. Some gill netters followed the bluefish out to the ocean and down the New Jersey shore. The fish usually remained within two hundred feet of shore.

Purse Seining for Bunkers

The third and final fin-fishing gear introduced in the 1800s was the purse seine, for catching schools of bunkers. Before the introduction of purse seines, haul seines and gill nets were used to capture bunkers. Fishermen set out gill nets ahead of the schools and easily caught many. The twine of the purse seine was made of cotton, and support pieces were made of hemp. Fishermen prevented the seines from rotting by tarring them after they were knitted and by sprinkling salt over them after each fishing day (Goode and Clarke 1887).

Purse seining in the bay was first described in the 1870s by G. Brown Goode (1880). There were five purse-seining sloops each, thirty-six to forty-five feet long, all from Belford. Each carried two purse boats, which in turn each carried half of the purse seine. They sailed out on the bay, sometimes before dawn, and waited for the schools of bunkers to show. When a crew spotted one, it lowered the two purse boats overboard and the crews rowed the seine, 1,500 feet long and 12 to 13 feet deep, around the school and pulled it into a tight circle. Then the crews transferred the bunkers into their boats with scoop nets holding about a peck. Next they transferred the bunkers to the sloop with the scoop nets and finally sailed as quickly as possible to the bunker factories in Belford to reach them before the fish decayed. Each sloop could carry about 375 bushels of bunkers, and the fleet of five landed as many as 1,000 bushels a day.

On 1 September 1886 the *Red Bank Register* reported that a sloop had surrounded a large school of bunkers with a purse seine, and the crewmen were congratulating each other on their good luck when they noticed several large sharks in the net. The sharks broke through the net and allowed all the bunkers to escape. One shark was ten feet long and aggressive. It attacked one of the purse boats and left some teeth in its planking as mementos. Fortunately, the men had an axe and, by using it vigorously, managed to drive off the shark.

Other Gear and Methods

Fishermen continued to catch fish with several haul seines at sites on the New Jersey side of the bay. Fishermen knitted their seines of cotton twine and dipped them in tar as needed to preserve them. The largest seine, at Seidler's Beach, just west of Keyport, was nearly a mile long. Every Sunday, a crowd of people from a small resort located there gathered at the shore to view the catch when the net was retrieved.

On a small scale, commercial fishermen from Staten Island, Belford, and Highlands used hand lines to catch bluefish, mostly in the nearby ocean but also in the channels at the eastern end of Raritan Bay. In the 1800s and early 1900s, the boats fishermen used in this fishery were bateaux and schooners. In 1909 a newspaper reported the following nightly catches of bluefish by individual hand-lining boats: 43; 110; 466; 539; none (*Red Bank Register,* 15 September).

Toward the late 1800s, the fyke net was one of the most important types of fishing gear used in eastern United States. For example, a census found that in 1894, 6,246 fyke nets in the state of New York caught 2,382,882 pounds of fish, and 1,562 fyke nets in the state of New Jersey caught 591,684 pounds of fish (Smith 1894). The same census found that fishermen had set 215 fyke nets, tended by 25 boats, around Staten Island, and 213, tended by 52 boats, in Monmouth County, New Jersey. Including 34 set in Gravesend Bay, perhaps 200 fyke nets were installed in Raritan Bay (Stevenson 1898).

By the late 1800s, fishermen used a fine-mesh cotton net, with openings about a half-inch square, to construct their fyke nets. They had substituted it for the larger mesh to catch eels, and afterward eels were the fish most commonly caught in them in the spring. Fishermen also dipped these nets and hoops in hot tar to preserve them.

The Belford fishermen experimented with fyke nets set up in gangs rather than singly. Each gang had a single leader, and two fyke nets were set opposite each other at a few intervals along its length (Stevenson 1898). In Belford, there were five such gangs, each with six to ten fyke nets. A local fisherman named Martin C. Lohsen designed a fyke with a leader, wings, and two hearts similar to a pound net. For a while, it gradually displaced the early fyke-net designs. Fishermen installed Lohsen-style nets singly, in pairs, or in strings containing from three to

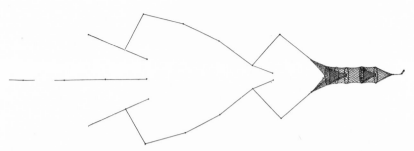

15. *Design of a type of fyke net used near Belford in 1880s and 1890s. From Hugh M. Smith,* The fyke nets and fyke-net fisheries of the United States, with notes on the fyke nets of other countries. *Bulletin of the U. S. Fish Commission for 1892 (Washington, D.C.: U.S. Government Printing Office, 1894).*

six fykes. They caught a wider variety and larger quantity of fish (Smith 1894). Soon after 1900, however, fishermen redesigned the fyke nets again, simplifying them and making them with only two wings.

To empty the fyke nets fishermen rowed out to them in bateaux at low tide and removed the fish from their heads with a heavily constructed crab net. Most fishermen had four fyke nets, which yielded fifty to one hundred pounds of fish a day. The fyke-net fishermen potted eels on the same days that they emptied their fyke nets.

Eel Pots and Spears

Fishermen continued to catch eels with pots and spears. Around 1900, meshed wire became available, and fishermen used it instead of wooden slats to construct the eel pots; thirty pots could be made from one seventy-five-foot roll of wire. Wire pots were much easier to construct and the fishermen did not have to put a weight in each one to hold it down. They found that the wire rusted, however, and they had to dip the pots in tar to preserve them. Instead of setting out each pot with its own buoy, the fishermen strung pots on lines laid out along the bottom and buoyed at their ends.

The abundance of eels varied in different periods, and catches varied accordingly. For instance, the daily catches of the eel spearers were about 12 pounds in winters of low abundance, 40 to 50 pounds in typical winters, and 150 to 200 pounds by the best fishermen in winters of extraordinarily high eel abundance. In typical years, the commercial spearers earned three to four dollars a day (*Red Bank Register,* 6 January 1915).

Marketing the Catch

Fishermen sold some of their catch from haul seines and fyke nets to local peddlers who used modified horse-drawn farm wagons for making their delivery rounds. Local people ate the fish fresh or smoked it for preservation; smoked fish lasted at least a year. The remaining fish were packed in barrels and shipped on sloops daily to markets in New York City. As early as 1804, ice was used to preserve fish sent there. The New York market received fish from various sources, only one of which was Raritan Bay. A market source listed twenty-three kinds of fresh fish in the market on a single day in 1783 and fifty-six kinds of fish, shellfish, crustaceans, and turtles on a single day in 1804 (Pearson 1972). In the 1820s some dealers sold fish and others sold produce along Fulton Street in lower Manhattan. By 1831 Fulton Fish Market was established as an independent market.

In the 1880s, fifty to sixty million pounds of fish per year were being marketed in New York City. Freight boats from Raritan Bay, fishing fleets from Long Island and New England, and freight trains from all parts of the Atlantic and Gulf coasts and the Great Lakes brought them there (Mather 1887). No records are available for Raritan Bay production of fish in the 1880s, but the bay produced at least nine million pounds of fish a year in the early 1900s (*Red Bank Register,* 8 March 1911), nearly 20 percent of the quantity consumed each year by New York City in the 1880s. The fish from Raritan Bay had the best reputation in city's markets because it was the freshest, having been caught on the day of delivery or the previous day.

Before the early 1900s, fishermen in Keyport, Belford, and Highlands supplied their own ice for fish shipped to New York City. They obtained it from shallow ponds, usually about one hundred feet in diameter, that they had dug using horses and scoops. Fishermen cut the ice when it measured at least six inches thick and packed it in wooden icehouses they had constructed in dunes ten to twelve feet high along the shores. The houses were about six feet high, six feet deep, and six feet wide. They had double walls and ceilings and door stuffed with salt hay. The sand on three sides and at least three feet on top insulated them from the summer's heat. When winters were relatively warm, however, fishermen had to purchase ice from schooners that delivered it from Maine. Since the early 1900s, locally manufactured ice has been available.

From the late 1800s to the late 1930s, Raritan Bay commercial fishermen shipped about 90 percent of their food fish catches to Fulton Market in New York City on freight boats running from Compton's Creek, Belford. Before 1900 the marketing boats were sloops and schooners in spring and fall, and a passenger-freight steamer, the *William*

V. Wilson, in summer. The steamer did not land at Fulton Market, and fishermen had to pay extra cartage overland from the steamer dock near the tip of Manhattan to Fulton Market. After 1902, a sixty-foot motorized boat, the *Lottie B.*, delivered the fish to Fulton Market during the entire season, March through October; before 1902, this boat was under sail and had been used, in part, for freighting Raritan Bay oysters to New York City. The first engine in the *Lottie B.* had only twenty horsepower, but, for more speed, its owner replaced it with a thirty-horsepower engine. The boat had a tall mast with a block and tackle suspended from it to hoist fish boxes gripped with tongs out of fishing boats. During the winter, the *Lottie B.* freighted coal from New York City to Belford.

Fishermen sold the remaining 10 percent of their fish catch to peddlers and to markets in Tottenville, Perth Amboy, Keyport, and Belford. They felt, however, that the peddlers paid them too little. Meanwhile, peddlers believed they should pay fishermen a little less than New York City prices because fishermen did not have to pay any freight and fish would never be lost when sold to them. The two groups argued over prices. The protest of one fishermen was recorded in the *Red Bank Register* (25 April 1888):

> The peddlers bought shad at 45 or 50 cents a pair (a male and a female) and sold them for a $1.00 and in some cases for $1.25. We should think that 100 percent profit on a staple item was pretty good in these hard times. The peddler with his horse, harness, and wagon hasn't one-fourth as much invested as the fisherman and yet the peddlers get most of the money the customer pays for shad, although the fishermen do all the work and the peddler only sells the fish.
>
> The peddlers gather on the beach before the fishermen get to shore, and will fix the price they will pay. When a luckless fisherman comes ashore with a small catch, too small to ship, the peddlers know that he must take their price. The fishermen simply want the current market price for their fish.

At times, the demand for fish in New York City was low, and when fishermen shipped fish to Fulton Market, they often got nothing in return after the freight charge was subtracted. When the market price remained low, some pound-net fishermen stored part of their catches of food fish in live cars, consisting of a wooden frame covered by netting. Each such car held from six hundred to two thousand bushels of fish. Crews sank the cars alongside their pound nets and often fed the fish to maintain their weight. In 1889, a newspaper cited an instance of a fisherman who put one thousand pounds of weakfish in cars when the market price was only 1.5 cents a pound and sold them at the end of the season in November for 6 cents a pound (*Red Bank Register,* 8 November 1889).

Bunkers: Bait, Fertilizer, and Food

Before 1850, bunkers were used only as bait by mackerel and cod fishermen and as fertilizer on farms. Crews sold them to farmers for seventy-five cents per thousand fish. Farmers plowed them into their fields to fertilize corn, potatoes, buckwheat, and cabbages (Akerly 1843). They could not plow in too many because the fish oil could build up to a concentration unfit for growing crops. Farmers put two or three bunkers in each hill of corn and laid them head to tail in the bottoms of potato rows (Goode 1880).

Briefly in the second half of the 1800s, bunkers were canned for food; they also were processed into oil and meal that farmers used for fertilizer; and they were used as bait. Four factories were constructed in Belford in the early 1870s to can bunkers for human consumption under the trade names of Shadine, Ocean Trout, and American Club-Fish. They were not labeled as sardines because bunkers rather than juvenile herring were the fish being canned. Nonetheless, the product was similar to canned sardines, except that the fish were larger. The plant of the American Sardine Factory was the largest, 360 feet long by 120 feet wide, and four to five stories high. The factory also had a boardinghouse for 180 employees. It made its own packing cans and kept horses and wagons for hauling cases of canned bunkers to the dock at Belford for shipment. The factories obtained bunkers seasonally from the five purse seiners sailing from Belford (Goode 1880).

After the bunkers arrived at the factories, they were scaled by machines. Then workers steam-cooked them and packed them in cans with covers perforated by two tiny holes. Workers then put the cans into a bath of pickle to fill them with it. Next, they cooked the cans of bunkers and pickle. When the cans were still hot and filled with steam, workers soldered the two holes closed. Finally, they glued labels on the cans. In 1870 the American Sardine Factory shipped 150,000 cans of bunkers to customers, some in Europe. By 1877, just several years after they were built, these factories were no longer profitable; they closed permanently in that year (Goode 1880).

Immediately, factories for reducing the bunkers to oil and scrap (meal) were constructed. The bunkers were caught by pound nets and the sloops using purse seines. Around 1900, Belford had three such factories and Atlantic Highlands had one. They occupied about five acres of land

16. *Bunker-processing factory in Belford (Port Monmouth), showing barrels of oil, scrap (meal) in bags, and factory crew, circa 1905. Courtesy of Kenneth A. Norton.*

each and operated from the end of March to the end of October (Frye 1978). The factories paid fishermen twenty cents a bushel for the bunkers. Farmers continued to buy the bunkers for fertilizer, but only after the factories had processed them into scrap. Farmers also purchased some bunker oil to make paint for preserving their barns and used red clay from bogs to color it.

To enable the pound boats to unload bunkers at all stages of the tide in Belford, one factory constructed an unloading dock two thousand feet out in the bay and a narrow pier to it from shore. It laid railroad track on it for running a hopper car that carried the bunkers. Boats brought the bunkers to the dock, and crews shoveled them into the cars. Workers pulled the cars along the length of the pier to shore and up a steep incline to a platform one hundred feet long and fifteen feet above ground. Eight cribs, ten feet in diameter, four feet deep, and made of heavy planking, were installed on each side of the platform for cooking and pressing the bunkers. A steam line extended through their bottoms to heat water (Murphy n.d.).

Workers filled the cribs with bunkers from the dump cars, and the bunkers were cooked in half an hour. Then the workers pressed the bunkers, using a flat wooden piston operated at the end of a long shaft by a cylinder suspended above the crib. They forked the pressed bunkers from the cribs into horse-drawn wagons that took them to a wooden deck area about an acre in size, where the bunkers were spread out for drying by air and sun to become scrap. The drying bunkers had a strong odor and attracted many flies. To facilitate drying, workers pulled a wooden-toothed harrow back and forth to turn and spread the fish out until they were ready for storage in the scrap house. There, workers bagged and weighed them for shipment, by rail or boat; local farmers carted some away for their own use (Murphy n.d.).

To obtain the oil, workers drained the gurry water (water and oil left behind after the fish were removed from the cribs) into storage tanks. With wooden scoops, they skimmed the oil from the surface into large barrels; about 90 percent of the oil was recovered (Murphy n.d.).

Each factory could process about 500 bushels of bunkers a day (Frye 1978), a quantity that yielded slightly more than five tons of scrap and 250 to 275 gallons of oil (*Red Bank Register*, 27 August 1890). The scrap was sold to farmers locally and on Long Island for thirty dollars a ton, the nitrogen-rich scrap being especially good for asparagus; it was also sold to fertilizer factories, which mixed it with phosphates and other substances before selling it to farmers. It cost about three thousand dollars a month to run a factory (*Red Bank Registery*, 1890s).

The manufacture of bunker oil had grown into a substantial business along the Atlantic coast. For example, in 1875, production from New Jersey totaled 87,747 gallons of bunker oil worth $30,711 and 4,545 tons of scrap worth $113,625. Total U.S. production of bunker oil in 1874 was 3,372,837 gallons, and in 1875 it was 2,618,487 gallons. U.S. production of whale oil totaled 2,505,137 gallons in 1875 (Goode and Clarke 1887).

Tanneries bought most of the bunker oil and used it for currying leather; some was shipped overseas for this purpose. The oil was also used in the manufacture of paint, rope, and soap, in coal mines as a lamp fuel, and on sheep farms where it was applied on sheared sheep to keep off ticks. In addition, some was sold as cod liver oil (*Red Bank Register*, 28 March 1883), and blacksmiths bought some for tempering tools.

In the late 1800s , besides selling bunkers to fish factories, pound-net fishermen and purse seiners in Raritan Bay sold some as bait. A fleet of about eighty smacks, or schooners, sailing from Fulton Market to catch bluefish and cod in the ocean bought five hundred bushels of bunkers a day from the pound nets (*Red Bank Register*, 2 July 1890). They paid about twenty-five cents a bushel for them, more than fishermen received from the farmers or factories (*Red Bank Register*, 2 June 1911).

Sport Fishing

The enjoyable activity of sport fishing grew in importance in the late 1800s but remained smaller than commercial fishing. The bay had a wide variety of fish to catch, including bluefish, croakers, eels, fluke, kingfish, porgies, sheepshead, spot, weakfish, winter flounder, and an occasional salmon. Of these, porgies were the most abundant (*New York Times*, 4 March 1878, 1 July 1888). Large sailing vessels took fishermen from places such as Manhattan, Hoboken, Jersey City, Newark, Elizabeth, Staten Island, Perth Amboy, and Highlands out on the bay (Barrett 1985). In 1842 J. E. DeKay had stated, "Porgies afford much sport to fishing parties, who go outside the harbor [of New York City] in vessels and take them in great numbers." In the late 1800s, engines were installed in some sailing vessels, a few of which were at least two hundred feet long, three decks high, and often crowded with fishermen; they fished in the bay and ocean (Barrett 1985). Some people also fished from small sailboats, trolling small spoons and sandworms hooked onto spinners (Zeisel 1988). They also fished from rowboats, piers, and from the shore (*New York Times*, 13 March 1892). Rowboats could be rented for a dollar a day; although most piers were free, some charged each fisherman twenty-five cents a day (Emmons 1907).

A phenomenon of the late 1800s was the founding of fishing clubs. About ten formed on Staten Island, and some formed in Monmouth County, New Jersey, as well. The larger ones bought clubhouses in which to meet and to stay on weekends when they fished in the bay. The smaller clubs met in cellars and back rooms of bars, perhaps once a month. The club members went out on fishing vessels, held fishing contests, and generally had fun together. These clubs have continued to be active into the 1990s.

A type of sport fishing that originated in the 1800s and continued through the 1940s was the catching of frostfish (whiting) along Staten Island and New Jersey beaches in November. Every year perhaps one hundred people did this. They were mainly commercial fishermen and farmers. Equipped with rubber boots and flashlights, they picked up the frostfish by hand when waves washed them ashore. Often each brought home half a potato sack full. Most of the fish were preserved by smoking and were eaten during the winter. Since the 1950s, frostfish have been scarce in the bay.

From the late 1800s to the 1950s, there was a fairly substantial commercial bait fishery on Staten Island and in Highlands to supply sport fishermen (*Red Bank Register*, 15 October 1890). Each summer, about fifty men dug sand worms, bloodworms, and nemertean "tapeworms" at low tide along the shore of Staten Island from Great Kills Harbor to Ward Point. Another fifteen to twenty men and boys dug these worms and also caught shrimp and killifish around Highlands for this market; these men earned most of their incomes from soft clamming.

The worms grew in intertidal and wading zones along the shores.

Sand worms inhabited the sloping area between the cordgrass and the flat. Bloodworms and tapeworms inhabited the flats and shallow zones with the soft clams. Fishermen dug the sand worms and bloodworms with garden forks using a "fork-and-a-half" technique as the worms were deep in the sand. First, they pushed the tines of the forks straight into the sand, and then pushed the handles back about a foot to determine whether wormholes appeared. If they did, fishermen dug out a fork full of sand and then another half fork of sand. Then they picked out the worms and put them in a flat box measuring about eighteen by thirty-six inches. Catches varied but each digger could get as many as twelve hundred sand worms and bloodworms on a low tide.

Shell Fishing

During the second half of the nineteenth century, shell fishing expanded. The oyster industry remained the largest fishery in the bay, and it developed further when railroads were built and could ship oyster meats to the Midwest and Far West and when the sloops were fitted with engines and power hoists to retrieve dredges. The invention of the long-handle rake and the sail dredge enabled fishermen to gather hard clams in deep water, and the invention of the churning hoe enabled them to gather soft clams subtidally. In addition, the lobster fishery grew somewhat, and the blue-crab fishery was founded.

Oystering

Far from being the common food of the poor man [as it was in the 1700s], so plenteous and vulgar that no feast ever saw its name upon the menu, the oyster became only a luxury for the well-to-do, and the prime feature of holiday banquets. Recovering from the scarcity [in the early 1800s] which had brought this change about, by means of the artificial cultivation of immense quantities [the importation of seed oysters from Chesapeake Bay to the beds of Long Island Sound, Raritan Bay, and Delaware Bay], oysters a second time have become abundant as an article of food, enjoyed alike by rich and poor. Those who live in the interior or abroad can hardly appreciate how extensive is the demand and supply in the coast cities. Oysters pickled, stewed, baked, roasted, fried, and scalloped; oysters

made into soups, patties, and puddings; oysters with condiments and without condiments; oysters for breakfast, dinner,
and supper; oysters without stint or limit, fresh as the pure air,
and almost as abundant, are daily offered to the palates of the
Manhattanese, and appreciated with all gratitude which such a
bounty of nature ought to inspire. (Ingersoll 1887)

So wrote Ernest Ingersoll, an agent hired by the federal government to
describe the shellfish industries of eastern Canada and the United States,
about the enormous growth of the oyster industry along the Atlantic
coast during the mid- to late 1800s.

The oyster industry, which extended from Canada's maritime provinces to Texas, was well known to residents along the eastern seaboard;
advertisements for purchasing oysters by brand name were common in
newspapers, and many recipes for cooking oysters appeared in booklets
and books. A well-publicized contest was held each year between the two
men whom the industry recognized as the fastest oyster shuckers along
the Atlantic coast. These contests were held at various sites, including
Grand Central Station in New York City; Keyport; and Norfolk, Virginia. They drew large crowds, the betting was heavy, and the results
were published in newspapers. In one contest held in Grand Central
Station in 1885, a shucker opened 2,300 oysters (about ten bushels) in
two hours, eighteen minutes, and nineteen and a half seconds, but he was
beaten by a contestant who opened 2,500 oysters in two hours, twenty-
three minutes, and thirty-nine and three-fourths seconds (*New York
Times,* 23 December 1885).

As Ingersoll implied, the residents of New York City were consum-
ing large quantities of oysters because supplies of beef, pork, and chicken
were inadequate. In addition, the city served as a distribution point for
oysters shipped both westward to the rest of the United States and
eastward to Europe. Since as early as 1816, oysters from Chesapeake Bay
had been delivered directly to the city. The two hundred vessels involved
in transporting them made about six hundred trips a month from September through February (Ingersoll 1881; *New York Times,* 2 August
1872). By the 1860s, about 500,000 bushels of oysters were being sold in
the New York market annually; their wholesale value was $500,000.
About 80 percent of the oysters originated in Chesapeake Bay: half came
directly from the bay; the remainder had been transplanted in the spring
as seed to beds in Raritan Bay and other northern estuaries for growth
and reharvesting (*New York Times,* 11 September 1870).

Wholesalers and eating places in the city referred to oysters by the
name of the locality where they were grown, and supposedly each had a
distinct flavor. There were perhaps twenty such names, and they were

famous in the trade; the oyster connoisseurs had their favorites. Oysters from Raritan Bay were assigned the names Prince's Bays and Keyports, and from the Navesink River came Shrewsburys. Popular oysters from Long Island were Blue Points; those from Virginia included Chincoteagues, Lynnhavens, and Rappahannocks. Of these, the Bluepoints and Chincoteagues had the strongest flavor, while the Lynnhavens and Rappahannocks were the blandest. Consumers much preferred those oysters with white shells on their insides to those partly colored black by being infested with mud-blister worms.

In Raritan Bay, the principal marketing season began around 1 September and ended in early January, when the supply was exhausted. Nearly all the oysters from Raritan Bay were handled through New York City or sold in towns along the Hudson River, including Albany. The remaining oysters were shipped from New York City to Europe. For example, in the fall of 1880, the Elsworth Company packed four hundred barrels (three bushels to a barrel) of oysters a week in Lemon Creek, Staten Island, for shipment there (*Richmond County Gazette*, 23 January 1881), and Perth Amboy planters also packed oysters for Europe (Ingersoll 1887). Before each marketing season, oyster merchants in New York City sent agents to Raritan Bay to buy oysters from various planters. They cruised the bay in vessels, examining oysters from individual beds. Planters also carried their oysters to New York City markets in their sloops for agents to sample; they sold them to the highest bidders (Ingersoll 1881).

Before 1860, the regular produce markets in Manhattan, especially Catherine Market, handled all the oysters. Afterward, the oyster dealers, numbering more than twenty, conducted their business mostly at two other centers. One was at the foot of West Tenth Street on the Hudson River, the other at the foot of Broome Street on the East River, nearly opposite. In addition, a few firms handled oysters at Fulton Market, also on the East River.

All the dealers sold their oysters from barges. These were flat-bottomed, two-storied, extremely durable boats, about seventy-five feet long and twenty-four feet wide; depth of their hold was six feet, height of their main room was eleven feet, and height of their attic room was nine feet. Except for their flat roofs, they resembled the Noah's Ark of Sunday-school picture books. The main room was where workers shucked and stored oysters and the manager transacted the business. The attic room was a storage area for barrels and baskets (Ingersoll 1881). Barges were securely moored side by side to the wharves and were generally permanent, although they could be moved by towboats. The dockage rent for each was $1.90 per day ("Report of the superintendent," 1907). They rose and fell with the tides, and since they always maintained the

17. Sloops unloading oysters at oyster barges, foot of West Tenth Street, Hudson River, New York City. From Ernest Ingersoll, "The Oyster-Industry," in The History and Present Condition of the Fishery Industries, *G. B. Goode, ed. (Washington, D.C.: 1881, U.S. Government Printing Office).*

same level as the oyster boats, they were always favorably situated to have oysters transferred from them. Sometimes the sloops carrying oysters lined up a dozen deep at the sterns of the barges.

Each barge was reached from the wharf by a broad, swinging platform. There were nineteen such barges at West Tenth Street and seven at Fulton Market; the number at Broome Street is unknown. Raritan Bay sloops delivered most of their oysters to the barges at West Tenth Street.

Use of the barges grew out of necessity, as suitable structures on local wharves were scarce. The barges were picturesque and familiar to New York City residents. Their ends, fronting on the street, were decorated attractively. A sign, usually extending across their entire front at the top, denoted the name of the company, and a flag flew just behind it ("Report of the superintendent," 1907).

Workers, known as carriers, laid planks between the boats and carried baskets of oysters from them to the barges. There were twenty-five to forty oyster carriers on each river. They earned ten cents for each thousand oysters carried, giving them twenty-five to thirty dollars a week (*Red Bank Register,* 15 October 1890). The twenty-six barges employed a total of about one thousand men as shuckers, and each barge could handle about seven hundred bushels of oysters a day. The shuckers earned a dollar for every thousand oysters they opened, and each could open from three thousand to seven thousand a day (*New York Times,* 2 September 1894).

Beginning in the 1880s, when the railroad companies developed

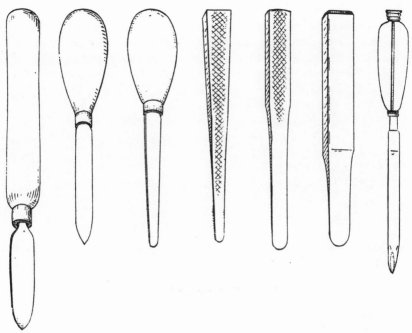

18. *Oyster knives used in various regions, from Ernest Ingersoll, "The Oyster-Industry," in* The History and Present Condition of the Fishery Industries, *G. B. Goode, ed. (Washington, D.C.: U.S. Government Printing Office, 1881).*

refrigerated cars, dealers shipped the oyster meats to western states by rail every day; about forty thousand gallons of shucked meats went from New York City to those states (*New York Times*, 2 September 1894). The refrigerated cars eventually led to the decline of the oyster industry along the Atlantic coast, however, because they made it possible to ship large quantities of chilled beef and pork from Chicago and Kansas City to eastern U.S. cities (Walsh 1982) and satisfy the need people had for protein. With a choice of meat and oysters available, consumers preferred the meat, and, since then, the demand for oysters has declined (*The Fishing Gazette*, 19 November 1898).

Some of the oysters were simply transferred through the barges unshucked for delivery by horse and wagon to New York City stalls, saloons, and hotels. These establishments, which served oysters raw, stewed, fried, or roasted, numbered in the thousands (*New York Times*, 5 May 1872). Each had its own shuckers. One type of stall was described this way:

> All along the East River are places, rude huts, paralytic shanties, where oysters are sold at a penny apiece. You can

stand on the outside and fish them up from the shells that are passed through the window to a ledge, or you can go in and have a 10-cent stew behind the red-hot stove. A man with a checked jumper on attends you and juggles the porter bottles containing catsup in so artistic a manner, that the thought of his being a base-ball player minus a position, will not be "put out." The frequenters of these *al fresco* oyster-houses are longshoremen, truckmen, stevedores, sailors, and others of that ilk, and a very large bowl of oyster soup, not stew, can be obtained for 5 cents. (Ingersoll 1881)

When the oysters were generally out of season in the warmer months, the barges bought hard clams from various bays, including Raritan Bay. The barges handled about a fifth as many bushels of hard clams as oysters ("Report of the shellfish commission," 1901).

During this period, the oyster industry in Raritan Bay was prospering and was a large employer. The number of Staten Islanders working as oystermen in the bay, the Arthur Kill, and Newark Bay was about 1,000 (MacKenzie 1984). Perth Amboy had 220 oystermen (Hall 1894), Keyport had 112 (23 planters with 89 employees) in the 1880s (Hall 1894) and 250 in 1914 (*Red Bank Register,* 23 December 1914), and about 100 men from Elizabethport tonged seed oysters in Newark Bay (Hall 1894). As noted, workers were most active on the Raritan Bay beds during the September to early January marketing season, somewhat less during the spring planting season, even less during the summer, and were inactive from early January until late February. Planters employed their men about six months each year (Hall 1894). Many of the Keyport men using sloops dredged blue crabs during January and February; along with many Perth Amboy and Staten Island men, they raked and dredged hard clams in the bay during the summer.

Most seed for Raritan Bay beds came from Chesapeake Bay, but some was also imported from the Arthur Kill, Newark Bay, Raritan River, and other local areas. The Arthur Kill seedbed extended for eight miles and was almost continuous; in the late 1800s, it was a never-failing supply of seed oysters ("Report of the shellfish commission," 1897) producing 50,000 bushels in some years. As in the other areas, the seed in the kill was attached to shells, but near the edge of the channel it was also on coal cinders dumped by steamships traveling between Perth Amboy and New York City. Tongers in Newark Bay worked about seven months each year. In 1881 seed production from the bay was 175,000 bushels; in 1882 it was only about 70,000 bushels (Hall 1894). New Jersey authorities believed that production was declining and blamed the tongers because they did not return shells to the bottom as cultch for

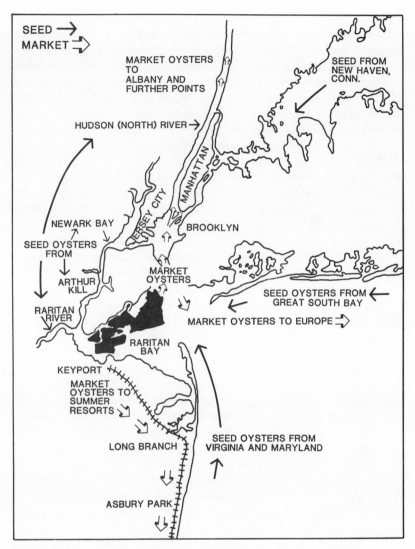

SEED →
MARKET ⇉

MARKET OYSTERS
TO
ALBANY AND
FURTHER POINTS

SEED FROM
NEW HAVEN,
CONN.

HUDSON (NORTH) RIVER →

MANHATTAN

JERSEY CITY

NEWARK BAY

BROOKLYN

SEED OYSTERS
FROM

ARTHUR
KILL

MARKET
OYSTERS

RARITAN
RIVER

SEED OYSTERS FROM ←
GREAT SOUTH BAY

MARKET OYSTERS TO EUROPE ⇉

RARITAN
BAY

KEYPORT

MARKET
OYSTERS TO
SUMMER
RESORTS

LONG BRANCH

SEED OYSTERS FROM
VIRGINIA AND MARYLAND

ASBURY PARK

19. Map of Raritan Bay and surrounding region. Black areas in bay depict location of oyster beds, from about 1830s to early 1920s. Single arrows show routes of seed oysters for planting in the bay. Double arrows show routes where market oysters from bay were shipped. A railroad line ran from Keyport to Long Branch and south along shore. Author's collection.

oyster larvae. In the 1870s and 1880s, annual production of seed oysters for Raritan Bay grounds averaged about 20,000 bushels from the Rahway River, 65,000 bushels from the Raritan River (where fifty men tonged seed), and 2,000 bushels from Cheesequake Creek (Lockwood

1883), besides the production from the Arthur Kill and Newark Bay. The total quantity being imported from Chesapeake Bay and local areas each spring ranged from 300,000 to 400,000 bushels a year.

Tongers living in local communities such as Elizabethport, Chelsea, and Sandy Ground (Rossville) rowed out to nearby beds to gather seed. Many hired boys, some as young as eight, for fifty cents a day to separate seed from shells and cinders. Each tonger gathered about twenty bushels of seed a day (Interview, William Pedro, 15 December 1985).

Sloops from Raritan Bay anchored in the local channels to purchase the seed. They were manned by a captain and a crew of four to six men, who loaded them and later shoveled the seed over their leases in the bay. B. J. Joline, a local historian of Tottenville, wrote the following anecdote about a sloop purchasing seed and planting it in Raritan Bay around 1900:

> My father owned a smart little sloop called the *Josephine* and, when I was a lad, I used to accompany him on some of his buying trips to Newark Bay. The custom, after the anchor was dropped, was to hoist an empty oyster basket to the masthead. This immediately attracted a noisy flotilla of small boats, each boat carrying from five to twenty bushels of so-called seed oysters. The small boats fastened themselves to both sides of the sloop, and often trailed a quarter of a mile astern. As there was no uniformity in the quality of the catch, each "jag" had to be appraised separately, causing much bickering and acrimonious bargaining. My job was to stand in the cabin-way, keep tally as each bushel was dumped on the deck, and handle the pay-off. The cash was safely kept below in the cabin locker. Our deck could carry four to five hundred bushels of seed. When we finished buying, our signal basket was lowered, and we broke anchor. Next morning, the load was taken out to Prince's Bay and planted. (Joline 1950)

For a number of years, some seed from Newark Bay and the Raritan River was transplanted to San Francisco Bay for growth and marketing (Ingersoll 1887; "Report of the shellfish commission," 1897). The railway cars carrying it had double walls to maintain a cool temperature. The freight charge was ten dollars a bushel. Any seed from the Raritan River was extremely small, and a barrel held 3,000 to 5,000 (Ingersoll 1881). In 1901, the J. and J. W. Elsworth Company, the largest planter in the bay, shipped 110 carloads of Newark Bay seed to San Francisco Bay. Nine days after the seed left Newark Bay, workers spread it over beds in

San Francisco Bay. About a year and a half later, those oysters had grown and fattened enough to be marketed. Townsend (1896) noted that Newark Bay seed also went to Willapa Bay, Washington, for planting.

The Civil War had a major effect on the Raritan Bay oyster industry because it prevented planters from obtaining seed from Chesapeake Bay. In addition, the supply of market oysters coming directly from Chesapeake Bay to New York City was curtailed. At the beginning of the war, Raritan Bay planters prospered, nonetheless, because their beds were nearly full of oysters and, lacking the Chesapeake supply, the New York merchants doubled their purchase price for oysters (Ingersoll 1881).

Early in the war, some Staten Island vessels ventured to Virginia to obtain seed but ran into various kinds of trouble, as this Staten Island newspaper report describes:

> Our boatmen on the north and south side of the island are not only sadly injured, but some are entirely ruined by the course pursued upon by the people of Virginia. Some schooners and sloops belonging here have been seized in the southern waters and appropriated, and the captains and crews imprisoned.
>
> We learned of an instance where a party waited upon the captain of a schooner, and informed him that he must leave in 20 minutes. He prepared to sail before the end of the time fixed, but his visitors meanwhile entered his cabin, and took about $300 in gold and silver, his tea, sugar, and other groceries, leaving him only some biscuits.
>
> A schooner, commanded by Richard Decker of Northfield, arrived on Thursday. He reports that while catching in Back River, Virginia, he observed that he was watched during the day by men with muskets on both sides of the river. He continued work, however, and had taken about 500 bushels, when he was waited upon by some persons from the shore, and requested to leave. He remarked that he could not do so without ballast, and proposed using oysters for that purpose. To this the leader of the gang ashore assented, and he proceeded with his labors, but shortly after, seeing some very suspicious movements on shore, he hoisted sail and came away as fast as possible.
>
> Capt'n Nicholas Bush, who has all his lifetime been engaged in the oyster business, reached here on Friday from Virginia, leaving a sloop and a schooner behind. He went down to look after his interests there, but was obliged to leave without arranging his affairs. He has between two and three

thousand dollars worth of oysters on the shore of the York River, which he will probably never be able to remove. He was a passenger on the sloop Arietta.

The schooner *Commander in Chief* belonging to Cap't Abraham Latourette, of Westfield, was sunk in the Southern waters last week.

The Virginians on the seacoast were almost entirely dependent for support in the trade in oysters with our northern men, and by driving them away, they have only bitten off their own noses. Thousands upon thousands of dollars in gold and silver coin were annually taken south from our island and used in the purchase of oysters.

The *Sherwood,* a schooner from Back River, Virginia, came north on Wednesday, with oysters for Mr. Analey Bedell, and was ordered to remain at her anchorage at Mariners' Harbor, until the authorities gave their consent to her departure. Several men in the vicinity of Mariners' Harbor, it is said, formed a plan of destroying the vessel in order that the Southerners would be "paid off in their own coin." But we are glad to learn that better counsels prevailed, and that the majority of our citizens are satisfied that the misdeeds of others can never justify them violating the law. (*Richmond County Gazette*, 18 December 1861)

Several Staten Island oystermen sent a letter to President Lincoln, and they also visited congressmen in Washington to explain how the war was interrupting their business and to ask for government assistance in obtaining seed. They wanted the federal government to supply troops to protect them when they sent down for oysters. They were willing to provide some schooners, skiffs, tongs, and extra men to gather the oysters themselves. They had heard that President Lincoln was not fond of oysters, however, and thus did not anticipate that their movement would be successful. It was not (*Richmond County Gazette*, 18 December 1861).

During the Civil War, the planters had to obtain all their seed from northern areas, including Connecticut and Great South Bay on Long Island. Following the war, the importation of seed from Chesapeake Bay resumed, and about three-fourths of the seed came from there (*Keyport Weekly,* 12 July 1879). For example, the beds on the New Jersey side of the bay received fifty schooner loads of Chesapeake oysters, about 135,000 bushels, in 1896 (*Keyport Weekly,* May 1896, date unknown).

While the oysters were growing on Raritan Bay leased beds, they were subject to theft by some of the poorer leaseholders, who, at night, dredged oysters off well-stocked beds and planted them on their own beds or they took them to New York City and sold them. Most "pirates" did not steal from beds in their own state but did so in the other state, where they would not be as easily recognized. A typical newspaper article in the late 1800s about such thefts noted:

> Another outbreak of the wars between Staten Islanders and Jerseymen over the oyster question took place on Wednesday last. Certain oystermen from Keyport trespassed on the planted beds belonging to the residents of Prince's Bay and began to dredge for oysters. The owners of these beds applied to the authorities of the county for protection. On Wednesday, Sheriff Brown and his deputies, the town constables of Westfield, and Captain Blake with a force of Richmond County police proceeded to the spot and found the New Jerseymen working on the middle ground in Prince's Bay in small sloops. Several vessels were captured and some of the crew were conducted before Justice Halle. The captain of one of the vessels— *Leonard*—was sentenced to pay a fine of fifty dollars and imprisoned for fifty-nine days. Others were also fined and arrested. (*Richmond County Sentinel,* 2 March 1878)

Poor people also stole some oysters from leases close to shore to eat at home. When tides were especially low, they could wade out to them and rake up oysters. This was debatable territory, however: were they in a public area, which meant the oysters were free for the taking, or were they in leases? Planters found it prudent not to contest these thefts, preferring to concentrate their efforts on stopping the oyster pirates who could dredge large quantities of oysters from their other leases (Ingersoll 1881).

In 1882 the oyster planters in Keyport formed a voluntary protective association to provide a collective means of policing the beds from oyster pirates. The association maintained at least one watch boat on the beds every night to scare off pirates (McCay 1984).

Another type of conflict regarding the leasing involved the hard clam diggers, who had developed rakes in the 1860s to gather clams in water ranging from about six to twenty-two feet deep. The diggers claimed that bottoms with clams, especially on the New York side of the bay, were being leased to the oystermen. The courts gave the clammers permission to remove clams from the leased grounds with the proviso that they leave the oysters there. This led to many infractions, however, and frequent arrests. Such incidents occurred as late as 1919 (*Red Bank Register,* 24 September 1919). The state of New Jersey had left most of its bottom, some 28,840 acres, for the clammers, even though much of it would have been good for growing oysters (Hall 1894).

In the 1880s oyster planters also objected to the operations of the purse seiners, who sought bunkers in all parts of the bay, including the sites of the oyster beds. Oystermen protested that the nets could disturb their oysters, because they reached the bottom when set and dragged along it when their bottoms were pursed. Moreover, sport fishermen charged that purse seiners depleted the bay of bunkers, a food of the bluefish and weakfish they caught. As a result, authorities temporarily prohibited purse seining for bunkers in New York waters of the bay (*New York Times,* 30 June 1886).

Perth Amboy had a slightly separate oyster industry. Oyster planting had begun there about 1840, sometime after the Great Beds had been depleted. Its grounds comprised about three hundred acres, lying off Ferry Point on the southern tip of the town and extending for about a mile toward Great Beds lighthouse. Average depth of water over the beds was about five feet. There were fourteen planters, each of whom had five or more leases, each five to ten acres in size. The planters owned a fleet of fourteen sloops and schooners and seventy-four tonging skiffs. Natural beds in the Raritan River supplied 80 percent of their seed ("Report of the shellfish commission," 1901); the remainder was from the Arthur Kill and Connecticut. When planters spread seed on leases, they left it undisturbed for about three years and then for its final season shifted it to their hardest bottom. There it grew into the desirable oval shape with a heavier shell. Two firms in Perth Amboy employed about sixty men for opening the oysters. In the 1870s, they sold thirty thousand gallons of shucked meats (equal to forty thousand bushels of shell stock) annually. The firms hired boys as young as ten to do light tasks such as sorting oysters (Lockwood 1883).

The original takeover of the Perth Amboy beds by leaseholders had been hotly contested earlier by poor oystermen without leases. These beds had contained oysters, which these commoners tonged for part of their livelihoods. Periodically, the commoners stole oysters from the leases (McCay 1984).

Each planter of Keyport had between six thousand and ten thousand bushels of oysters to sell each year (*Keyport Weekly,* May 1896, date unknown). The planters hired workers using tongs in skiffs to harvest most of them. On the deepest beds, under eighteen to twenty-two feet of water, workers also harvested them with hard clam rakes. The men rowed their skiffs to nearby beds, but sloops towed several at a time to distant beds. A typical man got about twenty bushels of oysters a day. Sometimes, he was paid 12½ cents a bushel for harvesting them (Ingersoll 1881), or else he was paid by the day. If he owned his boat and

20. *Tonging oysters for market at Round Shoal, Prince's Bay, from the* Illustrated News. *16 July 1853. Courtesy of the Staten Island Historical Society, Richmondtown Restoration, Staten Island, New York.*

tongs, he received $2.50 a day; if the planter supplied them, he received $2 a day (Hall 1894). Workers got some hard clams and conchs (whelks) with the oysters and were allowed to sell or keep them.

When oysters became scarce, planters with large beds hired sloops to dredge them, paying the vessels and their crews seven dollars a day (Hall 1894). Tonging was hard work for the men, but dredging was harder because the dredges were hauled up by hand, one-bushel dredges by one man, three-bushel dredges by three men. Eventually, crews fitted some sloops with hand winders for hauling the dredges to ease the work. But winding was slow, and thus some planters did not permit the devices on their sloops (Ingersoll 1887).

Western Raritan Bay was a scene of great activity when oysters were being harvested, as Ingersoll described:

> Almost innumerable crafts, with trim sails, crowd the bay on working days. The sailboats [sloops] used here are of good build, and often cost $3,000, while an unusually good quality of clinker-built, shallow-draft keel-boats, called skiffs, worth from $75 to $125 are used. A third sort of boat is flat-bottomed and straight-sided; this is known as a bateau, and costs $15 to $30. Two skiffs and a bateau may be counted for every regular oyster-sloop or cat-boat. These craft harvested oysters amidst a forest of stakes which were so numerous they were difficult to sail through. (1881)

After the hired tongers had nearly finished harvesting from small beds, scattered oysters remained on them. The planters then allowed

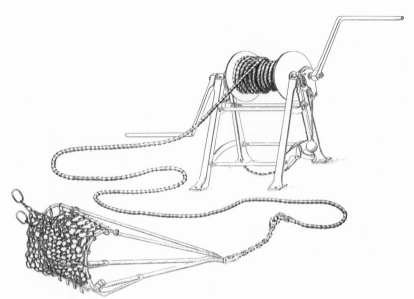

21. *Oyster dredge with hand winder. From Ernest Ingersoll, "The Oyster-Industry," in* The History and Present Condition of the Fishery Industries, *G. B. Goode, ed. (Washington, D.C.: U.S. Government Printing Office, 1881).*

these tongers to harvest the remainder and keep half of the oysters for themselves. While doing this, each man earned four to five dollars a day, a handsome wage in those years. Ingersoll commented "The principal of the good old biblical rule of not forgetting the gleaners is almost religiously observed in the last gathering of this harvest from the sea" (1887).

Before being taken to New York City, all the oysters had to be given "a drink" in brackish water. As noted, many sites were used for doing this, including the Hackensack River (by Snake Hill), Passaic River, the flats off Mariners' Harbor, the Rahway River, Mill and Lemon creeks on Staten Island, and Luppatatong Creek in Keyport. The Keyport planters had divided the shallow mouth of Luppatatong Creek into lots. They subdivided those into small squares by rows of stakes for holding different sizes of oysters. When workers brought in the oysters from the beds, they culled and graded them by size and shoveled them into the lots (Ingersoll 1881).

In 1865, George Thompson, an oyster leaseholder from Staten Island, developed wooden floats for "drinking" oysters. The floats measured twenty-five to thirty-five feet long, about twenty feet wide, and fourteen to fifteen inches deep (Powell 1976). Spreading oysters in these was much more efficient than spreading them on the bottom, because no oysters were lost and the work was easier. The number of floats used is known only for Lemon Creek; in the late 1800s, it had about twenty. Since oysters in the floats were always accessible, even at high tide, thieves occasionally stole from them at night, taking several bushels each time (*New York Times*, 2 August 1872).

Nearly the entire fleet of sloops in Raritan Bay carried oysters to New York City on the opening day of the oyster season, as the *New York Times* described in 1894:

> Fifty-two sloops returned yesterday from the oyster beds off Prince's Bay and Keyport. The sloops were heavily loaded with about 500 bushels of oysters each. They came into the North River at the break of day and made port at the oyster market, foot of West Tenth, Charles and Perry streets. With their arrival, hundreds of men were at work shucking oysters at the oyster barges moored along the shore. The shuckers sat in long lines and sang or whistled merrily as they worked. They placed the shucked oysters into a pail of clean water and the empty shells were dropped into a basket. As the baskets were filled, they were carried outside and emptied onto trucks waiting to cart them away. (2 September 1894)

When delivering oysters to the barges, the sloops got into trouble if the wind stopped. Head Captain Bill Wooley of the J. and J. W. Elsworth Company in Keyport told this story about such a time:

> I was taking a load of oysters to the market in a sloop. When I got nearly opposite the market, the wind died out and the water current carried us into a ferry slip and marooned us there. Before long, a ferry loaded with passengers from New Jersey came to get into the slip. The ferry captain upon seeing us, opened his cabin window, and began yelling at us to get out of there. I wanted to, but we were helpless with no power. My crew of four men were all young roughnecks. So, I said to them, "Tell him something, boys!" They went over to the rail and began yelling back all sort of obscenities. The ferry captain slammed down his window and left us alone. We finally got out about an hour later! (Interview, J. Richards Nelson, 10 March 1985)

Crews on the sloops had to count every oyster, because they were sold by the thousand. During the 1880s, wholesale prices of Raritan Bay

22. *Composite of oystering around Raritan Bay, showing tonging from ice and a boat (upper), shucking oysters in New York City (middle), and schooners delivering oysters to oyster barges in New York City (bottom); also, oyster shell with many small spat, oyster knives, tongs, dredge, drumfish, starfish, and oyster larvae.* From *Harper's Weekly, 16 September 1882.*

oysters were $15 to $25 per thousand for the largest ones, $7 to $10 per thousand for the slightly smaller box oysters, $3.50 to $5.00 per thousand for cullens, and 50 cents a bushel for the smallest (Ingersoll 1881). Considered by volume, cullens oysters, a common size, would sell for 80 cents to a dollar a bushel.

In addition, in the summer, Keyport planters shipped small quantities of oysters by rail to Long Branch, Ocean Grove, Ocean Beach, and other resorts along the New Jersey coast for sale to summer vacationers, who ate them on the half shell (Ingersoll 1881). Those oysters were originally from Virginia and remained fat enough to be eaten in summer.

The oyster industry in Keyport began to develop more around the turn of the century out of necessity: the various shipping interests in New York City had been claiming some of the waterfront being occupied by the oyster barges, and space for them dwindled. In 1899, the Elsworth company, whose main office was in New York City, erected a branch

23. *In the 1800s and early 1900s, oysters were sold by the thousand. Crew is shown here counting oysters on deck of their sloop. From* Fishing Gazette, *15, no. 42, 15 October 1898.*

office and plant alongside Luppatatong Creek to shuck oysters. It measured ninety feet long and forty-four feet wide and employed about forty-three shuckers; some were local and some were imported from southern states for the seasonal work. The company shucked its own oysters along with those of some smaller planters and, during the season of 1910–11, the plant shucked 101,000 gallons of oyster meats from 160,000 bushels of oysters (*Keyport Weekly,* 28 April 1911).

In the early 1900s, oyster beds in the New York waters of Raritan Bay were divided into 117 holdings, comprising 755 leased lots, which ranged in size from 2/10 acre to 95 6/10 acres, and totaled 1,554 acres. The mean size of lots was about 5 1/2 acres ("Report of the Superintendent of Marine Fisheries," 1911). The lots now rented for 25 cents per acre per year (State of New York 1896). Oyster beds in New Jersey waters were divided into eighteen holdings of which only five were under 10 acres; the others ranged from 18 to 328 acres (McCay 1984). The Elsworth company was the largest planter, leasing 868 acres of bottom; it also had oyster beds on Long Island and in Connecticut. The company

24. Oyster workers employed by the J. and J. W. Elsworth Company, Keyport, circa 1910. Courtesy of the Monmouth County Historical Association.

was obtaining most of its seed oysters from its beds in Connecticut, while the smaller planters were purchasing several schooner loads of seed oysters from Virginia each year. Around 1900, planters marketed about 350,000 bushels of oysters a year from New York beds (State of New York 1896) and 275,415 bushels from New Jersey beds in the bay (*Keyport Weekly,* 8 May 1904).

The Elsworth company also had an oyster packinghouse in Lemon Creek for shipping oysters to Europe. In the late 1800s, annual production from that packinghouse was eighty thousand bushels of oysters and five thousand bushels of hard clams (*Richmond County Gazette,* 23 January 1881). Elsworth's motor-powered oyster boats could not enter or leave the creek at low tide. If the tide was low at the end of the day, the boats had to anchor off the mouth of the creek; the crews rowed tender boats to get ashore.

To protect its oysters from theft, the Elsworth company had two watch boats anchored on the beds all night, one off Keyport and another off Prince's Bay. The watchmen often did some fishing to supplement their food supply. They slept on the boats in creeks during the day (Interview, Harold Moody, 15 December 1985).

25. *Packing oyster meats at the J. and J. W. Elsworth plant in Keyport, New Jersey. Cans of oysters were placed in wooden tubs which were filled with ice, they were sealed and then shipped, circa 1920. Courtesy of Steamboat Dock Museum, Keyport, New Jersey.*

Installation of Engines in Sloops

Raritan Bay planters converted the oyster sloops, one by one, from sail to engine power. By 1905, the planters had twelve engine-powered

26. *Lime kiln (right foreground) in Matawan, New Jersey, circa 1910. Shells were carried by barge from Keyport to dock on Matawan River (left background) and are being carried by horse-drawn dump wagons from the barge to the kiln. Courtesy of the Monmouth County Historical Association.*

vessels, eighteen sailing vessels, and forty-four tonging skiffs for their oystering (Wood 1906). Ten of the engine-powered boats belonged to the Elsworth company, which had given most the names of military titles, such as *Admiral, Captain, Commander, Commodore, General, Lieutenant,* and *Sergeant.* Though many people regretted the change from sail power, the development of motor-powered boats brought a great saving in time and money in handling oysters, as more trips could be made and larger loads could be carried ("Report of the Superintendent of shellfisheries," 1905). Engine-powered boats harvested oysters using eight-bushel dredges that were retrieved using engine power. A good catch for a dredge boat in a day was nine hundred to one thousand bushels. Only the small planters continued to harvest their oysters with tongs.

The oyster business brought a considerable amount of money to Prince's Bay, Tottenville, Perth Amboy, and especially Keyport. For instance, in the 1903–04 season, the 275,415 bushels marketed by the Elsworth company sold for $239,731. The seed had been purchased for $80,672, and wages paid to 256 men employed in planting the seed and 164 men in marketing them totaled $51,757 (*Keyport Weekly,* 8 May

27. *Dredging boat loaded with market oysters at Keyport, New Jersey, circa 1915. Courtesy of Mary Demlin.*

28. *Oyster dredge boat, circa 1916, used in Raritan Bay from about 1912 to 1925; its port was Keyport. Courtesy of the Monmouth County Historical Association.*

1904). The payroll of the company sometimes amounted to a few thousand dollars weekly, so the grocers and other merchants of Keyport received much benefit and at a time the farmers termed, "twixt hay and grass" (*Red Bank Register,* 23 December 1914). The oyster planters made a comfortable living but did not accumulate substantial sums of money to pass along to their children.

Hard Clamming

Fishermen did not know much about the abundance of hard clams in bottoms beyond wading depths until 1863, when George Eldridge, a retired whaler living in Highlands, developed the hand rake. This was a metal rake about thirty inches wide with about thirty curved teeth, spaced about three-fourths of an inch apart. It was attached to a wooden handle perhaps twenty feet long. Eldridge took his rake out in a rowboat and gathered far more clams than anyone had using short-handle rakes while wading in the shallows. For a week or two, he kept his rake and finds of clams a secret by raking at night, but others observed his large landings, had some rakes made by the local blacksmith, attached handles to them, and joined him. Several weeks later, some fishermen from Staten Island heard about the clams and the new rakes, had their own constructed, and ventured to New Jersey in their boats to rake them also. When the New Jersey fishermen tried to drive off the intruders, fights followed, and they called upon the local sheriff to help them defend their territory (Leonard 1923).

Fishermen used the hand rakes mostly during the spring, summer, and fall. They either rowed their bateaux to and from the beds, some of which were as far as two miles from the ports, or they paid catboats or sloops a small fee to tow them. The sailboats could each tow several bateaux at a time.

When they got to a clam bed, the fishermen began raking off the side or stern of their bateaux. With each jerk, they moved their rakes about two inches through the bottom, and they could feel and hear the clams collecting and rattling in them: "It's the kind of music we likes to hear," a fisherman said in the 1880s (Kobbe 1982). After pulling the rakes through the bottom about six feet, the fishermen had to empty them. They braced their knees against the side of the boat and hauled them up hand over hand, turning them 180 degrees as they did, to retain the clams.

When the rakes reached the surface, the fishermen pushed them back and forth to wash any mud off the clams, then picked them out and

29. *Hard clam hand rakes, shanty, and barrels on bayshore, circa 1870s. Illustration from archives of Sandy Hook Laboratory, Northeast Fisheries Center, National Marine Fisheries Service, Highlands, New Jersey.*

put them in separate half-bushel baskets according to the three size categories. Finally, they tossed out any empty shells and grass. When they filled the baskets, they dumped the clams into potato or onion sacks holding a bushel. They spent about two-thirds of their time raking and a third on the other steps. After fifteen to twenty rakings, the fishermen had usually drifted out of a clam bed and rowed back to about where they began.

Wind and water currents were important to hand raking. Winds of ten to fifteen knots were ideal because they kept the boats moving as the fishermen raked. During days when winds were around twenty knots, rakers put out an anchor tied to about two hundred feet of rope. They began with the rope short and let it slip under their feet as they raked. They could guide the direction of drift of their bateaux somewhat by putting the rope near the bow or stern. If a light wind blew against the current, raking was difficult because fishermen had to push their boats away from their rakes, and then they could jerk only about three times before they had to push back again. Strong winds much above twenty knots, usually blowing from the south on summer afternoons, made the water rough and forced the hand rakers to quit.

In rare winters when the bay froze over, fishermen cut holes in the ice to dig hard clams with their hand rakes. They carried the clams ashore in horse-drawn wagons in the late 1800s and early 1900s and in Model T Fords a few years later.

Within a few years after Eldridge had introduced the hand rake, fishermen designed a modification of it, the sail dredge. It was actually a rake similar to a hand rake, but slightly wider—forty inches—and its wooden handle was only about five feet long and two inches square. The teeth were spaced an inch apart, or about a quarter-inch more than that of a hand rake, to allow mud to pass through them easily. A rake full of mud did not collect clams and was heavy to retrieve. Fishermen used ropes about half an inch in diameter to tow them; thinner ropes hurt their hands when they retrieved them. The rakes were towed from catboats, sloops, and a few small schooners, and attached only on their windward sides. The length of rope between the boats and rakes ranged from forty-five to seventy-five feet; the ratio of rope length to water depth was about three to one. Most boats towed four dredges, but schooners towed six. Usually, boats with four dredges had two men in their crew; those with six dredges had a three-man crew. Keyport, Belford, and Highlands were the three main ports for the sail-clamming vessels as well as for the hand rakers. Sail dredging for hard clams is believed to have been unique to Raritan Bay.

The first description of sail dredging was in an 1875 letter written to Ernest Ingersoll:

They go after hard-shelled clams from Keyport in squatty, one-sailed vessels, called "cats" dragging clam-rakes, which are thrown out and drawn by the wind. The ground extends in Raritan Bay from Sandy Hook to South Amboy. A good day's catch would be from three to three-and-a-half barrels [nine to ten bushels]. The man who owns his boat and sells stock by the ten or twenty thousand at wholesale is sort of an aristocrat compared to those [diggers of soft clams] who go down to the shore daily, with a basket, get their somewhat precarious catch, take it home on their backs, open the bivalves, and then peddle the result in a can with a quart measure in the other hand. (Ingersoll 1887)

Sail dredgers worked in the middle and the southeastern end of the bay, in fifteen to twenty-five feet of water. The dredging area, from Union Beach to Sandy Hook, was about eight miles long; it increased from about half a mile wide opposite Union Beach to about two miles wide near Sandy Hook. The entire bottom was muddy, so the teeth of the rakes could be pulled through it. The dredges could not remove the clams from hard sand bottoms. In fact, dredgers had to be careful to avoid sand bottoms, because the teeth of the rakes would be bent outward and then need to be repaired by a blacksmith.

Fishermen positioned their boats nearly sideward to the wind when dredging, with the dredges tied along the windward side. They adjusted the sails to make the boats go faster or slower or, to maintain them on a bed of clams, forward or backward. The captain at the stern trimmed the "sheet" (mainsail), while his mate at the bow adjusted the jib. If the wind lessened, the mate pulled up the jib to put more wind in the sheet. If the boat traveled too fast, the dredges would not dig into the bottom, so the jib had to be lowered. If the crew wanted the sloop to fall backward, the captain let the sheet off all the way. To back off more, he let the peak drop. To go ahead, the mate let the jib out. If the wind came up strongly, the crew dropped both sails because the wind blowing against the hull was sufficient. Crews did not use the same side of the boat every day. Instead, they used the side that was best suited to the wind and current conditions each day.

When the wind was light, fishermen could tow only two dredges; if more were towed, the vessel would stop or move so slowly that the dredges would fill with mud and not catch clams. As the wind picked up, the men added the third dredge and finally the fourth (Interview, Louie Egnatovich, 14 February 1986).

A typical drift was one to two miles long and lasted about an hour, but these lengths varied by the size of the clam bed and the wind speed.

At the end of a drift, the captain sailed the boat back to the upwind end of the clam bed. In a day, boats might make as many as twenty drifts over the smallest beds or as few as two if extraordinarily long drifts over large beds were made. As a boat drifted, it pitched and rolled, pulling the rakes slowly and then quickly through the bottom, keeping the mud passing through. Since catboats and small sloops had more of the pitching and rolling motion, they were more efficient than large sloops and schooners for sail dredging. On days when a boat did not pitch and roll, the dredges filled with mud more often and were heavy when retrieved, tiring the clammers.

The two men spent most of their time pulling the dredges. Each pulled two. The men retrieved the two outside dredges together, then the two inside dredges together, back to the two outside dredges, and so forth during the drift. If dredges were retrieved differently, the vessel would go off line. If a dredge caught a horseshoe crab or a piece of sunken wood on its teeth, it sledded over the bottom and did not get any more clams. The worst area for hang-ups was in the southeastern part of the bay, which had accumulated so much sunken wood that the fishermen referred to it as "the lumberyard."

When a fisherman got a dredge to the surface, he took hold of its handle, shook it in the water to remove the mud from the clams, took out the clams, and then tossed it back, teeth down. A typical number of clams in a dredge was about twelve. If he got about that many, he began to pull in the other dredge immediately; if he got fewer, he waited a few moments. Sail dredgers got few littlenecks because the spacing of the teeth on their dredges was too wide to retain them.

At times, the wind was too light for the fishermen to sail. This was common in summer mornings; a lack of wind could last all day and even several consecutive days, particularly in August. The boats would move when the current ran with a light wind, but they would remain nearly stationary when a light wind and current were in opposite directions. When idle and waiting for some wind, fishermen tied their sloops together in groups of two to five and socialized; some played musical instruments to pass the time. A hazard for these becalmed fishermen were flies that accumulated on their boats and bit them: "We'd have to swat flies all the time. There were black and green-head flies and they'd both bite," said Lloyd Cottrell when he was interviewed in 1989. If a southeast breeze came up in the early afternoon, it blew them away and the clammers could dredge again (Interview, 9 September).

Eventually, about 150 fishermen earned a part of their livelihood hand raking and sail dredging, and by the 1890s Belford, the principal port, had about 100 boats for hard clamming. The boats included bateaux for hand raking and catboats, cabin sloops, and a couple of schooners for sail dredging (*Red Bank Register,* 23 March 1898).

Although it provided much employment, hand raking and sail dredging involved the hardest work of any type of fishery in Raritan Bay, and fishermen were nearly exhausted at the end of each day; their hands and forearms were especially tired. After pulling rakes for a few years, the clammers developed large, muscular builds, and the skin on their palms was as thick as cowhide (Interview, Jigs Apel, 11 March 1986).

There were hazards, as well. In 1886, sharks attacked two men digging hard clams with scratch rakes off Highlands. The men saw three sharks, each about ten feet long, and they jumped in their boat. The sharks bumped it. The men pelted them with hard clams and tried to pierce their thick skin with their rakes. The sharks became more violent in the attack, and the men, fearing their boat might be overturned, rowed ashore (*Red Bank Register,* 1 September 1886).

In summer, some fishermen treaded hard clams with their bare feet and hands at wading depths. While treading was first documentated in the late 1870s (Ingersoll 1887), it was an ancient practice, probably used by the Lenapes. In the late 1800s, it was most common in Highlands, where some women and girls treaded as well as men and boys (Kobbe 1982). Some treaded barefoot; others wore socks. Probably the technique changed little over the decades. Jimmy White from Highlands, who had treaded commercially in the 1940s and 1950s, described how it was done:

> We treaded when the water got warm. We put our feet close together and parallel, then twisted them as we moved sideward to feel the clams. We picked them up with our hands. There was no rake going that'll catch clams as fast as your hands can. Treading was rough on the feet, as it tore them up and there was no way to avoid it. We used mostly the heel of our feet because that's the hardest part, not our toes because shells in the bottom would cut them off. When we first began in the summer, we felt like we were walking on eggs as we walked down the street. By the end of the summer, our legs felt a foot shorter. The best treading was in water about knee deep. There were fellas here who could catch one thousand to two thousand clams in two hours!

White related that one of the regulars was nicknamed "Chowder Foot" because he treaded mostly chowder clams.

Nearly all the hard clams were sold in New York City, whose

markets sought them during the warm months when oysters were not handled. The city's wholesale and retail trade for hard clams and soft clams was estimated at $600,000 in the 1870s, hard clams being by far the more important of the two. About 100 sailing vessels carried hard clams from various bays to the city, with an average cargo of about 350 bushels. About 20 additional vessels supplied clams to towns on the Hudson (North) River. All 120 of these vessels carried oysters in the winter. The principal clam grounds were in Raritan Bay and Barnegat Bay in New Jersey and Great South Bay, Cow Bay, and Littleneck Bay on Long Island; some clams came from Chesapeake Bay. Fulton Market and Catherine Market in the city were the main depots receiving them. Including everyone, from fishermen to retailers and hawkers, the hard clam trade employed about eight thousand people. The city clam merchants handled other fish products as well and all the oyster merchants sold them (Ingersoll 1887).

The city wholesale dealers conducted their business by entering a contract to supply their customers with a certain quantity of clams at appointed times, with a penalty of one hundred dollars in the case of nonfulfillment. With an order from a wholesaler, a vessel captain sailed for one of the clam grounds, where he purchased the clams from fishermen and returned to the market. There he found the wholesaler with his wagons ready to receive his clams. The wholesaler delivered them to the retailers, who usually purchased the clams, like oysters, by the thousand (Ingersoll 1887).

For at least sixty years, from at least 1878 (Ingersoll 1887) and continuing through the mid-1930s, nearly all the sail dredgers in Raritan Bay sold their clams on the water to buy boats from New York City and other ports such as Newark and Rockaway. The buy boats usually made their purchases on Wednesdays and Fridays.

Customers in the hotels and restaurants in New York City preferred littlenecks to the larger clams (*Fishing Gazette* 1898). Littlenecks and cherrystones were eaten raw on the half shell. The shucker at a raw bar removed the upper shell of the clams with a knife, cut the two muscles from the lower shell, and presented the clam meat in the bottom shell, sometimes with lemon juice or sauce, to the customer.

Many of the steamer clams shipped to New York City were sold to saloons (*Red Bank Register,* 22 April 1896), which provided free soft clams and clam broth along with raw hard clams, meat sandwiches, and stews to lure their drinking patrons. To prepare the clams, bartenders put them in pots with a little water. After being steamed, a potful of clams yielded many cups of broth. It might seem that saloons could not make any money giving away clams and broth while charging only five cents a glass for beer (Interview, Ken Norton, 6 November 1985). A bushel contained about twelve hundred clams, however, and served many patrons.

In the early 1890s, New York City restaurants were pressuring legislators to ban the practice saloons had of serving free lunches, because it was hurting their business. In response, the New York State legislature passed the Raines Bill, which did ban the practice in 1896, and the sales of Raritan Bay clams declined substantially during the only year it remained in effect, as described by the *Red Bank Register:*

> The hard clam trade has not suffered as severely as the soft clam business. Hard clams are not used so extensively as soft clams for free lunches but the trade has felt the effects of the law. Last year at this time John Rickman [a produce dealer] was selling hard clams in New York to the amount of $50 per week; now his weekly sales average only about $30. About one hundred boats are engaged in dredging hard clams in the bay and their owners and sailors are as angry over the Raines Law as the soft clammers. (22 April 1896)

The demand for soft clams fell so much that only about ten men continued digging instead of the usual fifty or so at Belford, and fewer dug in the other areas as well. The demand for both types of clams returned after the law was dropped.

Annual production of hard clams from Raritan Bay in the early 1880s was estimated at about 150,000 bushels, worth $100,000, and in 1897 it was estimated at 200,000 bushels, worth $220,000 (Ingersoll 1887; *Keyport Weekly,* 7 August 1897). Around 1900, Raritan Bay fishermen received about $1.35 a bushel for littlenecks and 80 cents a bushel for chowders (*Keyport Weekly,* 7 August 1897).

Soft Clamming

Ernest Ingersoll described the soft-clam fishery in the bay during the 1870s. According to him, people dug soft clams when the tide left the intertidal flats bare. Strong northwesterly winds combined with full moons produced extra-low tides and exposed more areas for clamming than did ordinary low tides. At these times, hundreds of men and boys dug clams as fast as they could before the tide rose, "not exactly making hay while the sun shines, but clamming while the tide is out" (1887). Each fisherman brought the clams home, where he and his wife and children opened them. Afterward, the fishermen peddled them locally for twelve and a half cents a quart. In Keyport, some clammers picked discarded oysters from shell piles and peddled them also. Soft clams, sold in the shell, brought the diggers forty cents a bushel. The clammers had critically low incomes, lived a life of heavy labor, and had few luxuries and little variation in their lives. The *Red Bank Register* amplified Ingersoll's observations and listed some implements:

> During the warm days last week, while the tides were running low, there were hundreds of men and boys engaged in soft clamming on the flats west of Parkertown [Highlands]. They reaped a rich harvest for these days. Parties were there from as far away as Old Bridge and Cranbury [seven and eighteen miles away]. All sorts of vehicles lined the shore, and the diggers carried spades, corn hoes, pointed shovels, baskets, pails, and wash boilers. (23 December 1885)

Around 1900, the bare flats between Keyport and Belford were about one thousand feet wide on a normal low tide and as much as a mile wide on a "blow-out tide" (*Red Bank Register,* 28 February 1912). Soft clams grew all over the flats, but their abundance varied. Where fishermen dug, the density of market-sized clams (two to three inches long) was usually around fifteen per square foot, but ranged as high as about fifty. Fishermen dug them with a rake, or drag, consisting of four straight tines, each five to eight inches long, and a handle, about twelve inches long, perpendicular to it. Made for digging potatoes, drags originally had five-foot handles. Fishermen used mesh bags made from discarded pound nets or wooden baskets to hold the clams. Fishermen walked onto the flats, stomped to make the clams squirt, and began digging where the clams were most abundant.

In winter farmers joined the fishermen as diggers. Many living near the bayshore earned part of their livelihoods gathering soft clams, hard clams, and oysters and fishing with haul seines and fyke nets. When soft clamming, they arrived at the shore by horse and wagon (later by automobile) and walked out onto the flats to dig. Usually the farmers got only enough clams to make large pots of chowder at home. Winter digging yielded smaller returns for all soft clammers, however, partly because the days were shorter than in the summer; the diggers could not work the early and late tides as they could in the summer. Farmers also obtained clams by trading their produce with the regular diggers. In addition, a number of nonfishermen sometimes enjoyed getting out on the flats to dig soft clams for recreation and a treat of clams to eat when they got home.

The clammers began digging close to shore when the tide was just leaving the flats bare, went farther out as the tide fell, and moved in again when it rose. Most stood bent at the waist while digging; others dug on one knee to ease the strain on their backs. To initiate digging, each one made a hole in the sediment about two feet in diameter and nine inches deep with his drag and then hand-paddled out any water. Next, he reached forward four to six inches on one side of the hole with his drag and pulled the sand into the hole. He then picked out the adult clams in it and put them in his container, leaving behind any small seed clams, most of which were unbroken. Then he pushed away that sand to make another hole, stepped forward several inches, pulled sand into it, and picked out the clams. He kept digging like this in a straight line, forming a "drill" fifty or more feet long, until the clams became scarcer. Then he began another drill where the clam holes were abundant. The clammers had about three hours of good digging before the rising tide forced them to quit.

The quantity of soft clams a fisherman gathered depended on their abundances and size, his ability, and the distance the tide receded. Usually, one person could dig two or three bushels a tide. In freezing air, fishermen usually walked beyond the exposed flats to put soft clams in water so they would not freeze. They found, however, that if a soft clam froze it would survive, but if a hard clam froze it died and could not be sold. The clams had sand on them after they were dug. Diggers had to rinse it off, because otherwise it would get in the meats when the clams were shucked. They carried the bags and baskets of clams ashore on their backs by themselves, or with the help of their sons. Containers full of clams were often heavy for a small boy to carry perhaps a half mile to the shore. Ed Fisler, Jr., a fish peddler's son of Belford, heard stories that "their hands froze right off on the coldest days carrying them." "Pop, is that all?" a boy might ask. "Damn it, you get back here and carry them or you'll get a licking," was a typical reply (Interview, 28 January 1989).

Even though thirty or so fishermen may have dug over a clam flat extensively at low tide, leaving low mounds alongside their drills, the flats always appeared smooth when fishermen walked onto them the following day. Water currents and waves had nearly smoothed out any drills from previous diggings, which in any case contained only the siphon holes of seed clams.

Most of the clammers who dug in the area from Keyport to Belford brought their soft clams home and enlisted their families to help open and pack them for local sale, as Ingersoll wrote. In the kitchen of a typical home, the fisherman and perhaps an older son opened the clams, while the small children pulled the skin off the neck of each one. The skin covering a clam's siphon is only paper thin, but it is too tough for a person to chew. Housewives packed the clam meats in a large pot, or, from the late 1800s onward, in quart Mason jars. The yield from three bushels of clams was about twenty quarts of meats. Incidentally, the Mason jar was first developed by a tinsmith, named John Landis Mason, of Vineland, New Jersey; he patented it in 1856 (Pepper 1971). Fishermen discarded the clamshells in the marshes beyond their homes, spread them on driveways ("Didn't they stink when spread in damp weather!" [Interview, Bud Thompson, 7 January 1988]), or crushed them and put them in their chicken yards as a lime source for hardening the shells of eggs.

Fishermen peddled the shucked clams to customers around their communities. Some regulars bought one or two quarts every week. In the early years the fishermen delivered the clams in a pot and dipped out quart measures for customers. Later they sold them in the Mason jars and the customer returned the empty jars from the previous delivery. For many years, fisherman carried the clams in two-wheel carts or in two baskets suspended from a stick across their shoulders. The home shucking and peddling of soft clams continued from at least as early as the 1870s through the 1940s (Ingersoll 1887).

In the early 1900s, the largest buyer of clams in Belford was John Rickman. He bought unshucked soft clams and hard clams from thirty to forty diggers and transported them in his own boat to New York City. There, he owned a horse and a wagon with which he delivered clams to various saloons and hotel bars. He bought the clams for fifty to eighty cents a bushel and sold them for about twenty cents more. Some other diggers shipped their clams on freighting sloops or schooners or on passenger-freight ferries to commission merchants in Fulton Market.

Deeper-Water Clamming: Churning

Besides growing on the intertidal flats, soft clams also occurred in vast stretches of bottoms beyond them to depths of at least eight feet, mostly in the vicinity of Highlands and in the Navesink and Shrewsbury rivers. No one had gathered these clams until someone tried it using a hoe and a scap net (a crab net with fine mesh netting) or rake. The rake measured about two feet wide and was similar to a hard clam rake, but its teeth were shorter and closer together. Perhaps a mason was the first one to do it. He may have washed cement off his hoe at the shore when the tide was low and, by accident, lifted out some soft clams from the bottom. A method called *churning* developed, and men could then gather the soft clams beyond the tidal flats. In Highlands, the churning of clams was to provide continuous employment throughout the year for as many as one hundred fishermen and nearly as many female shuckers.

The churning hoe had a blade eight inches long and four inches wide. It was attached to a handle up to eighteen feet long. Clammers made the hoes themselves. The best were made from two-man bucksaws, which in turn were made of spring steel; the thinner the steel, the more efficiently they churned the clams.

To churn, a fisherman worked the blade about six inches into the bottom and then moved it rapidly up and down about six inches per stroke as he stepped slowly backward. He tried to keep the blade of the hoe beneath the clams to avoid breaking them. The churning action stirred the clams and sand into the water, and since the sand settled before the less-dense clams, the clams landed on the bottom surface and could then be gathered easily with a scap net or rake. Fishermen had to break into this work slowly because the churning rubbed against their shoulders, making them sore. They kept their muscles relaxed and used only their arms as they churned; otherwise, they tired quickly.

During the late 1800s and until World War II, most clammers churned from rowboats, a practice they called *long-rigging*. During economically depressed periods, as many as fifty boats were engaged in long-rigging. In the larger boats, termed skiffs, twenty to twenty-two feet long, clammers installed a churning board along their starboard sides. A churning board was a foot wide and a foot above the floor. Clammers stood on it when churning and piled their clams on the floor of their skiffs. The skiffs had sides about three feet high and were built almost vertically, so a clammer could stand on the board without tipping his skiff very far. Normally, one man churned from a skiff, but sometimes two did. The water was usually three to six feet deep at low tide where they did it.

Clammers did not get into water to churn except in the summer. They could get rheumatism or arthritis if they stood in cold water churning.

If fishermen did not know where the clams were abundant, they located them using a practice they called "sounding the clams." Standing in the bow of their skiffs, they held a sounding pole about ten feet long with a pointed end one inch in diameter. They used the pole to push the boat around and to determine whether clams were present. After bringing the boat to a stop, they put the pole straight down with the pointed end against the bottom and, using both hands, pushed down hard. If the bottom was hard, they suspected that clams were present, but to be sure they had to break some. If they broke several after a few minutes, they knew that the clams were abundant. Clammers could tell whether they were breaking shells or live clams and some could even determine the sizes of clams in a bed by feeling how far the pole moved down when the clams broke.

When they were over a bed of abundant clams, the fishermen tossed out two light anchors as far as they could—twenty to twenty-five feet—

30. *Model of soft-clam churning skiff with sounding pole, churning hoe, rake, and anchors made by Cris Kohlenbusch, a retired fisherman. Photograph by author.*

one straight off the bow and another straight off the stern, and tied their lines tightly. Then they tossed two others off the port side, one about ten feet from the bow anchor and the other about the same distance from the stern anchor, and tied them tightly. Next, they went to the bow with their hoe, reached it out as far as they could, and began churning down the starboard side. They worked to and beyond the stern, completing a drill in twenty to thirty minutes. They then gathered the clams with a scap net or rake and dumped them loosely on the skiff's floor. Rakes gathered clams more efficiently than scap nets, because they collected those partially buried and did not push any clams away as scap nets did. Usually drills yielded at least a bushel of clams; if the yield was less than a half bushel, the clammers moved to another site.

Most clammers churned alone, but if two went together, they began churning on the starboard side about ten feet apart. When the first clammer reached the point where his partner had begun, he went to where the partner had ended and continued. Meanwhile, his partner went to the bow and began taking up the clams.

After gathering the clams from a drill, the clammers moved their boats over about one and a half feet by resetting the anchor lines and churned another drill. On a bed of abundant clams, they did not have to take up the anchors and reset them that day. The long riggers usually worked five to six hours, and each gathered about eight bushels of clams, with largest catches being about twelve bushels. If two men went together, they dug less than double the quantities that one man dug. The churners easily outproduced men with drags on tidal flats (Interview, Cris Kohlenbusch, 11 January 1991).

Upon returning to Highlands with the tide nearly high, the clammers anchored near shore, culled out any broken clams and shells, and then shoveled the whole clams, carefully to avoid breaking their thin shells, into bushel baskets. The fishermen used wheelbarrows to carry the baskets of clams up the firm beaches. They sold the larger clams, at least two and a half inches long, to shucking shanties and sold the smaller ones to other buyers, who in turn sold them in the shell as steamers. Clammers were paid by the bushel, 45 cents in 1896 (*Red Bank Register,* 22 April 1896), 60 cents in the early 1900s, and $1.25 in the 1920s (Interview, Cris Kohlenbusch, 16 June 1986).

With the development of churning, Highlands had become the principal soft-clamming town of the bay, and it provided the only employment, besides a little eel spearing and work at the Fort Hancock army base on Sandy Hook, for its citizens during the winter. In 1889 Gustave Kobbe, a writer and journalist, wrote, "The soul of this . . . community is wrapped up in clams. They are to it what whales once were to Nantucket. Parkertown [Highlands] is clamming, shelling, stringing, or canning clams; devouring them, or dreaming of performing one or another of these acts . . . 'Clam' is said to be the first word lisped by its babies" (Kobbe 1982). The latter statement is apocryphal but to this day oldtimers talk about the clamming of yesteryear. One wonders whether *clam* is the last word they utter before they die.

In Highlands, most soft clams were shucked and shipped, strung on cotton strings in groups of twenty-five, by train to Fulton Market; these were called *string clams.* The shucking of clams in shanties built specifically for this purpose dates from at least the 1870s (Ingersoll 1887) and probably much earlier, and it continued from then into the 1940s. Some clams were also shucked in clammers' homes. In the early 1900s there were about twelve clam shanties, each measuring about twelve by sixteen feet, along the shore of Highlands. An owner-manager operated the business of each one. He purchased clams from the diggers, employed five to ten women as shuckers, packed the clam meats, and handled sales.

The women usually worked three to four days a week, for example, on Monday, Tuesday, Wednesday, and sometimes on Sunday for Monday's market. They often began shucking as early as 4 A.M. if the fishermen had brought in many clams late during the previous day and they had a large order to process. They finished late in the morning or in the early afternoon. At other times, though, they had to wait until mid-

31. *Churning boats upon their return to Highlands shore with soft clams, high tide. Four shanties where soft clams were shucked are on the shore, circa 1907. Courtesy of Irving Parker.*

morning or later for the fishermen to bring in the clams. Mothers began shucking after their children left for school and quit before they returned. The women sat on stools around baskets of clams to be shucked. They cut away the top and bottom shells of each clam and then split their necks to remove most of the sand in them, which the clams had sucked in during the churning. Finally, they removed the skin from the clams' necks and discarded it with the shells. They opened the clams rapidly, and "to watch them you saw shells in the air all the time" (Interview, Johnny Wallace, 15 October 1985).

After they had filled a bucket with clam meats, the women strung them on cotton strings. The string used was the same as that for making scap nets and was purchased in a ball. The shanty manager wound a length of it around a board of designated width and then cut it along one side. This way he cut all the strings the correct length for stringing twenty-five clams. The women looped the rim of each clam over one of their fingers and then ran the string through them and tied its ends. If they broke a rim, they could not string it; they brought these clams home and ate them. Each woman opened from two thousand to seven thou-

32. *Clambake at Richmond Valley, Staten Island, circa 1910. Note lobsters and cheesecloth sacks of other food, probably mostly soft clams and potatoes. Courtesy of Staten Island Historical Society, Richmondtown Restoration, Staten Island, New York.*

sand clams a day. Around 1900, they earned about fifty cents per thousand clams opened (Interview Mr. and Mrs. Irving Parker, 25 April 1987).

The manager collected the strings of clams from the women, sloshed them in a sink of fresh water to wash away the sand, and then put them around a piece of ice in a barrel. Finally, he nailed a burlap cloth over the barrel. A man whose business was carting freight with a horse and wagon in Highlands collected the barrels of clams from the shanties and took them to the railroad depot. At quitting time, managers loaded the baskets of clamshells onto wheelbarrows and dumped them on nearby beaches and in the water, where swarms of killifish nibbled at the remaining pieces of clam meat. Finally they washed down the floors, which would stink otherwise.

The shanty managers and the buyers of the steamer clams shipped most soft clams to New York City; some went to nearby summer resorts for sale (*Red Bank Register*, 22 April 1896). Bayshore residents ate the remainder. Fishermen also sold some soft clams to cod fishermen as bait (*Red Bank Register*, 17 October 1888). Annual landings of soft clams from the bay ranged from 47,850 to 121,000 bushels between 1897 and 1938 (U.S. Landings Statistics).

Ingersoll described the sale of soft clams in New York City and Newark, New Jersey, in the 1870s:

> Soft clams are to be bought in the markets raw all the year round; and in New York they are always sold in "strings" . . . connected by a cotton cord. In the spring, particularly, the region about Fulton Market is crowded with clam vendors, who came in wagons to retail their clams, both in the shell and by the string, with much chaffering and clamor. Both these and the quahogs [hard clams] are also sold from baskets, wheelbarrows, and crazy wagons, by the peripatetic vendors, whose prolonged howl—"cla-a-a-ams! fresh cla-a-ams!!" is so well known in the suburban parts of the city. In Newark, I used to hear a song drawled out by these street merchants of mollusks which would do well as the opening measures of a dirge. (1887)

Lobstering

In the 1800s and early 1900s, fishermen used catboats to lift their lobster pots. The boats were powered by sail. There were probably about ten such lobster boats in the bay, sailing from Keyport, Belford, and Highlands. Some fishermen went alone in their boats, some had a partner. The design of the lobster pots remained the same: semicircular, forty inches long, a funnel on each end, and open in between. Each pot contained two bricks to hold it down; fishermen had collected the bricks for nothing from houses which had burned down. Ropes and funnels, both made of hemp, had to be soaked in tar before use each spring to preserve them; they lasted one season.

Most lobstermen had about 150 pots. They strung groups of 25 to 35 pots along each of five or six lines, 800 to 1,000 feet long, and anchored them in the deep middle areas of the bay; shallow areas of the bay never had many lobsters. They laid the lines end to end and marked their ends with buoys made of saplings. Lobstermen usually set their pots in the bay around the first of May. If pots were set out earlier, catches were low and the pots collected a great many barnacles, making them difficult to handle. The pots were left in the same place during the entire spring and were lifted every day.

Around mid-June, some lobstermen shifted their pots out to the ocean, because catches in the bay often declined thereafter. They left the pots there until the end of the season in October or November. They did not have to scrape off the fouling organisms collected in Raritan Bay because the organisms died and sloughed off onto the deeper ocean grounds. Lobstermen used a compass and a watch to find their ocean pots. They ran a compass course and timed the distance to the pots from the tip of Sandy Hook as they left the bay. Lobstermen had difficulty finding their pots in foggy weather and when passing ships had cut off the buoys.

Lobstermen lifted pots seven days a week and, weather permitting, commonly went fifty or more days without a break. Stretches of bad weather could prevent them from lifting pots in the ocean for periods of a week or more, however. Lobstermen had to lift their pots early in the morning, because otherwise different fishermen might steal their lobsters. A thief could steal lobsters quickly, since he did not have to rebait the pots.

At 5 to 5:30 A.M., on the way to their pots, each lobsterman stopped at a pound net to buy about five bushels of bunkers to use as bait in his pots. Sometimes lobstermen bought enough bunkers for two days to save time; if so, bunkers for the second day had to be salted to prevent spoilage.

Lobstermen hauled the pot lines by hand. They began at one end of each line and worked down to the other end. When they got a pot to the surface, they grabbed its two-foot tail line, lifted it into the boat, removed its cover, took out the lobsters, crabs, and any fish, pushed two or three bunkers onto a stiff twelve-inch wire in the pot, replaced its cover, slid it back overboard, and then pulled up the next pot and repeated the sequence. The work was difficult even though the water was only fifteen to twenty-four feet deep in the bay, because lobstermen had to pull their lines in the direction opposite to which the current or wind was pushing their boat. They returned to shore around noon.

The work was even more difficult when pots were set in the ocean, because the water was from sixty to ninety feet deep. Lobstermen tied the pots about two hundred feet apart on the lines so there would be sufficient slack to lift one pot at a time. When there was a swell, the fishermen let the waves help them haul. They took in the line as the boat fell into a trough and held it as the boat rose in a swell (Interview, Bud Thompson, 7 January 1988).

Fishermen usually got about one large lobster and one to four small ones in each pot in the bay and ocean and sold them all. About 90 percent of the catch would now be described as "shorts"—less than the 1991 legal size of 3 5/16 inches, but legal in this period. The local market for lobsters was limited, and each fisherman had to ship them by freight boat, train, or buy boat to Fulton Market once every week or two.

Abundance of lobsters in Raritan Bay and the ocean varied annually

33. Part of the fleet of Raritan Bay shell-fishing sloops anchored in Keyport, circa 1915. Long dock in background served as partial protection from easterly storms. Courtesy of the Monmouth County Historical Association.

and was unpredictable. In some years lobstermen anticipated good seasons because they had had good catches during the previous fall. If severe spring storms stirred up the bottom, however, the lobsters sometimes migrated away from the area and were unavailable for an extended period, forcing the lobstermen into employment in another fishery.

Blue Crabbing

The beginnings of the blue-crab fishery are unknown. The first record of it is a December 1889 newspaper report, which states that many Keyport sloops were dredging for crabs in the southeastern part of the bay (*Red Bank Register*, 4 December 1889). Since then, fishermen have dredged for blue crabs there every winter. Raritan Bay is the northernmost bay along the Atlantic coast where blue crabs are dredged every winter, and most likely it has the smallest of the regular dredge fisheries for these crabs. The remaining winter dredge fisheries for these crabs exist in bays to the south—Delaware, Chesapeake, and bays in the northern part of North Carolina. Occasionally blue crabs are abundant enough in Great South Bay, Long Island, to support a small dredge fishery there.

Dredging for blue crabs was never a reliable source of winter income for Raritan Bay fishermen, because the crabs were scarce during some seasons, and during all seasons fishermen missed many days due to bad weather. In the worst seasons, commercial-size catches lasted only two to three weeks, and in extraordinarily cold winters, ice covered much of the bay, making dredging impossible. After the ice left, fishermen found that all the male crabs and nearly all the females were dead. In rare good seasons, however, commercial catches lasted until spring.

The dredging sloops, which sailed from Keyport, each had a crew of two. Until the mid-1930s, the crab dredges were three feet wide and had bags made with four-inch mesh netting. If smaller meshes were used, the bag would fill with mussel and clam shells, making the dredges heavy and the picking of crabs extremely slow. The large meshes did not retain many hard clams either. Undoubtedly, the first dredges were used for dredging oysters during the fall and early winter. Crews towed eight to twelve dredges off one side of their sloops as they sailed obliquely sideward. They retrieved them by hand; the dredges were not especially heavy unless full of live mussels. A U.S. government report published in 1887 stated that blue crabs were also taken with long-handled clam rakes in Gravesend Bay in winter (Mather 1887).

Much more than in any other fishery, crab fishermen had to spend considerable time searching for productive areas to dredge, because sometimes the crabs occupied relatively small, dispersed areas, and they often bedded in different areas each year. In addition, during the first few weeks of a season the crabs were slightly active and moved from one place to another, especially when their habitat had been stirred up by the dredging boats. The boats often got a good catch of crabs in an area one day and went back the next day and found that the crabs left behind had moved. As the season progressed, fishermen returned to areas where crabs had been scarce earlier and sometimes found that the crabs had moved there. When the water became colder, perhaps below 35° F, however, the crabs became dormant and did not move when boats dredged near them. The crabbing sloops each caught from twenty-five to one hundred bushels a day in good seasons; a bushel contained sixty-five to eighty crabs.

During the week, the sloops remained in the eastern end of the bay and the two crewmen slept and ate aboard. They stored their crabs in the holds of their sloops and ran them to New York City every two or three days to sell them. In freezing air temperatures, they had to keep a lantern or two burning in the holds to keep the crabs alive.

The crab fishermen had their own vernacular. They called the searching activity *spotting*. Usually a boat crew spotted with only two or three dredges and towed them for about ten minutes. When they caught some crabs, they termed it a *sign*. Once a productive ground was found, a crew deployed all its dredges. Some referred to a concentration of crabs as a *knuckle*. A male crab was a *jimmy;* a female was a *mommy*. Taking crabs off the deck by hand and putting them in baskets was *picking*.

Horseshoe Crabbing

During the 1800s and continuing into the 1930s, farmers collected horseshoe crabs by the thousands along the bayshore each spring. They walked along with a horse and wagon, picked up the crabs in baskets, and emptied them into the wagon. They fed the crabs to hogs and chickens and used some for fertilizing grapevines, apple trees, hills of corn, and other vegetables (Murphy n.d.). Fishermen using haul seines and fyke nets for fin fish also caught horseshoe crabs and sold them to eel fishermen for bait.

5

Working Lives of the Fishermen

By 1900, several generations of fishermen had accumulated experience fishing in the bay. Much knowledge about the seasonal abundances and behavior of various fish, lobsters, and crabs, about the bottoms, currents, and winds in the bay, and about construction and use of gear and fishing methods was stored in the heads of fishermen. Fishermen could find the productive channels, edges of shoals, and beds by lining up the multitude of structures available on the shores with navigation buoys in the bay.

Clothing

Fishermen wore a standard type of clothing; a wool vest was a common garment. In cool weather the vest kept their bodies warm while their arms were not encumbered as they would be by a coat, and its pockets were a handy place to keep a knife. Most fishermen wore hats and long underwear the year around also, the underwear being lighter weight in summer. Shirts buttoned to the neck. Such clothing was believed to ward off colds and other illnesses. During the 1800s and until the 1920s, when rubber-coated outer gear became generally available, fishermen used oilskin pants and jackets to keep dry. Oilskins were made of muslin cloth and had to be coated about once a week with linseed oil, which had a mild odor. A set of oilskins lasted about half a season. The rubber gear was heavier than oilskins, but did not involve any care, lasted much longer, and had little odor. Rubber boots had been manufactured since the 1850s (Miller 1971). Presumably fishermen began wearing them soon thereafter, but this is not documented. However, they were common by 1900 (*Red Bank Register*, 20 August 1902).

Versatility of Skills

During the warmer months, the main fisheries were pound netting, gill netting, eel potting, purse seining, fyke netting, hard clamming, soft clamming, and lobstering; during the colder months, oystering, blue crabbing, eel spearing, and, again, soft clamming were predominant. Most men worked at several fisheries during their working lives and sometimes engaged in as many as five each year. They could step right into any fishery and do well at it.

A feature of both hard clamming and soft clamming was ease of entry: little equipment was required, so a farmer or recent immigrant from Scandinavia or Germany could earn his living after obtaining only a rake and bateau for hard clams or only a drag for soft clams. To enter one of the other fisheries, a man had to work as a mate on a boat or purchase relatively expensive gear.

None of the fisheries had lent themselves well to mechanization, and the methods used in fisheries such as gill netting, soft clamming, and hand raking and sail dredging for hard clams did not change much throughout their history. Oysters were tonged most of the time. One fisherman characterized the work "as hard, but we had to do it to make a living. We kept at it and toughened up to it" (Interview, Otto Schnoor, 7 November 1987).

Schedules

For most fishermen, work began early in the day; they usually left their docks before dawn. An early beginning and early arrival back at shore had advantages. First, the water was normally calm in the mornings, whereas a stiff southerly breeze often made the water rough on summer afternoons. Second, the catch spent only the cooler part of the day in boats. Third, fish and shellfish could be landed in time to arrive fresh in Fulton Market on the day they were caught. Some fishermen, such as haul seiners, who could work only during high tide, soft clammers, who had to dig during low tide, and the hard-clam sail dredgers, had to arrange their schedules around the tides or were dependent on unpredictable winds.

If they could, clammers and lobstermen worked seven days a week to earn a decent livelihood, because some seasons were short. They also wanted to land sufficient shellfish to hold their market, because buyers depended on their catch, especially during periods of peak demand. If a buyer found that a fisherman was unreliable, he might drop him for another. The gill netters and pound netters did not lift on Sundays, though, because Fulton Fish Market was closed, the peddlers did not sell their fish, and the bunker factories did not operate.

Health

Fishermen had only a few special health problems or hazards. Some herniated from lifting heavy nets, boxes of fish, and other objects. Having their hands wet for hours every day resulted in hardened, cracked skin on their fingers. Occasionally, a fisherman got fish poisoning in one of his fingers from having an open sore and then handling fish. If so, the finger swelled to double its normal size and was extremely painful. In recent years, doctors have cured the condition with penicillin. Fishermen putting dredges over the side of a boat had to be careful not to allow their ropes to wrap around their ankles, or else they could be pulled overboard. Elderly fishermen affected by the cold avoided winter fisheries if they could.

A blister on the hand of a hard clammer could keep him from raking. Often one developed when he raked clams in especially hard bottom. If a blister raised and he continued to rake, his skin would tear, his hand would hurt and bleed, and he could lose a day or two of work. Rakers had a technique for preventing such a break. First, they quit raking before the blister broke. At home, they inserted a needle with thread on it in one side of the blister and out the other side and then snipped off the needle, leaving about half an inch of thread extending from each side. During the night, the liquid drained out, and the next morning, they eased out the thread and could rake without their skin splitting (Interview, Pete Glismann, 18 June 1987).

Attitudes Toward Work and Toward Each Other

As in other occupations, fishing had favorable and unfavorable aspects. The positive features were that: the work required little training, and, when fish and shellfish were abundant, a recruit could earn nearly as much as a veteran after only two or three days of learning experience; fishermen were independent and self-reliant, with no boss; they had a product to sell from their work each day ("gathering crops" satisfies basic human emotions); and fishermen had close contact with the processes of nature, viewing seasonal cycles of reproduction and growth of fishes and shellfishes and behavior of birds. The main drawback was that it was unreliable, because fish and shellfish were sometimes scarce for substantial periods, and adverse weather or ice sometimes prevented fishing. A bad-weather day was a day without fish, but also a day when a fisherman could rest. Two other drawbacks were that prices were nearly always low when catches were high, and that fishermen had to expend about the same effort whether they made large catches or small ones.

Fishing provided only a marginal living for most. One retired fisherman summed up his economic history, which was typical of earlier periods: "I've done all types of fishing, but never made much at anything." Fishermen's prosperity was limited because of the slack periods, poor fishing seasons (soft clams did not set abundantly every summer; bluefish, weakfish, and hard clams were scarce for periods of years; and lobsters were scarce in some years), and periods of low prices. And many soft clammers lost days when east winds kept the tide from falling low enough to bare the flats.

To reduce expenses, fishermen used secondhand gear whenever possible. For instance, hard clammers used secondhand burlap feed or potato or onion bags to hold their clams; soft clammers used discarded pound netting to make bags to hold their clams; and blue crabbers used secondhand bushel produce baskets to carry their crabs. Fishermen kept cloth patches, thread, and needles available to mend their sails. Any new fishermen's supplies, such as nets, rope, oilskins, and boots, were obtained from outlets at Fulton Market but fishermen purchased them through local hardware stores.

It is uncertain when baskets and barrels were first made to ship fish and produce. A number of small factories were operating in the area to make baskets for fishermen and farmers around the bayshore in the late 1800s and early 1900s. The towns of Tottenville, Keyport, Mattawan, and Red Bank had basket-making factories. A factory located about two miles north of Freehold sold some of its baskets to Keyport oyster planters (Beck 1984). Each factory employed two or three men to weave baskets, mostly bushel measures, year-round.

The first available records of barrel making date to the late 1800s and early 1900s. A newspaper described the making of barrels for marketing fish and soft clams along the Bayshore by the Thomas B. Sherman Company in a barn in Red Bank, New Jersey. The company assembled the barrels from wood cut in New York State; it also bought secondhand barrels from storekeepers in Red Bank and vicinity for repair and resale. The company made 4,000 to 5,000 barrels annually; 3,000 to

3,500 were new, the remainder secondhand. During a summer when fish were plentiful, twenty to thirty wagonloads of barrels left the barn every day (*Red Bank Register,* 13 October 1915). Barrels were also common shipping containers for all types of goods in this period.

As a matter of self-interest, fishermen generally had a strong attitude of conservation towards fish. Otherwise their economic future would be lost. Fishermen felt a common bond with one another and generally got along well together. Some were neighbors. In addition, they bought their sails, dredges, and anchors from the same blacksmiths, tied their boats in the same ports, worked in the same areas of the bay, and were all striving for a comfortable living. They were also all at the mercy of the same weather, the same equipment suppliers for prices charged, and the same buyers for prices paid.

Boys growing up heard their fathers and their friends' fathers talking about fishing almost constantly, and most believed that life as a fisher-men would be great for them. Boys as young as seven went along on boats daily in the summer, on Saturdays the remainder of the year, to see operations. At the age of twelve they assisted their fathers by doing light tasks, and by sixteen they were full-time fishermen.

Young men who were not brought into a fishery by their fathers had to ask veterans about methods. If they had come off a farm, the transition was easy because the work there was physical and out-of-doors. When the recruits followed veterans to good fishing areas, the veterans were resentful because sometimes they interfered with their operations.

Fishermen had to work in their old age to support themselves. For example, Charlie Schnoor of Belford continued pound-net fishing until he was eighty-nine, only two years before his death. During his last active years, he could hardly see, and when he was pulling nets, blue crabs hanging on them bit his fingers. In the fields, where the nets were dried, mended, and tarred, however, he mended nets better than younger men, because he was so skilled. Finally, his crew made him quit, because they were afraid that he would fall overboard or get hurt. Finally, fishermen had to retire when they could not do the work anymore.

The citizens of each town had a positive attitude toward the fish-eries, mostly because they provided much employment, and the relative abundances of shellfish and fish in the bay each season were common knowledge. The fishermen in each town were informally ranked. The hardest-working, most able fishermen ranked the highest because they caught the most and made the most money. There was a large middle group who earned a little less, and also a small group consisting of physically weak or heavy-drinking men, who missed many days, ranked the lowest, and were often held in scorn. When a young man entered a fishery, the citizenry wondered how good a fishermen he would become, and when a respected elderly fishermen approached retirement, they wanted him to continue fishing. When a fisherman died, people felt that some important history was lost. They hoped that at least his boat and gear would remain active in the bay (Interview, Ken Norton, 6 November 1985).

6

Life on the Bayshore: The Late 1800s to the 1940s

By 1900, the five smaller towns on the bayshore—Great Kills Harbor, Prince's Bay, Tottenville, Belford, and Highlands—had become fishing villages surrounded by farms. Tottenville had a population of about 500, many of whom were oystermen. Another source of employment in the town were shipyards, which constructed freighting schooners, catboats, sloops, and tugboats. Belford had a population of about 1,000, of whom about 350 were fishermen. Highlands, also comprised of about 1,000 people, was supported by soft clamming and the summer resort business; lobstering, eeling, and work at the Fort Hancock army base were secondary sources of employment. About 50 clammers and some lobstermen of Highlands purchased a three-acre stretch of land running between Miller Street and the waterfront to land their clams and store their boats and gear during the winter. The land became known as the Association Lot. The two larger towns, Perth Amboy with about 10,000 people, and Keyport with about 3,500 (Hall 1894), had a substantial number of fishermen, but other types of commerce were more prominent. About 240 men in Perth Amboy (Hall 1894) and 300 men in Keyport (*Keyport Weekly*, 28 April 1911) worked in oystering and other fisheries. Besides farming, other occupations around the bayshore included blacksmithing (Keyport had 7 blacksmiths), carpentry, conducting on ferries, trains, and trolleys, and service jobs related to the summer resort business.

From the 1870s onward, the principal commercial fin-fishing port in the bay was Compton's Creek in Belford. For many years the port was only a minimally developed marshland creek used for the transport of agricultural goods between northern New Jersey and New York City. The port expanded as the bunker-canning factories and then the reduction factories were built, and it expanded further as immigrants from Germany and Scandinavia settled there and worked as fishermen (McCay 1984). The main type of fishing from Compton's Creek was pound netting, which employed about 300 men during peak years. Belford fishermen also earned a living from gill netting, eeling, fyke netting, hard clamming, soft clamming, lobstering, and purse seining for bunkers. Bunkers, always predictable and abundant and thus a reliable money-maker, constituted over 90 percent of the fish landings by weight in the creek (McCay 1981).

The waterfronts of these towns had buildings, docks, and boats used by the commercial fishermen. Prince's Bay, Perth Amboy, and Keyport were mainly concerned with oystering. Prominent on the waterfront in Keyport after 1899 were Elsworth's oyster house and from one to three barges, where oysters were shucked until 1925. About 50 fishing sloops and several schooners were tied to anchored buoys in Keyport Harbor; the fishermen had to paint an identifying name on each buoy because there were so many. Fishermen left a rowboat tied to each one for coming ashore when they returned from fishing. Belford had about 28 pound-net boats, about 20 catboats for hard clamming and lobstering, and about 100 hard-clamming bateaux. In addition, it had 3 bunker-reduction factories. Another feature of Compton's Creek were 100 or so cats, which found shelter under fishermen's sheds. They lay in the sun around the docks most of the time, but ran up to boats when they docked to have a fish or two tossed to them. The waterfront of Highlands had about 12 shanties in which soft clams were shucked, nearly 100 bateaux used for soft clamming and eeling, and a few catboats for lobstering. Wheelbarrows and hand carts were common around all the waterfronts as well as on farms and in towns for carrying clams, farm produce, and other items (Interview, Irving Parker, 9 September 1989). During the off-seasons, lobster pots were piled in the yards of fishermen and eel spears were tied to numerous grape arbors. Each town also had several "smokers" (smokehouses) owned by fishermen for preserving fish (Interview, Wilbur Huylar, 9 October 1987).

The only descriptions of Gravesend Bay reveal that fyke nets, pound nets, and gear for catching crabs were present there (Bean 1897; Rathbun 1887). No reports exist of its waterfront or community life.

A few families lived in houseboats tied along the New Jersey bay-shore. Houseboats were twenty to thirty feet long, and each had a shanty covering most of its deck. The shanties were only about five feet high, allowing many women and most children but few men to stand erect. Inside was a stove, an eating table that could be folded against a wall, chairs, and cots for sleeping. Kerosene lanterns were originally used for light and possibly heat at night, but eventually the houseboats plugged into electric outlets. A plank provided access to shore, and a rowboat, tied on the water side, was used for hard clamming and soft clamming. Both clammers and summer people lived on the boats. The cost of living on houseboats was low; thus city people with modest means could use them for inexpensive vacations. They caught or dug much of their food from the bay and obtained water and some provisions from the towns. The houseboats moored in Sea Bright were towed up the Hudson River to serve as living quarters for local fishermen while they caught shad each spring and eels in the latter half of the summer.

In summer, the odor of the Belford fish factories ("the stink factories") permeated the air. It was a regular aspect of life for people living as far as ten miles away. The odor was not unpleasant when fresh bunkers were being processed but was noxious if they were partially spoiled. Because the principal occupations in the area were fishing and farming, neither fishermen nor farmers complained. Instead, "When the smell was in the air, the farmers knew that the fishermen were making money and were glad" (Interview, Ray Richardson, 20 November 1986). Nevertheless, summer people avoided Belford because they could not tolerate the smell. Marion Thompson, of Port Monmouth, wife of Bud Thompson and mother of Albert Thompson, both fishermen, and in her early 70s, experienced the odor for most of her life:

> If the wind was blowing from the factory toward us, we couldn't stay out in the yard because the smell was too strong. My curtains and all the cloth furniture in the house smelled of it. But they said it was a healthy smell and was even good for your lungs. It never hurt me and I smelled plenty of it. There was one story about this bald man who went to work in the fish factory. After a couple of years, he had a full head of hair. Everybody said that something about the smell must have made his hair grow, and they ought to find out what it is and sell it.
>
> The local people never complained about the smell, because the factory brought a lot of employment to the area, and it was a market for the bunkers. In the 1960s, the new people moving here complained about the smell and came around with petitions. I never signed one. I told them: "I've lived around here all my life and the smell never hurt me. Men around here make their living at that place." They looked at me and thought I was crazy! (Interview, 7 January 1988)

Farmers within ten miles or so of the bayshore shipped most of their produce, including apples, asparagus (the first crop of the season), carrots, corn, lettuce, melons, potatoes, strawberries, squash, and tomatoes, to Washington Market in Manhattan. This market handled the wholesale distribution of two-thirds of the produce and fruit consumed in New York City, which at the turn of the century had a human population of about six million. The produce was transported on passenger-freight ferries from docks along the Arthur Kill, and in Perth Amboy, Keyport, and Belford. Every weekday morning in late summer and early fall farm wagons were lined up nearly a mile from the docks in those towns waiting to unload onto the ferries. At times, so much produce was being shipped from Belford that the passenger-freight ferry *William V. Wilson,* which ran from 1880 to 1907, could not carry all of it; the ferry had to tow a schooner to take the remainder (Interview, Charlie Schnoor, 10 July 1977). Produce was peddled locally also.

The fertilizer used on farms was manure from local livestock and from horses in New York City. Besides manure, some farmers collected sea lettuce for fertilizer.

Much of the manure was delivered to the bayshore on railroad flatcars, schooners, and barges throughout the year. The barges were about one hundred feet long with sideboards for holding manure piled ten to twelve feet high. A humorous story concerned a three-man crew delivering a schooner-load of manure from the city to Belford in the late afternoon on a frigid January day in 1896. As they approached Belford, the tide was too low to get ashore and it was getting dark. To keep from freezing, the crew had to dig themselves into the warm, steaming manure and spend the night with only their heads exposed. The crew took much ribbing about their adventure, but the manure saved their lives (*Red Bank Register,* 29 January 1896). The importation of manure from the city ended around 1920 for lack of supply.

Fishermen and farmers were of necessity largely self-sufficient. With small incomes, perhaps five hundred dollars a year, they could purchase little. Most lived a hand-to-mouth existence. They and their families built or helped to build their own homes, made most of their clothes, raised and caught some of their food, and collected their own firewood. "People either rooted hog or died poor," was a common description of their way of life.

Before the 1920s, the water in people's homes was supplied from their own wells. Obtaining water from a hand pump or bucket for drinking and heating it for washing dishes and clothes and bathing were laborious chores.

Stews, potatoes, and bread formed the bulk of meals, but families of the poorer fishermen ate catches from the bay regularly. The pound-net crews, fyke-net fishermen, gill netters, and eel potters and spearers brought some of their catches home to eat almost daily; some families "ate eels by the yard" (Interview, Bud Thompson, 7 January 1988).

Fishermen often swapped their fish and shellfish for the produce a farmer or peddler had. In spring, the principal fish caught were alewives and shad, both members of the clupeidae family, famous for their many bones. Women eliminated the bones by "scoring" their fillets. Using a sharp knife, they made a series of deep cuts along the length of each one, about a third of an inch apart, cutting each bone in short segments. Afterward, they poured vinegar over the fillets to help dissolve the bones and add flavor, and then added onions and bacon for more flavor. Without these added condiments, the fish would have had little taste, because the scoring allowed the juices of the fillets to leave them when cooked. After the fillets were fried or baked, any remnants of bones remaining were undetected by the family eating them.

Shellfish were taken home also. Oyster tongers and blue crab dredgers brought home hard clams they had caught incidentally. In winter, fishermen dug soft clams and, to a lesser extent, hard clams to eat; the hard clams lived as long as two weeks on damp cellar floors. The soft clams were prepared as fritters, pies (clams, potatoes, and onions with a biscuit crust), and sandwiches. Marion Thompson of Port Monmouth recalled, "In the 1920s and 1930s our family made clam fritters by mincing the clams almost to a juice, mixing them with flour and a little milk to make a batter, and then frying them similar to pancakes" (Interview, 14 December 1987). In June, when lobsters were molting and had soft shells, a condition referred to as "tinny" (their flesh was also thin and watery and they could not be sold), lobstermen brought them home.

Winter was a "dead" time, when fishermen and farmers could earn little or no money. "Though we were short of money in the winter in the 1920s and 1930s, we were never short of something to eat," recalled the daughter of a former fisherman. A typical family bought a hundred-pound barrel of flour, about fifty pounds each of sugar and coffee (obtained from New York City), a few bushels of apples, and a few bags of potatoes, both obtained locally, to last the winter. Families also bought food from peddlers and grocery stores, termed "jot-em-down-stores" because most purchases in winter were on credit. Peddlers sold milk, meat, baked goods, vegetables, fish, soft clams, and ice, using horse-drawn, secondhand farm wagons for deliveries before they had trucks. In the fall, those fishermen with gardens preserved asparagus, onions, string beans, tomatoes, tomato juice, peaches, pears, and jellies; wild beach plums were used to make jams and dumplings. They stored cabbages, carrots, and turnips in sand beneath their porches. Some fishermen kept about a dozen chickens for eggs and an occasional roast, and a hog or two also. Fishermen butchered a hog in the fall, smoked its meat, and hung it in an attic or stored it in brine. Many families preserved fish in the fall for their winter table by smoking or salting them. Leona Crosby, the daughter of a fisherman, recalled, "My mother used to buy a bushel of ling at Compton's Creek, clean and bone them, get a butter tub, and put in the ling in layers with salt in between. She kept the tub under our porch. When she got some out for us to eat, she removed some salt by putting them in freshwater and changing it three or four times, and then she made fish cakes from them. My stomach would start to churn whenever she got some out, because I hated them" (Interview, 18 May 1987).

The fish hawk, or osprey, was familiar around the bayshore from about 21 March to about 20 September every year. For many bayshore residents, its arrival from the South at the same time shad first appeared in the bay signaled the onset of spring, and its departure the end of summer. Fish hawks were commonly perched on poles, where they nested and ate their catches of fish. Sometimes, while flying, they dropped a fish to the ground, where it could be picked up by a person. A newspaper described an incident when a man and his wife were walking to a fish market to purchase fish. As they were stepping from their front porch, they noticed in their front yard a large weakfish flopping vigorously. At first they thought the fish had been dropped by a fisherman, and they looked up and down the street expecting to see a man with a rod and line over his shoulder. Glancing upward, they saw some fish hawks circling over their house, and they deduced from the cries and actions of the birds that one had dropped the fish. The fish was a fine specimen and both agreed that it was just what they wanted. They took it into the house and ate it the next day (*Red Bank Register,* 29 June 1910).

On another occasion, a farmer invited a farmer friend to look at his tomato field. When they arrived there, the attention of the two men was distracted by shrill cries overhead. Glancing upward, they saw a struggle between two fish hawks. One bird had a fish in its talons, and the other was trying to take it away. After several minutes, the fish was dropped to the ground. One farmer picked it up; it was still alive. He took it home and his family had it for dinner (*Red Bank Register,* 18 July 1923).

The families of fisherman collected wood, available in ample supply on the beaches, to heat their homes; they could afford to burn coal in their homes only during January and February, and some not even then. The wood, which drifted down from greater New York City, was dunnage. Stevedores threw it overboard from freighters they unloaded, or from docks, buildings, and barges that had been taken apart. The most desirable wood was North Carolina yellow pine, because it contained much pitch and burned easily. Any wood having creosote produced noxious fumes and too much flame and was not collected. Often, fishermen's sons piled the wood on beaches after school and their fathers brought it home by horse and wagon, hand cart, or automobile.

The wives of fishermen and farmers did all the housework and cared for their children. With few labor-saving devices available, they had to use almost every waking minute to feed their families, wash and make clothes, and clean the house. Saturday was baking day, when they made bread (white, pumpernickel, and rye), coffeecakes, and cookies for the week. Some women baked extra bread and sold it to neighbors or a grocery store. Women and children also fed chickens and collected eggs.

Most clothing was made at home. Women bought inexpensive bolts of cotton cloth in dry-goods stores or from the mail-order catalogs that were introduced around 1900. Nearly every woman had a foot-powered sewing machine to make shirts, nightshirts, dresses, and children's clothes and to repair or remodel clothes to fit various family members, and she "patched and patched men's pants until they fell off" (Interview, Marion Thompson, 7 January 1988). Mothers and grandmothers knitted woolen socks, sweaters, gloves, hats, and scarves. Children wore hand-me-down clothes. A pair of shoes cost around two dollars, but many people found it difficult to spare that much money; the poorest boys went barefoot in the warmer months.

Children had to work nearly full-time when not in school. Girls crocheted or knitted if they were not doing some other work in the home. Boys worked more outside the home. As young as eight years of age, they began chopping wood for the kitchen stove. In the fall, some were sent to gather and bring home potatoes left over in the fields after farmers got through harvesting them. Some other jobs were stirring copper paint in a boatyard for a worker painting the bottom of a boat, whittling fishing net needles for fishermen, and helping men put on clam bakes. Boys also trapped muskrats and opossums, shot raccoons, and sold the skins in the fall.

When idle, boys played at the waterfronts. In summer, Keyport boys enjoyed diving off the roof of the Elsworth company's oyster house into Luppatatong Creek; Belford boys swam in Compton's Creek. When the sons of fishermen of about the same age got together, they recounted stories about extraordinary catches of fish heard from their fathers and they played around the docks watching the fishermen and making up nicknames for them. Some children in Perth Amboy and Keyport saved the newspaper comics for their fathers to read to them when they came home from a week of fishing in the eastern part of the bay (Interview, Betty Martin, 19 November 1987).

Grammar schools consisted of one or two rooms, housing all eight grades. Few children obtained more than a grammar school education. After leaving school, fishermen's sons went to work aboard boats.

Visiting one another's homes and playing cards were two of the most common pastimes for adults. Occasionally families took short rides on Sunday afternoons in the summer on horse-drawn wagons; fishermen used the wagons, ordinarily used for hauling pound nets from the docks to their fields and back, for this purpose. Once in a while a fisherman brought his family for a Sunday sail and picnic on his fishing sloop. In winter, ice skating was popular for adults and children.

Long winter evenings were dull, especially for children. They went to bed at 8 or 8:30 P.M., as there was nothing else to do except listen to the same stories repeated endlessly by adults.

Medical care was relatively primitive before the 1930s. There were few prescription medicines, no X-rays, and operations were rare. Contagious diseases were difficult to control and people had a great fear of them. If someone had a contagious disease such as chicken pox, measles, mumps, or whooping cough, the doctor quarantined the family for two or more weeks. Neighbors, friends, and relatives brought food and other essentials to the family and paid for it themselves.

In 1857 a small group of oystermen from Prince's Bay, disguised as American Indians, had burned down several buildings there that the New York Quarantine Commission had purchased to quarantine people with yellow fever. The quarantine site had been in Tompkinsville on the far eastern side of Staten Island, but in 1847 and 1848 epidemics within the site spread to nearby towns, "infecting hundreds and stampeding the population to the hills for safety." Local residents pleaded with the commission to remove it. The commission then selected Prince's Bay as the new site, but were dissuaded by the burnings. In 1859 the patients were moved to hospital ships anchored in the lower bay. In the spring of 1874, the quarantine facility was opened on two artificial islands, Hoffman and Swinburne, which had been built off the east side of Staten Island (Powell 1975).

Most babies were born at home with the assistance of the doctor. Elsie Werner, the daughter of a fyke net fisherman, described the birth of her sister: "The doctor came and delivered the baby. Then, my father went to the lady next door and said: 'We need a little help. We have a little youngster who just came into the world, and we'd like you to come over to give it a bath and dress it.' So, she came over, washed the baby, and took care of it. Afterward, my mother asked my father to go out in the chicken yard and kill a chicken and prepare some chicken soup for the lady because she'll need it. That's the way we were" (Interview, 18 May 1987).

Schools had programs that cared for children's teeth, while adults generally had poor teeth. A dentist charged a dollar to pull a tooth. Those who lost all their teeth had to go to New York City to get a set of dentures. People with poor eyesight bought glasses, which cost twenty-five to fifty cents in department stores (Interview, Ken Norton, 22 February 1988).

Before the Social Security Act was established in 1935, fishermen and farmers had to work in their old age. If they lacked the resources to care for themselves after they could not work, a man and his wife went to live with one of their married children. If the children did not have adequate room in their home, they "had room in their hearts" and made the room.

Crime was virtually nonexistent on the bayshore in the 1920s and 1930s (Interview, Elsie Werner, 18 May 1987). Fishermen did not steal one another's dredges, rakes, anchors, and other gear on boat decks or docks when they were idle, and nets were safe in fields and on drying racks. The enforcement officials were constables, who had regular jobs and were paid only when they carried out a civil action. One reason for the lack of crime was that if a criminal act became known, a stigma that could last a generation or more was cast on the man and on his family and relatives. Sometimes, lobsters were stolen from pots though, perhaps because there was little risk of being caught.

The bayshore was a popular summer resort. Vacationers by the hundreds came to Staten Island by train, horse-drawn stagecoach, and steamboat. Three Jersey Central steamboats, all just under three hundred feet long, were built in the 1880s and brought similar numbers of New Yorkers to New Jersey. A pier at Atlantic Highlands had four to six trains meeting the steamboats and carrying passengers as far as Bay Head to the south and Matawan to the west. Vacationers stayed in bayshore hotels, rooming houses, tent villages, and their own houses. They spent their time on beaches, fishing from piers and rented row boats, walking through woods, and at parties and amusement centers such as the one that developed in Keansburg.

This period is now often referred to as "the good old days," and people were said to be pretty happy. But today's bayshore residents would not want to live as people did then, mainly because there was more uncertainty and everything involved too much work: fish might be scarce during a summer and some summers were poor for growing crops; adults engaged in physical labor most of the time, and children had to work almost as much as adults did. In addition, people could not always depend on their neighbors and relatives for help in times of need; they were also malnourished, and were shorter in stature than they are now. On the other hand, they used to know everyone in their vicinity; everybody trusted one another and no one locked the doors of his house. The pace of life was slower then, there were more natural wilderness areas, the water was not polluted, and no matter where clams were dug, they were safe to eat.

PART
THREE

Peak and the Beginning of Decline: 1911–1991

7

Fin Fishing Before
World War II

The year 1911 was one of the most memorable in the history of the Raritan Bay fin fisheries because it was then that two brothers, J. Howard and Gilbert Smith, constructed a large bunker-reduction factory at the mouth of Compton's Creek, Belford. They named it the J. Howard Smith Fish Factory. It was the largest such factory in the United States, and for the next sixty years the bunker fishery was by far the largest in the bay, supplanting oystering. During that period, the majority of bunkers in the bay were caught and processed by this factory. Shortly after it was constructed, the three small reduction factories went out of business. The 1911–1939 period was also marked by the development of the motorized skiff, which supplanted the catboat as a working boat; an increased number of pound nets; the continued use of several fishing gears; increased transportation of food fish across Raritan Bay to New York City, where they were sold; the rowboat livery era in sport fishing; and fishermen involvement in the Prohibition Era of the 1920s and early 1930s.

During this period the states of New York and New Jersey imposed several laws to conserve fish in Raritan Bay from overexploitation. The first laws were passed in the early 1900s; others came later. During most of the 1900s, the principal laws were: no food fish, except strays, could be caught by purse seiners for bunkers and sold to the fish reduction factories; pound nets were restricted to certain areas; and otter trawling was not permitted.

Staten Island had only one warden. He oversaw laws protecting upland game, waterfowl, and shellfisheries. Only one warden was assigned to Monmouth County, New Jersey; he was present at the bayshore only part-time, had no formal training for the job, and had only an old boat with an unreliable engine for patrolling Raritan Bay. The two states did not make a strong effort to enforce the laws, except those pertaining to public health, while fishermen came to violate those regarding otter trawling, power dredging for hard clams, landing undersized lobsters, and others with little interference from the wardens. Before the 1950s, fish, hard clams, and lobsters were not declining in abundance, so enforcement was not a pressing issue.

Bunkers

Before constructing their factory the Smith brothers bought all the property bordering on Compton's Creek and also a substantial amount on either side, to ensure that no one else could set up a similar factory in the vicinity and compete with them. Then they rented berths along the creek at low rates—only about a dollar each per year—to all types of commercial fishermen, including the pound-net fishermen who sold bunkers to them. The fishermen never knew when factory officials might reclaim the berths and make them leave, however, so they spent little to improve the appearances of the docks and sheds. Besides the factory buildings, the Smiths constructed a dormitory and dining commons for about seventy-five people who came up seasonally from the South to work; a caretaker's house; a loft for repairing seines; and reels for storing the seines. The factory also hired about thirty local men to work during the bunker season. Later, when it automated some processing, it needed fewer workers. The factory enlarged through time and consisted of several buildings.

During the plant's first years of operation, pound nets in the bay supplied most of the bunkers. Purse seine boats, most still under sail but some using primitive engines, supplied the remainder.

When workers brought bunkers into the plant, they put them into several steam cookers, each of which could each handle about 350,000 fish per hour. Next, machines pressed oil, water, and blood from the fish. A separator removed the oil from the water and blood, with the latter two going into an evaporator. Their product was fish solubles, called *stickwater;* it was sold to the hog industry as a feed ration.

In the early years of the factory, the scrap was dried outdoors on concrete platforms, where it had to be covered with waterproof sheets at night to prevent dew from moistening and rotting it. Flies and maggots feeding in it were a nuisance, so the factory manager paid a local farmer to keep his flock of domesticated geese at the factory every summer to

34. *Brailing bunkers from a pound net to a pound boat, circa 1950s. Courtesy of Louis Booz.*

control them. In later years, the factory dried the scrap in scrap houses, which had rotary driers, and then put it into scrap rooms, where workers had to turn it regularly to prevent spontaneous combustion. Afterward, it was put through hammer mills, which reduced it to meal; then it was bagged.

In the 1930s, the factory paid workers about thirty-two cents an hour, and in the peaks of the seasons each worked as many as ninety-six hours a week. Workers who handled the fish and scrap absorbed their smells. One former worker remembers, "When my job was to carry the hundred-pound bags of scrap from one place to another, the smell got into my skin, and even a bath wouldn't remove it. So I smelled of it all the time" (Interview, Walt DeGrote, 4 August 1989).

The factory could process as many as 10 million bunkers a day. It processed 200 million in an average year and 350 to 400 million in years of high bunker abundances. It used a better process to extract oil from bunkers than had the earlier factories, and it obtained a yield of twelve to eighteen gallons per thousand fish. The bunkers yielded more oil in some seasons than in others, probably because more of the oil-containing plankton they filtered and consumed was available. In 1911, the first year of operation and the only one for which data are available, the factory sold oil for forty cents a gallon and fish scrap for thirty-six dollars a ton (*Red Bank Register,* 3 May 1911). In subsequent years the oil was used in the manufacture of paint, rope, and soap, and for currying leather; in the 1950s and 1960s it was used in the manufacture of cosmetics, linoleum, and paint. The average yield of scrap was 350 tons per million fish. In the beginning, the factory sold the scrap to farmers as fertilizer, but during the 1930s and thereafter poultry and catfish farmers bought it as feed. The factory once experimented with making flour from the scrap, but it tasted like fish when baked as bread and no attempt was made to market it.

The odor from the J. Howard Smith Fish Factory, like that of the smaller ones, was an environmental problem. Bayshore residents as far away as Keyport, six miles from Belford, could smell effluents from the factory. In addition, the paint on a hotel and homes adjacent to the factory turned black because of the discharge from its smokestacks.

Pound-net crews sold nearly all their bunker catches to the factory. In a five-week season in April and May, each pound-boat crew made from one to four trips a day, carrying as many as 350 bushels of bunkers each trip from their pound nets to the factory. Bunkers often entered pound nets as soon as fishermen emptied them, and each net could be emptied up to four times a day. When the crews were running three or four loads of bunkers from their pound nets to the factory each day, they had to work on the alternate nets in their fields until dark. After June, when the bunkers "quit running" and "began schooling," they went into pound nets in much smaller quantities, but could be taken then by seine boats.

The usual quantity of bunkers each pound-net crew sold to the factory during a season was twenty thousand to thirty thousand bushels, and, in an extra good season, fifty thousand to sixty thousand bushels. A typical seasonal total from all the pound nets was about three hundred thousand bushels (twenty to forty million bunkers; one bushel contained about sixty-five bunkers). Soon after it opened, the factory paid fishermen 12.5 to 15 cents a bushel for the bunkers (*Red Bank Register,* 3 May 1911). The price generally rose through the years, but it fell to only 10 cents a bushel during most of the 1930s. The factory paid the pound-net owners a lump sum in October or November, after receiving payments for the oil and meal it sold.

The pound-net fishermen also sold bunkers to lobstermen for bait. Some crews sold about fifty bushels each morning to about ten lobstermen, for 30 to 50 cents a bushel, much more than the factory paid. They took the remaining bunkers to the factory.

From its beginnings, the factory maintained excellent relations with the pound-net fishermen. Besides leasing them the berths at low rent, it bought nearly all the bunkers they caught at a fair price when there would have been no other sale for them, and did favors for them. Bud Thompson, a Port Monmouth fisherman, who had the reputation of being able to clean a blowfish in two seconds, explained the relationship in the 1930s and 1940s:

> Old man Smith, he'd always do something for you. He was a good man. A lot of people didn't like him because he was making money, but he'd give you most anything he had and you never had to pay for anything. If something broke on our boat, we took it down there and got it fixed by their mechanics. It wouldn't cost us a penny. Once, we broke part of the bow stem on our pound boat. Mr. Smith himself made us a new one and put it on for us. (Interview, 7 January 1988)

At the end of the bunker season in June, about a third of the pound-net crews pulled out their nets and went lobster fishing. The remaining fishermen took out one of their pound nets, leaving two. They had to do that because the nets became fouled so rapidly with animal and plant growth and mud after that, that they needed changing every nine to fourteen days; a crew could not handle three nets.

Gradually the factory acquired sixteen motorized seine boats, 140 to 200 feet long. They were wooden, run by 220-horsepower engines from surplus World War I submarine chasers, and they carried from eight hundred thousand to one and a half million bunkers each. Their seines, made of tarred cotton, were from 1,200 to 1,400 feet long and 65 feet deep with mesh sizes either 2½ or 3 inches. The seines had to be salted every night after use or they would rot quickly; crews spread twelve fifty-pound bags of salt on each one. The boats had a captain, pilot, cook, two engineers, and a crew of twelve, who lived aboard. They caught fish in Raritan Bay and in the ocean along the Long Island and New Jersey coasts as far away as twenty miles. They had to return to Belford every afternoon with their catches or the fish would begin to spoil. During a good season, each supplied forty to fifty million bunkers to this factory and others the company had subsequently constructed at three sites along the Atlantic coast. At any particular time, eight to ten seine boats were bringing bunkers to the Belford factory.

Vessel crews, who consisted mostly of black men imported seasonally from the South to work, ate extremely well on the seine boats; the good meals attracted many to the job. While the boat crews paid for their own food, the factory guaranteed the grocers that the food would be paid for and, as another gesture of local good will, ensured that the purchases were spread around about equally to each grocer in the Belford vicinity.

The length of time required for a seine boat to make a set depended on the size of the bunker school. The entire operation with a small school took only about half an hour, from the time the purse boat went out with the net to encircle the school with it to the time the bunkers were emptied from the seine. If the school had about a million bunkers, which was an exceptionally large number (each boat usually had only about five such sets in a season), it took three or four hours because the seine had to be drawn up slowly or the weight of the fish could tear it open. The main boat had a fifteen-bushel brail net lifted by a power winch to transfer the bunkers from the seine to its hold.

In typical years about 90 percent of the bunkers the factory processed came from its seine boats; 10 percent came from the pound nets in Raritan Bay. Prior to 1950, the seine boats and pound boats were emptied at two elevator stations at the fish factory. The elevators consisted of chains of buckets that carried bunkers out of the boats. The state of New Jersey had a law that no food fish could be processed by a fish factory. Only stray scrap fish, such as a sculpin, could be used (*Red Bank Register*, 27 August 1890).

The factory shut down every season about a week after the baseball World Series was played. The seine boats then went to Virginia, where they caught bunkers until Christmas. After that they went to Beaufort, North Carolina, seining them there until March.

From Sail to Engine Power in Boats

From about 1905 to 1915, fishermen installed engines in their catboats and sloops. For several years, they retained their sails, however, because the engines were unreliable. Nevertheless, they took delight in the engines, and their pride suffered when they had to resort back to sail. If, after a sail had been hoisted the engine started again, the boat captain usually made the excuse that his sail had gotten wet and he was only drying it. With engine power, fishermen could handle gear much better and lost much less fishing time; trips were faster; and getting in and out of ports was easier. Previously, for example, crews on sloops and schooners had had to launch a rowboat when entering and leaving Compton's Creek and tow their vessel, or else pole it.

The first boat constructed with only a motor was the lapstrake skiff, which quickly replaced the catboat as the commercial fishing boat for hand lining, gill netting, eeling, and lobstering. Skiffs were constructed by Petersen's yard in Keyport and the King Boat Works in Highlands. They ranged from eighteen to twenty-four feet long and had a beam of about six feet. Skiffs used for lobstering had a water-well built amidships to hold lobsters. The well had two holes in its bottom for water circulation. Skiffs had open decks; when they headed into rough water, water sprayed over them, making fishermen duck every wave. Though much more efficient than catboats, skiffs lasted only about ten years, because the rivets holding their planks loosened and then their hulls leaked. The planking could not be caulked, so the skiff had to be abandoned. Skiffs were used in the bay from about 1915 to 1950.

The pound boats constructed with motors were about thirty-six feet long and ten feet wide, with smooth sides. Built in Belford and on Staten Island and Long Island, they had a small pilothouse in the stern and a relatively large, open midsection holding 300 to 350 bushels of fish.

Fishermen began to install secondhand automobile engines instead of marine engines in their boats starting in about 1920. Junkyards charged only fifteen to twenty dollars for them. Automobile engines were superior to any marine engine made and had much more power, but marine use was hard on them and they occasionally broke down. So as not to lose any time, almost every fisherman had a spare engine available, which he could install in his boat in only a few hours.

Pound Nets

With engine-powered boats, pound-net crews were able to increase the number of pound nets they could manage from one or two to three, and they could also install them farther from Compton's Creek. Those off Belford were installed one-fourth to one-third of the distance across the bay; some were off Union Beach and along the shore of Sandy Hook.

Pound boats with motors had a boom and a brail net to transfer fish from the pound-net pocket to the boat; this supplanted the hand scoops that fishermen had used earlier. The brail net held about one and a half bushels and was suspended from the boat's boom by two blocks; a thin pole about eight feet long was attached to its side to guide it. After the fish had been concentrated in the pound pocket, one man holding the pole pushed the net through them and another lifted the net full of fish out and over the boat. The first man then emptied the net by releasing a drawstring at its bottom. It took about twenty minutes to transfer three hundred bushels of fish. In the late 1930s fishermen installed winches in their boats to lift their brail nets (see page 174). One man handled the rope around the winch, while the other handled the brail net, which had been enlarged to hold about five bushels.

Since the early 1900s, the state of New Jersey had required that each pound net have a license. The owner had to print his license number and his name and address on boards about twelve inches square and nail them to one of the poles of each pound net. For years the license cost ten dollars for each pound net. In addition, each pound net, or a row of up to four pound nets, had to have a white light on its offshore end and a red light on its inshore end, in order to show their presence to passing boats at night. Under federal law, pound-net poles were removed for the winter by 1 December.

The number of pound nets installed in the bay varied. In 1911 the bay had about fifty pound nets (*Red Bank Register,* 8 March 1911). During the Depression, when demand for fish became low, however, there were only about twenty-five pound nets.

During the 1800s and early 1900s, sharks (species unknown) were common in Raritan Bay. A pound-net fisherman once counted fifteen sharks within sight of his boat (*Red Bank Register,* 24 July 1912). When sharks were caught in pound nets, they usually damaged them. The largest shark ever recorded from a pound-net catch weighed 486 pounds and was 16 feet long (*Red Bank Register,* 24 September 1913). Pound-net fishermen gutted the large sharks they caught and sold them in Fulton Market. Fishermen, interviewed by newspaper reporters, attributed any high abundances of sharks to several causes: a scarcity of their natural food fish, which made them come closer to shore than usual; the absence of most ocean liners from their regular trips during World War I, leaving the sharks without the refuse normally thrown overboard to eat; and the possibility that the Gulf Stream had come closer than usual to the New Jersey coast, bringing the sharks closer to the bay (*Red Bank Register,* 19 July 1916).

In 1937, pound-net fishermen profited from the largest run of shad they had ever seen. The run lasted about three weeks, and pound boats came in daily with nearly full loads. In normal years, daily catches for a crew had been only 50 to 150 shad. On two of the days, however, the boats made two to three lifts a day from their pounds, returning nearly full each time. The *Red Bank Register* (15 April 1937) described the shad run:

> Fishermen and other persons could scarcely believe their eyes when they saw boat after boat pull into Compton's Creek laden to the gunwales with the valuable fish. Like the blizzard of 1888 and other unusual incidents, the great run of shad is securely anchored as a criterion in the local history of this section. Nothing like it, so far as monetary returns are concerned, had ever occurred in the past, and it is most improbable that even an approximation to it will happen in the future.
>
> Perhaps shad were equally as prevalent in the bay in 1888. Old folks recall that the pound nets yielded tremendous quantities of fish for a few days, but a comparison cannot be made because sailboats were then in use and it was not possible to make more than one lift daily, whereas with motor boats three could be made.
>
> In one short week, some of the fishermen made larger profits than for the past six years. Last year, they had a fairly profitable season, but the five prior seasons were very discouraging ones. No one will begrudge them the sudden good fortune. They will pass a good part of it along because of their increased purchasing power. They work hard and invest large sums in the pound-net fishing and their day in the sun is more than earned by their record. Now, if only some similar stroke of good fortune would befall the farmers, Monmouth County's recovery from its Depression would be complete.

Occasionally during the 1930s a few robbers stole fish from the pound nets. They dropped the net of the pocket and concentrated the fish to remove them as the owner and his crew did, but left the ropes untied. To stop the stealing, one owner hired a suspected thief to guard his pounds from robbery.

Pound-net owners paid crews a weekly salary rather than shares from the sales of the fish catch. Crewmen received fifty to sixty dollars a month, about five hundred dollars a season. Owners laid off their crews without pay from November through February or March and usually hired the same men back each spring. An owner did not like to break in a "green" man in the spring, because he had to teach him every operation. Mending holes in the nets and replacing worn sections of net required the most skill of the various tasks. While laid off, nearly all the men dug soft clams and sold them locally, or raked hard clams, which were shipped to New York City.

Four Ancient Fisheries

Haul Seining

Commercial haul seining continued at several sites on the New Jersey side of the bay throughout the early twentieth century. During the 1920s and 1930s, about seven crews operated haul seines. Some used horses to help haul in their seines, while some frequently got hauling help from local people who expected to get some free fish for their tables. A typical catch was eight to ten bushels of fish, and a haul of eighty bushels of weakfish was considered newsworthy (*Keyport Weekly*, 8 August 1924). Some farmers operated a few of the seines, mainly to obtain bunkers for fertilizer, but other farmers purchased bunkers for fertilizer from haul-seine crews for twenty-five cents a bushel. The farmer-fishermen also took the horseshoe crabs to feed their hogs and chickens and sold the remaining fish as food.

Fyke Netting

While fyke netting was important in the early 1900s, the number of fyke nets slowly began to dwindle after that, because the catches in the pound nets were so much larger. By the 1920s and 1930s, only three fishermen in Keyport and three in Belford had three or four fykes each, and Highlands fishermen had several fyke nets along the west shores of Sandy Hook installed in the spring and fall. Apparently all the fykes had been discontinued along the shores of Staten Island and Gravesend Bay. The fykes were installed singly, rather than in gangs as some had been in the late 1800s. Fishermen still rowed out to them and scooped out the fish every day using a heavily constructed crab net. It took about an hour to empty four fykes.

The fish caught were bluefish, croakers, eels, flounders, herring, mullet, sculpins, and weakfish, the most abundant being eels. Each fisherman still got fifty to one hundred pounds of fish a day from his fykes. In the spring, horseshoe crabs were part of the catch also, and while difficult to remove, they were useful as eel bait and were saved for this purpose in floating cars. Most fyke fishermen lifted fifty to sixty eel pots each day besides emptying their fykes.

Major storms with winds from the north occasionally dislodged fyke nets, and could cast them ashore. Fishermen had to reset them. At times, boys playing along the shores vandalized them, mainly by slashing the netting with knives.

Hand Lining

The hand-lining fishery, which operated mainly at night, was made easier by the use of motorized skiffs. Hand lining was practiced mostly in the ocean, where about five crews from Belford and two from Highlands did it regularly. They were often joined by several others when times were slack in other fisheries. In addition, crews on about thirty-five schooners (smacks) whose port was New York City hand-lined in the same area. The schooner crews each put out five two-man dories, each of which caught bluefish.

Hand liners lured bluefish to their boats using a chum line of minced bunkers. Chum lines had to be maintained without gaps or the bluefish would leave for another boat, and since currents ran fast in the bay, it was not a good place for hand lining, because chum lines broke up frequently. Each skiff from Belford and Highlands had three fishermen; one ground bunkers and maintained the chum line while the other two— the "fish pullers"—worked the hand lines.

Every day, bayshore crews purchased the eight to ten bushels of bunkers they needed each night from pound nets and purse-seine boats. The bunkers had to be fresh; bluefish were not lured to partially spoiled chum. Crews checked their freshness by cutting open two or three bunkers and tasting their flesh with their tongues; if the taste was tangy, the bunkers were partially decayed and would not be used.

On their way to the fishing area, one crewman began making chum by mincing the bunkers through a hand grinder, which had a mouth about eight inches in diameter. Fishermen recall, "You couldn't mince the heart of a bunker; they went right through the grinder intact" (Interview, Irving Parker, 22 July 1989). Meanwhile the two fish-pullers cut three strips from the backs of about fifty bunkers, to be put on their hooks as bait. The strips were larger than the minced pieces, because bluefish would select the largest pieces available.

Hand-lining crews arrived at a fishing site about two hours before dark. Then one man started the chum line by dipping chum out of a tub with a cup and scattering it in the current, while the fish-pullers, standing on either side of him, let out their lines about sixty feet. The steam-tarred lines were twenty-one thread and had a ten-inch wire leader holding the baited hooks, which were size 8/0 or 9/0. Fishermen had removed their barbs by filing or bending them in, because they could not afford to lose time unhooking fish if a school was biting. The line did not have a weight on it, and the current held it near the surface. After dark, a lantern was lit to enable the crew to see their chum line and other boats to see them.

When a school of bluefish came close to the skiff, the fish-pullers shortened their lines to about fifteen feet and caught a bluefish every few moments. When a fisherman caught one, he pulled it in and threw it and a wire leader over the unhooker, a stationary piece of wood about waist-high and twelve inches wide with a wire fastened horizontally across a V cut in it. He pulled the line and the bluefish dropped off into a bin. He had to put on another piece of bait after each fish was caught. Typically, a school of bluefish remained near the skiff for about two hours. The two fish-pullers competed with each other for the larger catch, and the three men often shared a bottle of wine during the night.

If a school of bluefish did not appear when the crew arrived at a site, they waited a few hours for the current to change and tried again. While it was briefly slack, the fishermen often weighted their lines, let them fall to the bottom, and caught two or three bluefish and perhaps a fluke there. Normally bluefish bit just after the change of current.

Lester Nelson, who had the reputation of being one of the best fish-pullers, related, "We caught bluefish weighing as much as twelve to fourteen pounds, but that was miserable fishing, because you ruined your hands pulling them. I had my fingers worn so much, you'd see the bones. I hated them things; five to seven pounders was ideal" (Interview, 2 March 1990) Some fishermen tied finger stalls, knitted by local women, on their first two fingers to keep from getting sores. If they did get an open sore on their hand, they urinated on it each morning to keep down infections.

Besides bluefish, other species, such as bonitos, porgies, sharks, tuna, and weakfish, appeared in chum lines at times. Sharks and tuna snapped off the hand lines. When several sharks appeared, the bluefish always left. Sometimes porgies took all the chum, also making bluefish disappear. Hand liners could not catch the porgies, because their hooks were too large for porgies' mouths.

When bluefish were abundant during the 1930s and 1940s, the usual nightly catch ranged from 800 to 1,000 pounds per skiff, but catches ran as high as 2,500 pounds. Crews gutted the fish on their way back to port; they often saved some of the roe and took them home to eat. Like the roe of other fish they saved, such as herring, flounder, and bunkers, they were extremely tasty.

The hand liners normally returned to Belford just after daybreak, packed their fish in ice, sold them, bought bunkers for the next night, and then went home to sleep. Their working day lasted fourteen to fifteen hours. They slept until midafternoon and went out again. Fishermen considered hand lining for bluefish hard work; one said, "We walked around like zombies all the time because we had to be awake such long hours" (Interview, Fred Johnson, 1 October 1989).

When the bluefish left for southern waters in October, the hand liners switched to mackerel fishing and caught mackerel until Christmas. Mackerel were caught only in the daytime and a little farther offshore, from north of Scotland Light to Shrewsbury Rocks. A chum line with bunkers was used, but less chum was needed than for bluefish. Fishermen cut out the hearts of bunkers to bait their hooks, "because mackerel went crazy for them." Often, thousands of mackerel schooled around each skiff, and as many as a ton were caught by each crew in a day. When the fishing was good, the fishermen remained warm, but when it was slow they "froze to death" (Interview, Walt DeGrote, 14 August 1989).

Eeling

About thirty fishermen (five from Lemon Creek, eight from Keyport, six to eight from Belford, and ten to twelve from Highlands) potted eels in the bay. The prime eeling areas were off the southwestern side of Staten Island and off the New Jersey coast from Keyport to Highlands. Fishermen attached eel pots at about sixty-foot intervals along trot lines and strung them along the bottom, anchoring and buoying their ends. From five to fifty pots were on a line. Full-time eelers each had about one hundred pots. For bait, they used horseshoe crabs or broken clams they obtained from the shucking shanties in Highlands. The bait had to be fresh because eels, like other fish, were not attracted to rotting bait. Fishermen lifted the pots daily. The catch from one hundred pots was fifteen hundred to eighteen hundred pounds of eels a week. Fishermen held them in cars and took them in tight wooden boxes to Fulton Market in their skiffs, or shipped them there on a freight boat.

During the second half of each summer, some Belford and Highlands fishermen went up the Hudson River from Nyack, New York, north to West Point, New York, to catch eels. They towed houseboats to live on and came home on weekends. They stored their bait supply of horseshoe crabs and waste chicken parts in cold rooms at Fulton Market, picking up new bait when they went there to sell their eels.

Each winter, about fifty fishermen speared eels (Interview, Joe Irwin, 8 May 1987). Some speared from rowboats before ice formed and during winters too warm for ice. Usually, two men were in a boat. They found the eels in one of two ways. Either they tossed out their anchor in an area where they had caught eels in past years, drifted about 120 feet from it, pulled their boat slowly back toward the anchor while spearing on each side of the boat, and stopped when they came to a concentration of eels, or they rowed to such an area, lowered a cement block until it just scraped bottom, and drifted slowly. One man was in the bow and the other was in the stern, and they speared continuously. When they got to a concentration of eels, they let out sufficient line on the block to anchor the boat and speared there. Spearing from boats was less efficient than from ice, however, because water currents and winds moved the boats around too much. Some of the veterans could judge the weight of eels within a quarter of a pound before bringing them out of a hole, or so it was said.

The commercial eel spearers earned three to four dollars a day in the early 1900s (*Red Bank Register*, 6 January 1915). One interviewed fisherman said he once speared eight thousand pounds of eels from the ice during a winter (Interview, Lester Rogers, 29 October 1987). Another man said he paid all his taxes with the eels he speared each winter.

Several fishermen speared eels on summer nights. Night spearing was called *jacking*. In rowboats, the fishermen drifted over bottoms two or three feet deep, spear in hand ready to jab. They lit the bottom with a bright jacklight set in the bow. When they saw an eel, they speared it. Jacking had to be done on still nights, because fisherman could not see the eels if the water surface was rippled. One fisherman said he caught a total of one thousand pounds of eels, weighing from one to four pounds apiece, in three consecutive nights.

Another method for catching eels was bobbing. For about a month, from late March to early April, about twenty fishermen caught eels using bobs of worms. Fishermen made the bobs of thread and sand worms, or sometimes night crawlers from their lawns. Each fisherman needed about sixty worms for a night of bobbing, thirty for each of two bobs he used. To make a continuous string about five feet long, a fisherman took a mattress needle, or made a needle from a bicycle spoke about eight inches long, put a long piece of linen thread in it, inserted the needle just behind the head of the worm, and ran the needle and thread through its body. The needle could not be inserted in the head or the worm would be turned inside out. Then they wound the worms into a bob about the size of one of their fists. Eels appear to be extra hungry in the spring and come into the shallows to feed at night, and they will bite such bobs. Fishermen bobbed in eelgrass beds in the bay, and in creeks such as Compton's Creek, but mainly in the Navesink and Shrewsbury rivers; a favorite area was just above Red Bank in the Navesink.

At dusk on a rising tide, fishermen went out in rowboats to where the water was two to three feet deep. They went alone because more than one man in a boat would be "throwing eels into each other's face" in the dark, and they had to remain quiet in their boats to avoid scaring away the eels. Bobbing had to be done after dark or else the eels would not bite, and it could not be done in deeper water because most eels would come loose from the bobs. Each fisherman usually put out two anchors to hold his boat cross-tide and then tied each bob onto the five-foot threaded lines weighted to bring the bobs to the bottom. Some fishermen tied their lines on the end of five-foot bamboo poles instead.

Eels bit the bob and their teeth caught on the thread. Fishermen had to pull them in as soon as they bit because a large eel could worm its tail into the mud, anchor itself, and be pulled free. They pulled them in slowly and shook them off in the boat. As the eels were caught, the bobs became smaller. Usually fishermen could bob for only about two or three hours; after that the tide rose too high and the bobs became too small and ragged. Each fisherman caught as many as one hundred pounds of eels, although usually about 80 percent were undersized. Eels were in the boats overnight. The next morning, the small eels, still alive, were thrown overboard and the remainder sold (Interview, Jimmy White, 16 May 1986).

After mid-April, the water warmed more and the eels became too active for bobbing; they tore up the bobs too quickly. The fishermen then set out pots for eels during the remainder of the spring. Fishermen bobbed for eels during the 1800s and into the 1950s, but this fishery disappeared afterward because sand worms became scarce and the local market for eels became weak.

Gill Netting

Drift gill-netting for weakfish and bluefish was an active fishery in this period, but it was not as long-established as the previous four. There were thirty-four crews in this fishery from New Jersey ports: two from Perth Amboy, fifteen or sixteen from Keyport, five or six from Morgan, eight from Belford, and three from Highlands. They had switched from using catboats to using skiffs; each skiff had a crew of two. With skiffs, they were able to lay their nine-hundred- to one-thousand-foot nets in a circle. This capability was important during the 1930s, when the main fish available was weakfish, which weighed from one to one and a half pounds. Weakfish would not gill themselves in numbers in a net unless the fishermen scared them into it, and thus it was much more effective to circle them. To scare the fish, fishermen tied the ends of the net together, ran their skiff inside the circle, and either took a pan on a stick, inverted it into the water, and let air bubbles escape, or splashed the water with an oar. Gill nets with three-and-a-half-inch meshes were used.

Whenever fishermen saw a school of breaking bluefish, they also set the net in a circle, ran the boat inside, and splashed the water with oars. The scared fish were gilled over the entire net. When crews did not see signs of bluefish, they set the net out in a straight line and the bluefish were gilled near its bottom. Usually the nets were left out for only about ten minutes and then retrieved. Some croakers and porgies were also caught in the gill nets; porgies "were a pain because they were hard to get out of a net." Typical daily catches were two hundred to four hundred pounds of fish (Interview, Bill Morrell, 10 November 1987).

Gill netters landed their fish in Belford, arriving there by 3 P.M., when the market boat that freighted fish to Fulton Market had returned. Fishermen put their fish in boxes obtained from this boat, took ice from its hold to preserve them, and put labels on the boxes. The boat left for Fulton Market about 9:30 A.M. the next day. If gill netters got some fish early in the morning, they loaded them on the freight boat before it left or while it was on its way across the bay.

Marketing Food Fish

Fishermen continued to ship about 90 percent of their catches to Fulton Market in New York City on freight boats running from Compton's Creek, Belford. From about 1910 onward, two boats, the *Lottie B.*, captained by Tony Gibson, and the *Alexine Davis* and later the *Edith*, both captained by Will Dennis, freighted the fish. The *Lottie B.* was taken out of this service in the early 1920s when Gibson retired, and the *Edith* freighted by itself. The *Edith*, seventy-five feet long with a green hull, was a converted schooner that had been cut in half, then lengthened from fifty feet to carry larger loads, the maximum being about six hundred boxes full of fish and ice; the boxes varied in size but most held about four bushels. The *Edith* had only one and a half feet of freeboard when fully loaded.

Most of the fish were loaded on the *Edith* at a dock near the mouth of Compton's Creek. At times as many as six pound boats loaded fish onto it simultaneously; three were on each side. Two men from each crew remained on their pound boat, shoveled the fish into baskets, and lifted them onto the *Edith*, where a third crewman shoveled crushed ice into the bottoms of boxes. The fourth crewman emptied the fish into them, the third covered them with more ice, and then they nailed on covers. Will Dennis nailed on dealers' tags, which had the name and address of the fisherman. Dennis's two crewmen stacked the boxes four or five high on the deck, arranging them so the *Edith* remained level.

A normal trip to Fulton Market for the *Edith* took about two hours. Fulton Market closed at noon, and it had to leave Compton's Creek

Loading Fish for the New York Market, Port Monmouth, N. J.

35. Pound boats loading fish aboard market boat, which would take them to Fulton Market, New York City. At stern of pound boat, a man in bateau with hard-clam rake rowing out to a bed, circa 1915. Courtesy of Kenneth A. Norton.

around 9:30 A.M. to arrive in time. The Edith did not have much power; it chugged at about seven knots across the bay. Often Will Dennis stopped to take on late boats' catches in the bay as he headed north. If Dennis had to buck the Hudson River current to the market, he went up between Hoffman and Swinburne islands and Staten Island, and crossed the main channel, skirted along the Brooklyn shore, and then crossed it again to Fulton Market. At times, Dennis also carried a few passengers on the Edith to New York City and back again.

At the market, workers off-loaded the boxes on the dock, stacked them on two-wheel dollies, and carried them to the sheds belonging to the various commission merchants. The crew of the Edith loaded on two-hundred-pound blocks of ice and stored them in its hold for preserving fish on the return trip. At times, however, ice was obtained from a plant that made it in Red Bank. In the 1930s, the only period for which data are available, Dennis charged fishermen two dollars per four-bushel box, or about one cent a pound for the fish, to transport their fish (Interview, Bill Schnoor, 7 February 1991).

The freshly caught Raritan Bay fish were often in such demand in Fulton Market that some of the merchants sent agents to Belford to persuade the fishermen to drop their regular buyers and sell to them.

They even offered to help transfer the fish from the pound boats to the *Edith*.

Because they did not have portable scales, fishermen could not weigh their fish when they loaded the *Edith*. Instead, the fish were weighed by commission merchants in Fulton Market. The fishermen believed they were sending far more fish than they were being paid for, and they referred to the *Edith* as "the Santa Claus boat." The merchants took out 12.5 percent of the sale price as their payment for handling the fish, then paid Will Dennis directly for freighting the fish, and finally mailed a check for the balance to the fishermen. Fishermen also had to pay about fifteen cents for each wooden box (Interview, Bill Schnoor, 11 December 1985).

Sometimes pound-net crews with extra-large catches of food fish carried them to Fulton Market in their pound boats to avoid the freight charge on the *Edith*. Monday was the usual day for this, since the pound nets had not been lifted for a day or two. Because porgies sold for only about one cent a pound, fishermen often carried them when they had a large load; otherwise they would receive nothing in return after the freight charge was paid. The more valuable fish carried there were bluefish, weakfish, croakers, and butterfish. When pound boats took fish to Fulton Market, they did not ice the fish, because the two-and-a-half-hour trip was begun just as the sun was rising and air temperatures were cool. Upon arriving at Fulton Market, the crew shoveled the fish into baskets; a crew from the market hoisted them onto the dock, put them on dollies, and wheeled them to their sheds.

In the late 1930s, Will Dennis, then in his seventies, lost his business when trucks took over the freighting of fish from Belford to Fulton Market and other points. The *Edith* was hauled onto a marsh in Compton's Creek, where it decayed; the freighting of fish across the bay to New York City had ended for good.

The food fish that were not carried to New York, about 10 percent of the total caught by fishermen, were sold to seven to ten peddlers in Belford. They had horse-drawn covered wagons and waited every morning at the docks for the boats to return. Each bought from two hundred to three hundred pounds of fish of a few varieties, laid them on ice in his wagon, and then sold them house to house within a radius of about ten miles (Interview, John Fisler, 20 October 1988). The peddlers covered a different route each day. They had fewer customers in Belford, Highlands, and Keyport, where so many residents were fishermen, than in other towns. The wives of nonfishermen in Belford could walk down to Compton's Creek and buy fish cheap off the boats.

Peddlers sold to about fifty customers a day. The peddler, or his son if he went along, rapped on customer doors and yelled, "Fish man." After a customer placed an order, the peddler usually cleaned the fish for a small extra fee, but some customers bought whole fish to save a little money. The peddlers chatted with customers and were useful in communities as purveyors of local news and stories gathered along their routes. Peddlers saved the fish heads, guts, and scales in buckets for friends who used them for fertilizer. At least one recipient used them to fertilize his grape arbor (Interview, John Volk, 2 February 1990). After automobiles became available, peddlers began using them for carrying the fish. During the 1920s and 1930s, two men used motor boats to peddle Raritan Bay fish and hard clams along the Hudson River to a dozen or so towns, from Hoboken, New Jersey, to Albany, New York. Both had iceboxes on their decks to preserve the fish and clams, along with weighing scales. They bought fish and clams on Mondays and sold them during the week. They had initiated their peddling by stopping at docks at certain times and days. Business started slowly, but soon lines of customers formed when it became known by word-of-mouth that fresh fish and clams were available there. One or two boat peddlers from Belford also went to Perth Amboy and New Brunswick, New Jersey, carrying fish, clams, and lobsters. Boats could not travel easily to New Brunswick selling seafood before they were motor-powered.

Eel fishermen also sold skinned eels locally to peddlers, markets, and men who smoked them. Fishermen and helpers cleaned and skinned the eels at the shores. Wilbur Huylar, an octogenarian and model boat-builder living in Keyport, remembered:

> Us kids used to go down to the shore when the eelers came in, sit in the sand, and skin their eels. We'd dig a hole and dump the eels in it. The sand clinging to them gave us a good grip. We cut off their heads, skinned, and washed them and then put them into a pan. The fishermen gave us a quarter or half dollar for doing it. The old-timers could clean eels faster than we could. They ran their knives down an eel's belly and the eel's guts would come out at the same time! (Interview, 9 July 1986)

Schoolboys peddled skinned eels for some fishermen. They carried the eels, tied in bunches of four or ten, with ice on their play wagons and sold twelve to fifteen bunches a day. The smaller bunches sold for fifty cents each and the larger ones for a dollar each. The boys earned five cents for selling the smaller bunches and ten cents for the larger bunches (Interview, Pete Rosenberg, 7 January 1988). Local people ate the eels fried, smoked, or in stews.

A brief sketch of the working history of Ed Fisler, the last fish peddler in Belford, provides more details about the operations of peddlers.

> The first vehicle Fisler owned in the 1920s was a horse-drawn wagon. On cold winter days, he was warmer walking alongside than sitting on it. In the 1930s he switched to a secondhand automobile; he removed its back seat and put in two washtubs for holding the fish and ice. In the winter, he also delivered shucked soft clams. He purchased the clams from diggers, and he opened and packed them in quart jars with the assistance of his family. On early summer mornings, while waiting for the fishing boats to return, he often spent about an hour collecting wood off beaches to bring home for fuel. During the 1940s and thereafter, he used panel trucks for selling and his wares included eggs from his large flock of laying hens. During World War II, when the government rationed meat, he also sold dressed chickens from his flock.
>
> Fisler peddled in the towns of Port Monmouth, New Monmouth, Middletown, Leonardo, Red Hill, Holmdel, Lincroft, and Red Bank. Most customers paid him in cash, but some were on credit. Two customers had twenty or so cats each, and for lower prices they bought all his leftover fish that were two or three days old to feed them.
>
> Fisler did not need a license for peddling until the 1940s. In the 1960s and early 1970s, his final years, he also sold more expensive items such as lobsters and shrimp, but by this time, peddling had become difficult. Local ordinances required that peddlers park off the roads when they stopped to sell, and places to park were scarce. Authorities also required board of health inspection of trucks and certification of weighing scales. When Fisler died in 1975, his son, Edward, Jr., did not carry on the business; he had a more profitable job, unrelated to fishing. Fish peddling had ended in the Bayshore. (Interview, Ed Fisler, Jr., 28 January 1989)

Smoking Fish

Smoking eels and other fish was an ancient practice along the bayshore. Eels and other fish were smoked in "smokers" (also called smoke boxes or smokehouses). These were usually constructed of wood or cement blocks, but fifty-five-gallon drums and abandoned refrigerators were also

36. A "smoker" (smokehouse) for fish. Note thermometer above
door, flue at top rear, and fruitwood on ground. Photograph by
author.

used. A well-constructed wooden smoker stood about six feet high; the
largest were ten feet wide and ten feet long, the smallest three by three
feet. Smokers had pitched roofs with a flue on top and several holes
about an inch in diameter on each of their sides just above the bottom.
These holes could be closed if the fire burned too high. One side of the
box had a tightly fitting door. The fire was contained in brick boxes or in
cut-down metal barrels. The fish hung by their tails or heads on about
twenty-six nails spaced along each of several racks set two to four feet
above the fire.

Several steps were involved in smoking fish. First they were gutted and their gills removed, but they were not skinned. Next they were washed and soaked for twelve to fourteen hours in brine to harden their flesh. The brine was prepared by mixing one pound of salt with one gallon of fresh water, or mixing salt into water until a potato floated in it. The fish were then drip-dried and put on the racks in the smokehouse. The fire of small logs had been made ahead of time. The wood used was fruitwood—apple or cherry—or hickory, whose smoke added sweetness to the flavor of the smoked fish. The fire was periodically smothered with wet wood chips to keep it smoking. If the box had a thermometer, the temperature was held at 120° F for six hours, then raised to 200° F for about two hours to cook the fish. Otherwise, the smokebox operator had to use his judgment, based on years of experience, to smoke the fish properly. After that, the burning wood was removed from the box and the fish were allowed to cool. They were then ready to eat and were stored in a cool dry place (Interview, Lou Defonzo, 27 July 1991).

Highlands had about ten such smokers in the 1920s and 1930s; other towns around the bayshore had several each. Most were commercial. The owners bought fresh fish and sold them smoked (for five cents each during the 1930s); they also smoked fish for people for a small price per pound.

The Rowboat Livery Era in Sport Fishing

The period from 1911 to 1939 was the heyday of rowboat liveries, when recreational fishermen could rent boats for fishing in the bay; liveries continued afterward but on a reduced scale. Sport fishing also continued from piers and the shore, and some people fished from sailboats trolling small spoons and sand worms hooked onto spinners (Emmons 1907). Fishing was excellent for porgies, fluke, croakers, bluefish, and weakfish. One old-timer recalled, "In the 1920s there were so many lafayettes in the bay that you could go down to one of these piers, put out a line with seven or eight baited hooks on it, wait a couple of minutes, and you'd have one on every hook. They were fabulous. They were small, but edible" (Interview, Arnold Petersen, 17 November 1989). There were about ten sport-fishing clubs on Staten Island and some were founded in Monmouth County, New Jersey, but commercial fishermen still far outnumbered sportfishermen.

The rowboat liveries operating in Raritan Bay included Shoals Dock in Great Kills Harbor; Sandy's at the mouth of Lemon Creek in Prince's Bay, Staten Island; and Bahrs, Johnny's Landing, Julian's, and Roxy's in Highlands. Keyport and Belford also each had a livery. The number of

37. Sport fishermen's catch of bluefish in Raritan Bay, in port of Prince's Bay, circa 1930. Courtesy of Pete Glismann.

rowboats in each livery ranged from about thirty to a hundred; nearly all were floating and tied to piers or slips, but the one in Belford had its boats hauled onto a beach. People rented rowboats for half a day or a full day; they could also rent fishing rods. Most people arrived between 5 and 9 A.M. and rowed the boats out on the bay. At Sandy's and Roxy's, motorized skiffs were available to tow them out and in for a small fee. The day usually ended between 4 and 6 P.M., but some fishermen stayed out into the evening. The liveries rented boats from April through October and were busiest from June through August.

Sandy's, which had about seventy rowboats, was "one of the most famous fishing liveries on the East Coast for weakfish." It opened for business in 1918 and stopped renting boats in 1967. To stimulate business at the beginning of each season, Sandy Cuthbert, the owner, gave a new rod and reel to the fisherman who brought in the first weakfish, and throughout the season he advertised his livery in newspapers in New York and New Jersey, where he drew his clientele. Many fishermen got to his livery by car; New Yorkers also came by train from the Manhattan-Staten Island ferry. His livery was so popular that when the weather was nice all the boats were rented every Sunday. Fishermen reserved many of them the previous Sunday or by telephone. Many people arriving without reservations had to wait in line for a boat to return at midday. Sandy's charged $1.00 for a boat all day during the week and $1.50 on weekends. Tows to and from the fishing area of Round Shoal nearby the livery cost an additional 75 cents; when a fishing party wanted to come in, it signaled by standing up an oar in its boat.

Sandy's sold bait, including shrimp and killifish, caught by his helpers in a local creek, sand worms dug locally and in Maine, and bunkers obtained from Belford. Killifish sold for fifty cents a quart, sand worms for thirty-five cents a dozen, and bunkers for a dollar a bushel (Interview, Margaret Wittich, 8 February 1988).

Fishermen caught mostly porgies, fluke, and weakfish; they also caught winter flounder, lafayettes, and blowfish. Only two or three species were usually available at any one time. Some fishermen chummed for weakfish, using shrimp. They threw a few large handfuls into the water to attract the weakfish and when the fish came they continued the chumming, but with fewer shrimp. Then they put shrimp on their hooks and began catching them (Interview, Everett Walle, 9 December 1987). When commercial hand rakers were gathering hard clams on Round Shoal, the fishing for fluke and porgies was best because the digging lifted burrowed invertebrates out of the bottom, attracting fish. Catches for a boat usually ranged from ten to twenty fish per trip. Some fishermen also went crabbing up Lemon Creek beyond the livery in the rented boats.

Sandy's also had a twenty-eight-foot head boat, which took out parties of up to six fishermen at a time. The fish sought were bluefish (chummed with minced bunkers), fluke, porgies, and weakfish (chummed with shrimp) (Interview, Everett Walle, 9 December 1987).

Sandy's was especially busy during World War II, because for security reasons the federal government did not allow party boats to go out fishing. Sandy's boats were all rented every weekend and frequently during the week.

Sandy's had a small restaurant serving lobster and fish dinners as well as ice cream cones and candy. It also had a fish market that sold fish, mostly eels, and lobsters that Sandy had caught in pots in Prince's Bay, as well as other fish that he purchased wholesale from Belford. He used an old twenty-one-foot oyster-tonging skiff fitted with a motor for lifting his eel and lobster pots.

Sandy stopped renting boats, in part because its business had declined. Many fishermen had obtained their own boats and motors, leaving Sandy's with only berths to rent. Moreover, patrons often

38. *An early type of head or charter boat used in Raritan Bay, in port of Prince's Bay, circa 1930. Courtesy of Staten Island Historical Association, Richmondtown Restoration, Staten Island, New York.*

damaged rented motors, and after fishing they frequently left the boats on beaches at distances from the livery. In addition, the U.S. Coast Guard decreed for safety reasons that only four people were allowed in such rowboats, but people wanted to take out more, usually their children. The Coast Guard held the liveries responsible for any infractions. Rather than hire more help to make repairs and retrieve its boats and be liable for penalties from the Coast Guard, Sandy's went out of business (Interview, Margaret Wittich, 8 February 1988).

Head Boats

By the 1930s the bay had only three head boats for sport fishing. Each was busy, however, because many people were out of work and found that a fishing trip was a great way to obtain cheap food. They went out "meat fishing" and caught quantities of fish for food, mostly porgies in summer and ling in winter. Frequently, neighbors gave them a quarter to help pay their way if they would bring them back some fish. Head boats charged each fishermen two dollars a day and carried about ten thousand people a year.

8

Shell Fishing Before World War II

The 1911–1939 period was marked by the end of the oyster industry due to pollution, by a huge set of hard clams during the early 1930s, and by the continued prominence of the soft-clam fishery. It also featured the development of the winch on boats, which made lobstering, blue crabbing, and pound-net fishing much easier.

During this period, New York and New Jersey imposed laws to protect the public from eating unsafe shellfish by prohibiting landings from polluted beds. They also imposed laws to conserve shellfish: hard clams could not be dredged from a boat driven by motor power; soft clams could not be dug using motor-driven propellers; and small lobsters could not be landed. There were no minimum size limits on hard clams and soft clams, however, and no limits on the quantities of shellfish that could be taken.

Oystering

In 1912 the first substantial notice that pollution might be a problem in raising oysters came when the New Jersey Health Department prohibited the Elsworth company from using Luppatatong Creek for "drinking" oysters. It found that the creek was unsanitary and would contaminate the oysters. The company then devised a means of accomplishing what "drinking" had done, by bringing the oysters directly from the beds into the plant and, after workers had shucked them, emptying their meats into tanks of pure fresh water for several minutes. The meats were washed clean, and they bloated with fresh water.

Workers put the washed oyster meats in clean pails and then put them in a chilling room for twenty-four hours, taking every care to keep them clean. Next, they put them in five-gallon cans and sealed them, so the customers would receive them without further handling. Finally, they put the cans into barrels packed with ice. Up until a few years before this, workers had put the ice in the same can with the oysters, but this resulted in a loss of oyster flavor and some contamination. The oyster meats were shipped to the Midwest and the Pacific coast; they brought the company $1.15 to $1.40 a gallon, the lower prices being for smaller oysters (*Red Bank Register,* 23 December 1914).

In 1914, after transferring two oyster barges from New York City to Keyport, the Elsworth company more than tripled the size of its shucking force to about 140 men. Most shuckers were imported seasonally from southern states. They were paid twenty cents a gallon for oyster meats shucked and earned from thirty to forty dollars a week. The company shucked 2,500 gallons of oyster meats (about 2,800 bushels of oysters) daily, and 200,000 gallons (about 220,000 bushels of oysters) a season. It also employed a few men throughout the year to make bushel baskets. These men constructed the baskets entirely from strips cut from oak logs. The Foster Oyster Company of New York City also transferred a barge from the city, bringing the total to three. Whenever Foster's shucking barge in New York City could not handle all its orders, the orders were supplied from Keyport (*Red Bank Register,* 23 December 1914).

During the early summer, Elsworth workers transferred the empty, shucked shells, usually 100,000 to 150,000 bushels piled near the plant, onto its vessels. They took most of the shells to Connecticut and spread them on the company's seedbeds there for collecting oyster sets (*Red Bank Register,* 23 December 1914). They took the remaining shells to a lime kiln in Mattawan or used them to fill local roads (Interview, Bill Richardson, 5 October 1985).

The oyster industry in Raritan Bay continued to operate briskly until about 1915, when the western end of the bay began to become polluted. Authorities found that some shipments from the bay were making people as far away as Chicago sick with typhoid fever and intestinal diseases. Afterward, New York dealers became reluctant to purchase oysters from the bay. The industry declined, and finally in 1925 oyster planters abandoned the bay amid much negative newspaper publicity about polluted oysters being sold.

The Elsworth company transferred its ten oyster boats to its oyster plants in New Haven, Connecticut, and Greenport, New York, on Long Island, where they remained in use through the 1960s. The small leaseholders either transferred most of their vessels to Belford, where they used them for dredging hard clams and blue crabs, or they sold some as freight boats; the oldest ones were hauled onto marshes and abandoned. Authorities permitted the larger planters, mainly the Elsworth company, with beds in Gardiners Bay in eastern Long Island, and Narragansett Bay, Rhode Island, to transplant their oysters from Raritan Bay to the other beds for cleansing and marketing. Head Captain Bill Wooley of the Elsworth company established an oyster farm in Barnegat Bay, which he operated for a number of years.

The closure of the oyster industry forced the local oystermen into an economic depression, accentuated after 1929 by the nationwide Depression. The closures displaced oystermen and their families, eliminated shore-based enterprises, and generally diminished the quality of bayshore life in the western part of the bay. For example, one prosperous planter from Tottenville became a house painter, and the Elsworth family of Keyport lost its money. Mrs. Elvira Cunningham, of Tottenville, whose father was an oysterman, recalled: "The oyster industry was like a part of you. It was a dreadful loss because many of the men weren't that young. They'd gone into it from grammar school and that's all they knew. The boats were dear to their hearts and their families" (Interview, 26 September 1989).

An unusually abundant set of oysters was discovered on some beds off Keyport in 1930. Several boatloads of the seed were dredged and transplanted to beds in eastern Long Island, where the Elsworth company grew them to market size (*Keyport Weekly,* 18 April 1930).

Hard Clamming

Hard clams varied in abundance through the years. For example, in 1884, a sloop from Keyport dredged forty-nine bushels of clams in one day; it was the largest catch reported up to that time and sold for forty dollars. Hard clams must have been relatively scarce between 1884 and 1899, however, because by 1899, catches of fifteen, sixteen and a half, and twenty bushels of hard clams by three sloops in one day were the largest catches reported in many years. In 1911, another report stated, "The bayshore clammers are having the best clam season which they have had in years and many residents who quit the clam industry two years ago have bought a boat and rake and gone offshore clamming. Most of the clammers got discouraged two years ago, sold their outfits and hired out with pound fishermen at $60 a month. They are now returning to the clam business and some of them have made as much as $15 a day this summer raking clams" (*Red Bank Register,* 26 July 1911).

During the 1920s, hard clam abundance was low; during the 1930s it was extremely high, and then it declined again.

In the 1911–1939 period, several implements were used for gathering hard clams. The most important were hand rakes and sail dredges. Short-handle rakes and tongs were used on a small scale; treading was also common.

The Tools

George Porter, an eighty-one-year-old who had been a blacksmith in Keyport from the 1920s to the 1960s, described how he had constructed a hand rake (Interview, 29 September 1985). He made its twenty-eight teeth from 10/30 carbon-steel rods twenty feet long and three-eighths of an inch in diameter. The first step was to cut the rods to the length of a tooth, fifteen inches. The teeth were heated in a fire about five inches from their ends and made oval-shaped by hitting them with a hammer. After being cooled and tempered by a dip in oil, they were sharpened on a grinding wheel; sharpening twenty-eight teeth took half an hour. The next step was to heat the entire length of each tooth and bend them over a curved form. The attachment end of each tooth had to be heated and hammered to make it thicker, for a stronger weld on the tooth bar.

The tooth bar was made of one-inch-by-half-an-inch steel. The places where the teeth were to be welded on it were marked with chalk, and the bar was clamped onto the anvil. Next, the two "crabs" (sharply curled teeth at each end of the rake to hold in the clams) were welded onto the two end teeth, and then each tooth was welded onto the bar spaced a little less than an inch apart. The shank of the rake was welded on last.

To align the teeth parallel to each other, strings were tied across them in three places. A rake set, consisting of two iron pieces eighteen inches long and a half inch in diameter, was used to pull the teeth in line.

Porter cut and made all the pieces for two rakes in a morning and welded them together and lined up the teeth in an afternoon. He produced his rakes on order and on a cash basis. In the 1920s and 1930s, he charged twenty cents a tooth for his rakes. His price gradually went up to seventy-five cents a tooth by the 1940s and to a dollar a tooth in the 1950s.

Raking wore the teeth and often they became paper-thin at their tips, and bent. When a fisherman had worn down the teeth of a rake half an inch, it would not catch clams well. He brought the rake to Porter, who reconditioned it simply by bending and reforming the teeth, done without heating. For doing this, he charged one dollar for a rake in the 1920s and 1930s and two dollars in the 1940s and 1950s. The teeth could be

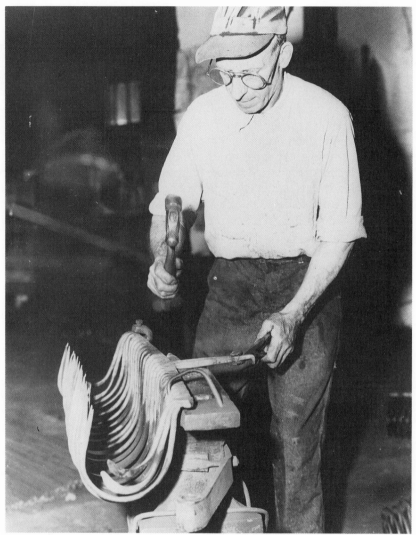

39. George Porter, circa 1950, one of seven blacksmiths in Keyport. He made hard-clam rakes (shown here) for about forty years until the beds became polluted in 1961. Courtesy of George Porter.

reconditioned twice; after that, they were too short and the rake was discarded. If used in a sand-mud bottom, a rake lasted three or four years; if used in a mud bottom, a rake could last fifteen to twenty years.

One source of handles for hard-clam rakes around the turn of the century was Florida. The *Red Bank Register* (11 April 1900) reported that a local man sailed a schooner to Florida to get longleaf yellow pine for clam rake handles. In this instance, he returned without any because the water was so deep in the swamps where the pines grew that they could not be cut. He planned another trip within a few months.

Urban Hancock of Belford made rake handles during the 1930s and 1940s. Longleaf yellow pine was the only wood he used; it contains much pitch, which kept the handles moist. A dry handle made of other wood snapped easily, as did a handle with knots. Moist handles also sank, keeping a rake against the bottom, whereas a buoyant handle tended to lift a rake out of the bottom, making digging less efficient.

Hancock and his friends collected the pine as driftwood from local beaches. At times they found square logs as large as forty feet long and twelve inches on a side. Eight handles could be made from one of these. The logs were trucked to Hancock's shop, where they were cut into two-inch-by-two-inch square pieces using a crude circular saw powered by an old steam engine. Hancock then planed all the corners repeatedly by going along the full length of the handle without lifting off the plane. He did this many times, until the handle became round. Most handles were about thirty-two feet long. If a handle was too short, he cut a long taper on two pieces and fastened them together with nails and marlin line.

Each handle also needed three splices, ranging in length from two to eight feet. Fishermen had found that the angle between their rakes and the bottom was critical and had to be about forty-five degrees; if more, the rake would anchor; if less, it would not catch clams. Since the clammers raked at various depths, they needed the splices to adjust their handle lengths. Hancock could make a handle and its splices in half a day. Fishermen called the handle a *but*.

The handles of the clam rakes used on Staten Island were also made from longleaf yellow pine. Some of the longleaf yellow pine came from the bottoms of abandoned barges in the Arthur Kill. The old barges were beached, their sides were torn down and used for firewood, and some of the bottom planks were used for making rake handles. Planks were ripped down with saws into the same two-inch-by-two-inch square lengths, then made round by planing (Interview, Pete Glismann, 18 June 1987).

If a fisherman cared for his rake handle, it lasted five or six years. Whenever his rake was heavy and nearly full of clams, he had to bring the handle straight up as far as he could before the rake reached the surface. This made for less curve in the handle and less stress on it; it could snap under too much stress. A fisherman also had to be careful on windy days. If the wind bent the handle sharply or a rogue wave hit the boat when it was in the air, it could also snap (Interview, Al Sonic, 16 April 1986).

When he came ashore, the fisherman took the handle off his rake, laid it in the water, and lashed it to his boat to keep it straight and wet.

Some fishermen tied the handles straight up alongside a piling at the dock, but that way the upper part dried and could get splintery. If a fisherman stored the handle on land for some time, he had to soak it in water before use. During the off-season, he kept his rake handles out of the sun, usually under a building (Interview, Pete Glismann, 18 June 1987).

The Work

Hand raking remained the most difficult fishing task. Jerking a rake through the bottom and then lifting it, heavy with clams and mud, to the surface was hard work. Whenever the clammer did not work, his rake did not get any clams. This was not the case with some other gears, such as fyke nets, pound nets, gill nets, and eel and lobster pots, which caught fish and lobsters by themselves after the fishermen left them. Several clam fishermen recall, "We were 'pounding' all the time, " and they jokingly said that they called it "hard clamming" because the work was hard, rather than because of the hard clam's harder shell (Interview, Jigs Apel, 19 September 1988).

The primary boat used was the bateau. In the 1920s and 1930s those fishermen who raked off the stern of their boats fastened a foot-long hard rubber roller obtained from an abandoned washing machine on their sterns. When they pulled a rake to the surface, they laid it on the roller and pushed it back and forth to wash the mud from the clams. The roller prevented the handle from wearing.

Fishermen raked hard clams around the bay in wide transition zones between hard sand in shallow water and soft mud in deeper water around the bay; the water ranged from ten to twenty-five feet deep. The owners of skiffs towed the rakers to and from the beds for fifty cents a day. The rakers carried oars with them for rowing back to the towing skiff at the end of a day and to the beach whenever a sudden squall roared down the bay.

Hand rakers from the New Jersey ports of Keyport and Belford normally got out of bed about four each morning, dressed, ate breakfast, prepared their lunches (perhaps two sandwiches or a chicken leg and some raisin buns), filled their quart thermos with coffee or tea, put on a pair of short rubber boots and a cap, and left for their docks. Few wives got up that early to prepare breakfast or lunch for their husbands. Hand rakers usually left the dock at daybreak. They ate their lunches after they had been on the water for about two hours.

During a typical day, winds and currents were ideal for perhaps only about one and a half hours, and rakers got nearly half their catch of six to twelve bushels during that period. Each fisherman made from sixty to eighty-five rakings, after which he was usually too tired to continue. The rakers all quit at about the same time, about one in the afternoon, after six or seven hours on the water, and were towed back to port. Some "bulls" dug a little longer and rowed home, but they became old men before their time. In summer, rakers could work almost every day because the weather remained good, but it was impossible to rake on summer afternoons—the southern breezes were too strong. In fall, the weather worsened, forcing them to miss some days. From November onward, they could rake only two or three days a week.

The most difficult area for raking clams was off Great Kills Harbor, where the bottom is relatively hard, currents relatively strong, and swells come in from the ocean. Fishermen had to rake off the sterns of their bateaux, which drifted too fast if they worked off the side. Al Sonic, a former clam digger from Great Kills, described hand raking there:

> If the wind was against the current, it was pretty hard. Sometimes, the rake wouldn't go in the bottom right, or the boat would only go around in a circle and we wouldn't get much. When the wind and current were in the same direction, we put out a four-prong drag anchor to slow the boat down. We let it way out and kept shortening it until we had the right slow speed. On some days, though, no matter how we set it, we'd go too fast. Sometimes, I got so annoyed that I just packed it in and went home with only one or two bushels. I could have stayed and battled it, but I'd be burning myself out.
>
> Ordinarily, I lost two or three days a week, sometimes four, from bad weather. I rarely got in six straight days. If the day was good, I stayed out a little longer because I might lose the next day. I used to get five to eight bushels on a good day. Some days, the weather might be good, but I didn't feel good and couldn't get as many as usual. My highest was ten bushels. We never hit any bonanzas. We broke our backs for what we got. When I was through a day of clamming, all I wanted to do was to hit the sack and go to sleep. I didn't go clamming by choice. No other jobs were available. It was hard work! (Interview, 16 April 1986)

The clams were most abundant in the bay on Round Shoal off Prince's Bay. Each day, fishermen there had to dig only four to six hours to obtain ten to twelve bushels of clams. Typical catches were three bushels of littlenecks, four bushels of cherrystones, and five bushels of chowders (Interview, Pete Glismann, 18 June 1987). The largest reported catch there in one day was the astonishing total of seventy-three bushels

40. Rakers unloading their hard clams at Great Kills, Staten Island, circa 1939. Photograph by Anthony Lanza. Courtesy of Staten Island Historical Society, Richmondtown Restoration, Staten Island, New York.

by Charlie Badke, whose son pulled up his rake every time with an attached rope. The catch occurred in 1939, the year the state of New York opened the beds for gathering the clams.

Besides wind, ice sometimes prevented hand rakers from working. Bill Braun, a former clammer from Keansburg, New Jersey, described his experience with ice on a still night in winter while raking illegally in Prince's Bay:

> Ed Quinn from Keyport and I were clamming about thirty feet apart. It was dead calm. I'm raking away and all of the sudden the noise on the handle sounded funny. It also felt as though the water was getting heavy. I said to Quinny: "Boy, is that water heavy." He says: "Ya, I can feel it on my handle." He said: "Do you know what it is? Its ice." I knew it was cold because when I pulled in the rope it froze to the floor, but I wasn't thinking of the bay freezing. I put my hand overboard and the ice was about an eighth of an inch thick. I said: "Holy smokes, I'm getting out of here. If we freeze in solid, we're not going to get out." I remembered about the guy who bought a boat and tried to run it up Compton's Creek with a thin sheet of ice on it. The ice cut through the wood and the boat sank right there in the middle of the creek.
>
> So, I said to Quinny: "I'm going to turn this boat around

and go home backward, and I'm going to break the ice all the way. I'm not going by power." So, I took my cross-head and a long splice, broke the ice ahead of me, and pulled through the broken ice. It was about four miles across, but we were young.

I was worried about Quinny. I thought that he would get tired of doing this and take a chance and try to go under power. I broke all the way, got to the dock, and tied up. We left Prince's Bay about 2 A.M. and I got ashore about 5:30 A.M. I jumped into my car and drove fast up to Keyport, thinking about Quinny. There was his boat tied to the dock. He told me later that he didn't try to power through the ice. (Interview, 12 December 1986)

During the 1920s, hard clamming was depressed in the bay. The state of New York had prohibited all further shellfishing in its half of the bay in the mid-1920s, after the oyster industry was terminated because of pollution. At that time, only about twelve fishermen were digging hard clams in New Jersey, mostly because the clams had become somewhat scarce and also because more land-based jobs were available.

The Huge Set of Hard Clams

In the early 1930s, the situation in New Jersey changed dramatically, for two reasons: there was a huge set of seed hard clams in vast areas of the bay, and the country had fallen into a severe economic depression, leaving a great many people without jobs. Fishermen reached down in knee-deep water along various shores of the bay, picked up handfuls of sand, and saw dozens of white pea-sized clams in it. Quickly, markets were found for the clams and several hundred unemployed men soon purchased clam rakes and bateaux and began digging the clams. Most clams were sold to leaseholders in Chincoteague Bay and Barnegat Bay for rebedding and additional growth. They paid $1.00 to $1.50 a bushel for them. The remainder were sold to coal truckers from Pennsylvania, who brought the inch-long clams back with them for resale to people who ate them even though they were unusually small (*Red Bank Register,* 17 October 1935).

To collect the seed, fishermen inserted coarse metal screens in their rakes. Each gathered several bushels a day, with some daily catches ranging as high as twelve bushels per digger. Many earned about ten dollars a day, and some even as much as twelve to fifteen dollars a day, extremely high wages for the time. Five hundred to six hundred fishermen raked clams in any one day (*Red Bank Register,* 17 October 1934). Nearly all raked in rowboats, but some skiffs carried as many as three clammers (Interviews, Harry Sage, 9 September 1988; George Kaveleski, 15 October 1991). The *Red Bank Register* estimated that about one thousand men were hard clamming and soft clamming in the mid-1930s. As a result, unemployment in the New Jersey bayshore was almost negligible (*Red Bank Register,* 28 November 1935). Work picked up considerably for blacksmiths, who were busy making rakes and anchors for the clammers.

Calamity struck in the mid-1930s, however, when most of the seed clams attained littleneck and cherrystone sizes. New York City had imposed a ban prohibiting the importation of hard clams from Raritan Bay in the mid-1920s, because city authorities feared they were polluted. Thousands of bushels of market-sized clams began to glut the local New Jersey market and some spoiled for lack of demand (*Newark Evening News,* 14 October 1935). In 1935 the New Jersey clammers formed a Bayshore Shellfisheries Association, electing Will Dennis, the captain of the fish freight boat *Edith* as president, to deal with the ban. The association was joined by local businessmen, who stood to gain by increased retail business from the clammers if the ban could be lifted. The association wanted to present a united front of fishermen and to collect enough money to hire a lawyer to get the ban lifted. On 10 January 1935 Congressman William H. Sutphin, representative of the Third Congressional District (the New Jersey bayshore), conferred in New York City with Mayor Fiorello LaGuardia, urging that he order it lifted. Mayor LaGuardia requested the congressman to submit data pertaining to the purity of shellfish in the bay, stating that city authorities were concerned only about public health (*Red Bank Register,* 10 January 1935).

In 1935 the association appealed to the U.S. Public Health Service in Washington to make a survey of the clam beds. The service found the beds to be safe for harvesting the clams, and on 15 October 1935 New York City agreed to lift the ban, if two conditions were met: New Jersey authorities had to maintain a sanitary patrol of Raritan Bay, and each bag of clams had to have a red tag on it (*Red Bank Register,* 3 October 1935).

Hundreds of clammers along the bayshore communities were jubilant over the news. The world's largest market was open again. Clammers were upset about the red tags, however, because they tainted and stigmatized the clams in the minds of the buyers (*Red Bank Register,* 24 October 1935). Clammers believed the tags were a warning to consumers that they had to cook the clams to kill any germs; also, the clams sold for less. On 1 January 1937 New York authorities removed the red tag requirement (*Red Bank Register,* 10 December 1936). This action led to a better market and slightly higher prices for the clams.

When the ban in New York City was in effect, 2,430 people in

Middletown, Atlantic Highlands, and Highlands were on relief or working for the Works Progress Administration (WPA). But after New York authorities removed the ban, that number fell to 957; the decline was attributed mostly to the lifting of the ban (*Red Bank Register,* 10 December 1936). Landings of market-sized hard clams from the bay rose from 11,560 bushels worth $13,029 in 1933 to 141,167 bushels worth $164,930, in 1938 (U.S. Government Landing Statistics).

In the mid-1930s many men were unemployed on Staten Island. The large hard-clam fishery in New Jersey inspired a few to sample the Staten Island bottoms with rakes; they found those off Prince's Bay, at least, to be almost paved with clams. They asked state officials to reopen the beds and to open New York City as a market for these clams, but the officials refused to do it. Not to be denied, the men enlisted the aid of a bacteriologist from Wagner College on Staten Island, who found that the quantity of bacteria in the clams was well below the acceptance level for direct marketing. The men then brought the data to a politician, who directed state officials to open the beds for clamming in 1939. As a compromise, it was ruled that the digging had to be at least a mile offshore to assure that the clams were safe for consumption.

The fishermen landed the clams in Great Kills Harbor, where buyers had constructed four clam houses, and Prince's Bay, where they built two. These houses were simple shanties with cement floors pitched to a central drain. The clams could be stored for a day or two until collected by trucks.

Sail Clamming and Tonging

After 1900 the three main ports for the sail-clamming boats— sloops, catboats, and one or two small schooners—were Keyport, Belford, and Highlands; two sloops were from Perth Amboy. In Belford, the clam-dredging sloops tied up on the east side of Compton's Creek and the pound boats on the west side. The eight sloops in Highlands anchored along a channel running close to its shore. During the week, the Keyport and Perth Amboy sloops remained in the eastern end of the bay anchoring overnight. Johnny Wallace, who used to gill-net fish in Florida in the winter, remembered:

> From about 1917 to 1921, during school vacations when I was a kid, my father took me on his sloop to the eastern part of the bay for the week. I used to pick big tapeworms [nemertean ribbon worms] and hermit crabs out of his rakes as he was taking out the clams. I saved them in a bucket of water and sold

41. *One of the last working sailing sloops on Raritan Bay, in port of Perth Amboy, circa 1951. Courtesy of Louis Booz.*

them to sportfishermen when we got back to Keyport on Saturdays. That's how I got my spending money.

On some weeknights, my father, his mate, and some of the other Keyport crews went into Highlands to drink and socialize in a saloon. Afterward, they'd come staggering down the dock to get back to our sloops.

When we sailed from Keyport to the clam beds on Monday mornings and then back again on Friday afternoons, we had trouble avoiding the pound nets because there were so many in the bay. (Interview, 6 December 1985)

The fleet of sloops from Keyport made a race of their return home on Friday nights and Saturday mornings to determine who would arrive first. The fishermen put on all the sail they could.

The number of boats in the sail-clamming fleet from 1915 to 1925, the earliest period for which data are available, was about forty (most were from Keyport), and in the late 1920s and 1930s there were twenty-five to thirty; most had transferred to Belford by then after the oyster industry closed down (Interview, Johnny Wallace, 19 October 1987). At times, lobstermen joined the fleet by adding temporary sails to their skiffs when the weather was too bad for them to go offshore and lift pots: "Quite a few of us lobstermen threw on three rakes and went sail dredging to get in a day's work" (Interview, Johnny Mount, 29 November 1988). Though the sail-clamming boats had added engines, a New Jersey state law required them to tow their dredges by sail. Fishermen used the engines only to steam back into the wind after a drift instead of sailing as they had before. Fishermen sometimes used their motors to pull dredges in small beds where the clams were abundant, however. To disguise this action from wardens, they screwed an extension pipe on their exhaust pipe to direct its smoke underwater where it would not be visible.

Bill Richardson, of Keyport, a retired fisherman, described some other aspects of sail dredging:

> I sail-dredged out of my pound boat after the bunkers quit running about the Fourth of July. That was the nicest, cleanest work on the water. You didn't have to listen to a motor. Most everyone had a radio playing. It was great listening to the World Series. I always went alone and I pulled four dredges, which kept me hopping. My dredges felt heavy when they had only eight or nine clams in them, but as light as a feather when they were half full of clams. The work was hard, though, and I was always tired at the end of a day. (Interview, 5 October 1985)

While returning to port at the end of the day, most fishermen greased the teeth of their four dredges so they would not rust overnight. Some did it by pushing a pork rind over them. If they did not grease the teeth, it took a drift or two the next day to remove the rust. Fishermen believed that the rust slowed the speed of the boat, making catches smaller.

Typical daily catches for each boat ranged from fifteen to thirty bushels of hard clams. One-man boats got about ten bushels. The highest known catch for a boat was fifty-three bushels.

Fishermen alternated this fishery with winter dredging for blue crabs. After the sail-clamming season ended in October, the crews spent two to four weeks getting their boats repaired and rakes ready for the crabbing season. If blue crabs were scarce, some fishermen sail-dredged for hard clams all winter.

Fishermen tonged clams mostly off Staten Island. Blacksmiths made the wood handles of ash, in lengths from eight to twelve feet. The two-foot-wide iron "heads" had about sixteen two-inch teeth, which lasted forty-five to sixty days of clamming. To operate tongs, fishermen put them straight down to the bottom and opened the handles widely by fully extending their arms. Then they brought the handles together in about four quick, increasingly closer movements, sweeping the teeth through the bottom. Then, with the handles squeezed together, they brought them straight up smoothly to retain the clams in the "basket" of the tongs. Next they washed the basket sideways in the water by moving the handles back and forth against the rail of the bateau. Then they took out the clams, opened the basket to let any shells and grass fall into the water, and put the tongs to the bottom again. Tonging was usually less efficient than raking, because the clams were more abundant in deeper water where it was difficult to operate tongs. Usually the tongers got from three to nine bushels of hard clams a day.

While waiting for buy boats to come once or twice a week to purchase them, some of the clammers stored their hard clams in floating cars that measured about ten feet by twenty feet by two and a half feet deep. In the cars, sulfurous black spots developed where the clams touched one another, and the remainder of the shell accumulated a layer of slimy brown algae. Although the black spots did not injure the clams, fishermen referred to them as the kiss of death, because customers resisted purchasing spotted clams. To keep the clams stirred and clean of black spots and slime, the clammers kept two or three large horseshoe crabs, which walked constantly, in the cars.

The sail dredgers of Keyport and Belford continued to sell their clams on the water to buy boats from New York City until the mid-1930s. Sales were made on Wednesdays and Fridays.

A fish wholesaler named Dan Seeley bought the hard clams from the sail dredgers in Highlands. With a motorized buy boat, named the *Maud*, he went to each sloop and purchased clams when they were anchored in Highlands. He then emptied the clams into two large floats. When he had a large supply, he reloaded them onto the *Maud* and took them to Fulton Market for sale.

Some sail dredgers obtained leases, each about an acre in size at wading depths off Belford, to hold their catches of chowder clams in summer, when the demand for them was low. Each lease had as many as five hundred bushels on it. The dredgers took them up with hand rakes and sold them in winter, when housewives commonly made clam chowder. Clams were frequently stolen from the leases, however, and thus the practice was not especially profitable. The thieves were not other leaseholders, but "some guys without nothin' who would go out there and rob them" (Interview, Bud Thompson, 14 December 1987).

Soft Clamming

This fishery continued to be prominent, although in the Keyport to Belford area the number of soft-clam diggers varied with economic conditions. During the 1920s, for example, only five or six people dug soft clams regularly with drags off each town in winter. During the 1930s, however, the number swelled, ranging from twenty to sixty; the soft clam catches were their main source of income and, in many instances, food. Some regulars also spent the summer months digging. About nine of every ten diggers walked onto the bare flats from shore; the remainder got to them by rowboat, saving a long walk to shore carrying the clams.

At times, digging soft clams was difficult or impossible. If, because of an extended, strong easterly wind, the tide did not recede, fishermen could not work. Only a few fishermen bothered digging clams when the tides were neap because the available digging time was too short; many did dig when full-moon tides left wide areas of the flats bare. During unusually cold winters, ice formed over the flats, sometimes lasting a month or more, preventing most clammers from digging. Some cut large slits in the ice, though, and churned the clams. They could not get as many clams, but usually received a higher price for them. On rare occasions, the surfaces of the flats were frozen for a few days, making digging impossible.

During unusually cold winters, drifting ice on the outer areas of the flats gouged out some hard clams growing there. By walking between the ice cakes, a man could gather as many as four bushels on a low tide. On a really cold night if the tide left them bare, the clams could freeze and die, however, and this supply was lost for the season.

Because the level of water in the bay has been rising about a foot a century due to higher worldwide ocean levels (a consequence of the melting of the polar icecaps), after 1900 the clammers had less time to dig than their forebears had before 1900. For example, a comparison of the years 1880 and 1930 shows that the water level rose about six inches.

42. *Fisherman's family, circa 1930s, in their kitchen opening and packing soft clams for sale. The fisherman and his son are opening the clams, one daughter is pulling the skins from the clam necks, and another daughter is carrying a pail of clam meats to her mother, who is packing them in quart Mason jars. Source: Author's collection.*

Thus in 1930 the water on the flats, which are wide and slope gradually, did not leave the flats bare for nearly as long as in 1880, and did so less frequently than in 1880.

Most fishermen from Keyport to Belford brought their soft clams home and enlisted their families to help open and pack them for local sale. In the kitchen of a typical home, the fisherman and perhaps an older son opened the clams; the small children, six to twelve years of age, pulled the skin off the neck of each one. Leona Crosby, who skinned clam necks as a child, remembered it as

> . . . a dirty job. Juice ran down our forearms and dirt got under our fingernails. Our knees hurt because we kneeled on the floor. But we had to do it. I felt like killing my father when I came home from school and saw that he'd been clamming. We

had to stay up until the job was finished, sometimes late in the evening, even though we had to go to school the next day. My girlfriend used to come over after school to help me once in a while. (Interview, 18 May 1987)

Because they did not have a New York State Board of Health sticker, soft clams shucked in the homes of fishermen could not be shipped to New York City. Instead, fishermen peddled the clam meats to regular customers around their communities for twenty-five to thirty-five cents a quart. The customers bought one or two quarts of clams a week and returned the empty Mason jars from the previous delivery. Fishermen peddled their clam meats in their automobiles when autos became common. Fishermen also took clams to grocery stores and traded them for produce such as butter or flour or traded clams with farmers for potatoes or another crop.

The clams were a favorite food along the New Jersey bayshore, as Henry Pulsch of Port Monmouth, an octogenarian whose hobby is local history, recalled:

People around here went crazy for soft clams. They were beautiful, almost white. You'd put two fried clams between two pieces of bread and make a delicious sandwich. I used to go to school regularly with a clam sandwich. Some kids turned up their noses at them, but they didn't know what they were missing for good taste and nutrition. They weren't soggy. They were real good! (Interview, 25 February 1988)

Albert Poling, a Keyport resident who was the first to put armor plating on rumrunning boats in the bay in the 1920s, recalled shucking and peddling soft clams:

My father dug the clams on the local flats. He brought them home and opened them on the kitchen floor. After my brothers and I skinned the necks of the clams, he put them in a five-gallon can which had a little fresh water in it; the clams absorbed the water. My father would get four or five cans of clams and on a Friday morning, he'd hop on a trolley car, go to South Amboy, transfer to the public service [a fast trolley car], and go to New Brunswick where he had a route for selling them. He got thirty-five cents a quart for them, whereas in Keyport he got only twenty-five cents a quart. He made all that trip to gain only ten cents a quart. He'd take one of us kids along to help carry the cans. We liked that because we could go to a bakery shop and buy some cookies or a cake to eat on the way home. (Interview, 19 November 1986)

Tools and Techniques

In Highlands, besides "long-rigging, " fishermen began shoal-water clamming—that is, gathering clams while wading in water, using a churning hoe with a seven-foot handle, a scap net, and a floating basket, by the 1920s and 1930s. The fishermen worked in pairs at low tide. The man with the hoe would step slowly backward as he churned a drill, while his partner scooped the clams into the basket. In good weather, a pair got six to ten bushels of clams a tide, but in bad weather, which was common in the fall, a pair might get as few as two bushels. As many as 150 men clammed this way. They got to the beds in rowboats, rowing themselves or being towed by a motorboat, which could tow as many as ten clam boats at a time. During the winter, the churners had to line their boots and waders with newspapers to insulate their legs from the cold. This was only partially effective, and their legs were numb by the end of a day.

In the summer, dense stands of eelgrass inhibited fishermen from shoal-water clamming in some areas. The clams were abundant in it, though, and the fishermen surmised that the eelgrass must have held the clam larvae. They cut the grass with small scythes before starting to churn.

In unusually cold winters when ice covered the bay, groups of eight to ten Highlands fishermen churned clams through long slits they cut in the ice. They churned in water that was two to ten feet deep. Some of the group spent their time cutting ice; others churned the clams and scooped them up. They carried baskets of clams, in improvised devices, such as an old bedspring with boards laid on it, or several children's snow sleds towed by a borrowed horse. They divided the money equally from the sale of the clams (Interview, John Seminski, 19 April 1988).

Another implement used for digging soft clams was the four-tine garden fork. During the 1930s, some Staten Islanders dug soft clams for home consumption and also got some hard clams with these forks along their shores. The practice was illegal because of pollution, but the warden overlooked it because the people were desperate for food (Interview, Margaret Wittich, 8 February 1988). Fishermen in Keyport also dug soft clams with garden forks. In both locations, they dug at low tide in water about knee-deep.

Fishermen in Highlands also used motorboats for digging clams in the Navesink and Shrewsbury rivers. This practice had begun in 1911 when a pleasure party went aground in its motorboat off Highlands and

43. *Jimmy White of Highlands demonstrating how churning hoe is held when digging soft clams. Photograph by author.*

the occupants observed that soft clams covered the furrow where the propeller had washed the sand. Word spread, and some clammers in Highlands began using their boats to dig soft clams in this manner. State authorities felt that the method was too efficient, however, and they banned it.

Economics and Marketing

Fishermen received about $1.25 for a bushel of soft clams in the 1920s; during the 1930s the price was as low as 50 cents for steamers and

75 cents for the larger shucking clams. Frequently during the 1930s the clams fishermen sent to New York City were returned because they could not be sold; sometimes dealers without money sent postage stamps as payment to fishermen. A number of people dug or bought a bushel or two of clams and took them to New York City on ferries and peddled them on the streets to earn money.

Highlands had about twelve shanties for shucking clams along its shore; each measured about twelve by sixteen feet. Kerosene lamps originally amplified the light coming through the windows, and in the late 1920s electric lights were installed. About ten diggers sold to each shanty. The men dug on orders from the shanty manager, who informed them a day in advance what quantity he would purchase. The Highlands clammers also dug on orders from the buyers of the smaller "steamer" clams. Thus, at all times, the clammers had to be aware of the quantities and sizes of the clams in every bed.

In 1923, to ensure that clams being shipped to New York were pure, the New Jersey Board of Health and the Bureau of Local Health Administration drew up the following set of sanitary standards for the shucking shanties:

> 1. All rooms where soft clams were opened were required to have concrete floors and an adequate supply of fresh water. Floors, receptacles, and all tools used for opening soft clams had to be clean and sanitary. During the fly season, all doors and windows had to be screened.
> 2. Clam shells had to be removed from the shanties daily.
> 3. Shucked clams had to be washed in clean fresh water before shipment.
> 4. Containers for shipping the clams had to be clean and sanitary.
> 5. All shuckers of clams had to have clean hands and wear a white oilcloth apron from their shoulders to the top of their shoes.
> 6. All clams had to be packed in machine-made ice made from pure water.
> 7. The shanties had to be open for inspection by a representative of the state board of health at all times. (*Red Bank Register,* 22 August 1923)

The shuckers were women. Each opened from 2, 000 to 7, 000 clams in a normal day. Around 1900 shuckers earned about 50 cents per 1,000 clams opened; by the 1920s and 1930s the rate $1.00 per 1, 000 clams opened. After washing the sand away from the clam meats in a sink of fresh water, the manager packed them in cans, sixteen strings (400 clams) per can. He then put the cans into barrels with ice around them (Interview, Johnny Mount, 29 November 1988). The procedure was much more sanitary than that practiced before 1900, when the strings of clam meats were placed loosely around ice in a barrel. Margaret Kendrick, a retired shucker, described the work further:

> I began opening clams when I was sixteen years old in the mid-1920s and did it for eighteen years. There was competition amongst us as we opened. We'd get jealous if one of the girls got much ahead of the rest of us, although one woman in our shanty always had to open the most or she'd be upset, so we let her. Each of us wanted to get the largest clams so we'd make more money. The sizes of clams which came in were according to the tide; if there was a big tide off, the fishermen got bigger clams. Sometimes, in the winter when the men dug though the ice, the clams we opened had ice in them.
>
> We worked so hard, and it was tiresome, but we had some fun while we opened. Somebody'd say something foolish and we'd all laugh. Our backs would be killing us by the time we quit. Sometimes a man would come down to our shanty, play a guitar, and sing for us. Somebody else might bring a pie or some buns and coffee. We went home for lunch. Our homes were nearby.
>
> Lent was a heavy demand time for soft clams, when the Catholics couldn't eat meat. We worked long hours then. Sometimes during Lent we'd finish up in one shanty and go to another. (Interview, 18 October 1985)

Men with teams of horses collected the barrels of shucked clams from loading platforms at the shanties in the early afternoon and put them on the five o'clock train to New York City. From one to three train cars loaded with barrels of shucked clams left Highlands nearly every day during the entire year, except when ice covered the clam beds (*Red Bank Register*, 28 February 1912). The clams were at Fulton Market when it opened the next morning. Small quantities of clam meats were also sold directly to local residents, who came to the shanties with quart milk bottles to carry them home.

Every Saturday, the shanty managers traveled to Fulton Market to collect their money from the dealers. In summer they went up on the passenger-freight ships *Sea Bird* or *Albertina* which left from Highlands; in winter they went by train. Usually, they came back with five hundred to six hundred dollars apiece and paid the clammers and women shuckers later that day.

The smaller "steamer" clams made up about a third of those dug in Highlands. Each buyer had floats, or, in the case of one buyer, running water tanks, to "give the clams a drink, " as the oystermen did, except in this case their intent was to allow the clams to pump out any sand they had drawn into their necks when they were being churned. Each float and tank held fifty to sixty bushels of clams. Buyers shipped these clams to Fulton Market, to Long Island, to resorts as far south as Atlantic City, and to local clambakes. Before automobiles, men using horses and wagons delivered clams to the clambakes; two or three wagonloads were needed to feed 100 to 150 people. In addition, some peddlers bought as many as 100 bushels of clams a day and delivered them to various outlets. Buyers sold any broken soft clams to eel fishermen, who used them for bait.

Cris Kohlenbusch of Highlands described how his father and he became clam buyers:

> My father had the business before me. He started in business in 1912 by floating the clams he dug and selling them to a large restaurant. Then he began buying from other clammers. That's the way all small businesses got started. I began clamming in the summer when I was twelve years old and sold to my father. When I was thirteen, I worked all summer clamming. When I was fourteen, I left school and was a full-time clammer thereafter. I had no further education. When my father retired, I took over the business.
>
> About ten clammers used to sell to us in the summer; maybe five or six in the winter. We had one hired man who helped put the clams in and out of trays. We sold a lot of clams to Lundy Brothers in Sheepshead Bay on Coney Island. Every day during the summer, they sent a truck over and picked up thirty to fifty bushels. In the winter, it would be three times a week. Lundy's redistributed some of the clams over in Sheepshead Bay to various restaurants. We also sold to clam bars in Atlantic City. I ran the clam business for twenty-five to thirty years. (Interview, 16 June 1986)

Pollution began to affect the harvests and sales of soft clams in the 1920s. When oystering was terminated in the bay as a result of sewage pollution in 1925, the state of New York also prohibited any further soft or hard clamming on its side of the bay. In 1923 the state of New Jersey condemned small areas off Highlands for soft clamming because of pollution, and, in 1926, the intertidal area from Belford to Highlands was also condemned. In four of the five years from 1925 to 1929, the New York City Board of Health imposed intermittent bans on importing soft clam meats from Highlands, stating that they were unsanitary; each ban lasted one or two months (*Red Bank Register,* 18 September 1929). In 1932 the area from Keyport to Atlantic Highlands out to 1,300 feet from shore was closed to soft clamming (*Red Bank Register,* 30 March 1932). This ban should have eliminated all intertidal digging, but the fish and game warden was aware that hundreds of people depended on the clams for their livelihood and food; besides, no one on the bayshore had contracted typhoid fever or other illnesses from eating them. Thus, the warden did not enforce the ban (Interview, Dave Thompson, 19 May 1987).

Lobstering

Potting lobsters was easier work after the development of the motorized skiff. Fishermen could run the skiffs along their lines as they lifted the pots. When using catboats, they had had to pull them along the lines against the wind or tidal currents. In the 1920s and 1930s, there were about forty-two lobster skiffs in Raritan Bay ports (two from Great Kills Harbor, one from Lemon Creek, six from Keyport, ten from Belford, and twenty to twenty-five from Highlands)—probably more than fished for lobsters previously.

Most lobstermen did not work at other fisheries during their off-seasons, although some dug soft clams, raked hard clams, and speared eels sporadically. In the late fall, they hauled their skiffs ashore and spent most of the winter overhauling their engines, repairing and painting the skiffs, and cleaning, repairing, and making new pots. They purchased the hoops for pots from coopers and the remaining wood from lumberyards. Fishermen used wet (green) oak for the frames and lathing of pots, so they would sink. After they had cut all the wood parts to the correct sizes, two men could assemble thirty to thirty-five pots a day. A man could knit thirty to fifty funnels a day or about five each evening in his home, usually working in his living room. In the spring, the pots were dipped in tar to inhibit "worms" (actually a mollusk in the shape of a worm) from boring into the wood.

It was at the beginning of this period that the parlor pot came into existence; it had a funnel on only one end and another in its middle dividing it into two sections. The "kitchen" was the funnel end, where the bait was placed; the "parlor" was where most of the lobsters went

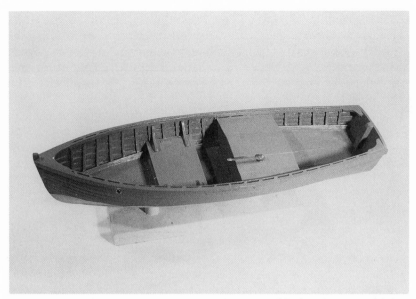

44. *Model of lapstrake lobster skiff, made by Cris Kohlenbusch, a retired fisherman. Photograph by author.*

after they had been in the kitchen for a while. The earlier pots had a funnel on each end and none in the middle.

Lobstermen put two secondhand bricks in pots permanently to stabilize them on the bottom. Since the wood had dried while being stored on land in winter, they had to put about eleven extra bricks in them temporarily to counter their buoyancy in the spring.

Lobstermen from Keyport and Highlands tied their boats to moorings and got to them in rowboats. Beginning in early May, lobstermen placed their pot lines along the banks of the navigation channels in the bay, where they always obtained their best catches. They believed that lobsters occupied burrows they made along the channel slopes. Government authorities did not allow fishermen to set pots in the channels, because the lines could entangle the propellers of passing vessels.

As they had done earlier, some fishermen left their pots in Raritan Bay only through June and then shifted them out to the ocean for the remainder of the season. Severe storms were often a problem, however, because they could roll the pots and lines into a tangle. The lobstermen had to try to find them with a grapnel. Most lobstermen had about one hundred pots, which they lifted every day when lobsters were abundant. Thus about four thousand pots were lifted by the forty or so lobster crews every day.

45. Bill Richardson, a fisherman of Keyport, constructing a lobster pot in the basement of his home during the winter off-season. Photograph by author.

Lobster catches varied over the years. In some years individual boats got from 100 to 150 pounds a day during peak periods, but in others catches were only 30 pounds a day forcing the lobstermen to quit and engage in another fishery (Interview, Bill Kendrick, 1 October 1985). Lobstering was not as profitable in June as in other warm months, because the lobsters were shedding; perhaps a quarter of those caught were "tinny" (soft-shelled) and could not be sold. Lobstermen took them home to eat.

The first laws regarding the minimum size of lobsters that could be landed were enacted between 1910 and 1920. Total length of the lobster was the original dimension used, but it was later changed to its carapace length. In the 1920s the fine for possession of short lobsters was twenty dollars per lobster (*Red Bank Register*, 2 June 1926).

Lobstermen did not immobilize the claws of lobsters for many years. As a consequence, they damaged each other to a small extent. Beginning in the 1930s, lobstermen immobilized the crusher claw by forcing a whittled wooden plug into its joint, as it did the damage (Interview, Bill Richardson, 5 October 1985). The slicer claw has a relatively small muscle and does little damage. It will not even hurt a person's finger if it

46. *Joe and Bill Kendrick at the shore of Highlands with their lobster catches, circa 1940. Courtesy of Monmouth County Historical Society.*

closes down on it. The plugs discolored the meats and made the lobsters bleed, however.

The local market for lobsters continued to be limited, so fisherman had to ship keeper lobsters by freight boat or train to Fulton Market or sell them to a buy boat, which took them there. Each fisherman had five or six live cars for holding lobsters until he had enough to ship. The live cars, made of a wooden frame and laths, resembled lobster pots. They measured about four by four by two feet. Fishermen weighted them with bricks and anchored them on sand bottoms in about fifteen feet of water in the bay. They had to tow a grapnel to recover them. They put their daily catches in the cars, and when they had an order for lobsters, they counted out the oldest ones from the cars. This was a hard day's work for lobstermen: it meant lifting the cars after hand-hauling about one hundred pots in the ocean.

Fishermen believed that some commission merchants to whom they sold lobsters in Fulton Market were dishonest. Merchants could cheat the fishermen by telling them that many of their lobsters arrived dead in the market and pay them for only the live ones. Moreover, the merchants could sell the lobsters for perhaps twenty-five cents a pound and tell the fishermen that they had sold for twenty cents a pound. Thus the merchants got five cents a pound plus their 12.5 percent commission (Interview, Bill Kendrick, 1 December 1987).

Fishermen sold shorts locally and to New York buyers. In the 1920s and 1930s, local fish markets purchased fifteen to twenty dozen shorts per fisherman daily for about a dollar a dozen. Fishermen kept the remainder in cars temporarily and sold them to buy boats from Staten Island and Brooklyn, which paid fifty to seventy-five cents a dozen for them (Interview, Bill Kendrick, 1 October 1985)

Development of the Winch

In 1935 the motorized winch, which replaced hand hauling of lobster pots, hand lifting of brail nets, and hand hauling of crab dredges, was introduced to the bay by Arnold Pedersen, a Belford fisherman, then nineteen years old. The winch saved so much labor that many fishermen viewed it as a gift from Heaven. Before he began lobstering in 1935, Pedersen had worked a few summers on ocean pound-net boats in Sea Bright. He believed that the winch used on those boats could be adapted for use on lobster skiffs. He used the transmission and rear end of a Ford automobile to construct his winch, then installed it in the bow of his captain's skiff and powered it with the skiff's motor. To use the winch, he wound each pot line around it two or three turns and then simply took in the slack as it rotated, and thus it did the heavy lifting. Soon, all the other lobstermen installed winches similar to his. A disadvantage of the winch was that the oilskins worn by lobstermen could get caught in it and cause them serious injuries. Most solo lobstermen soon took on a mate for safety's sake.

With the motorized winch, lobstermen set out more pots, because they were able then to lift as many as three hundred a day. In the late 1930s, some lobstermen shifted to a two-day system of lifting: they had six hundred pots and lifted three hundred each day.

In 1936 Pedersen worked with a pound-fishing crew in the bay. To save the labor of lifting the brail net by hand, he bought an air-cooled engine with a winch head on it, set it on the pound boat, and used it for brailing. The winch could not be attached to the main boat engine because its propeller would turn when the boat was next to the pound net and entangle it. The other pound-net fishermen quickly copied it. Within a year, blue crab fishermen also installed motorized winches on their boats to haul in their dredges (Interview, Arnold Pedersen, 13 July 1989).

Blue Crabbing

The fishermen who sail-dredged for hard clams alternated this warm-weather fishery with blue-crab dredging in the winter. A captain and a mate comprised the crew on most crab boats, as they did on the sail-clamming boats. In the 1930s, about forty motorized sloops and skiffs dredged for blue crabs.

When fishermen installed power winches on their boats in the mid-1930s, they redesigned the dredges, making them five to six feet wide; by state law, the width could not exceed six feet. Dredges weighed seventy-five to a hundred pounds and resembled oyster dredges, but with longer teeth. Each boat crew had dredges for mud bottoms with six-inch teeth and dredges for sand bottoms with five-inch teeth. Most boats towed four dredges.

In some cold winters, fishermen connected a hose about fifteen feet long to their engine exhaust pipe, so if ice formed on their winch they could run warm exhaust water over it to melt it; otherwise they could not wind in the dredges. During especially cold spells, ice formed on the ropes, making it impossible to wind in the dredges. Fishermen then had to switch to sail dredging for hard clams.

Fishermen did not consider blue crabbing hazardous, but once every year or two, a fisherman, nearly always the mate, had a rope wrap around his leg as the empty dredges were going out for a tow and was pulled overboard. The captain reversed the direction of the boat and pulled him back aboard. Bill Richardson, a fisherman of Keyport, recalled that it was dangerous for a man to dredge alone:

> One time Paul Turner was crabbing alone, and when he threw over one of his dredges the rope caught on his leg and pulled him overboard. Luckily, one dredge was over on one side and two were over on the other side, because they made the boat go around in a circle. Usually, he didn't tow his rowboat behind, but that morning he did. When the boat came around, he missed it by six feet, but the rowboat came along and he was just able to grab it by the stern. He pulled himself back into it and got back aboard the dredging boat. Otherwise, he would have been lost. He came ashore soaking wet and nearly froze. He never went out alone again. (Interview, 5 October 1985)

During the 1920s and 1930s, when crabs were abundant, good typical daily catches were 20 to 30 bushels of crabs per boat (Interview, Elmer Peterson, 1 March 1990). The highest reported catch was 150 bushels. Usually about seven females to three males, or eight females to two males, were caught. Most males remained in the western part of the bay and in rivers. During this period, fishermen continued to store their blue crabs loosely in the holds of their boats and bring them directly to Fulton Market every two or three days.

Johnny Wallace, who dredged crabs with his father on a sloop during the 1930s, described this operation further. They sailed from Keyport and slept on the sloop anchored off Highlands during the week.

They took their crabs to Fulton Market in the afternoons, arriving there about 4 P.M., to tie up for the night and sleep aboard. They tried to get there earlier than most other boats in the crab fleet, so they could tie up next to the dock instead of against another boat. If so, they would not have to carry the sixty-pound baskets of crabs across other boats to the dock. The next morning, about an hour before the market opened, they began putting the crabs in baskets, which had been purchased beforehand at the market. His father had taken a dozen or so crabs from the hold of the sloop to its galley to warm them. Then he took those up to a buyer to show him that their crabs were active and in good condition.

After the sale, Wallace and his father left immediately for the bay so they could spend most of the day dredging for more crabs. Thus the run to Fulton Market did not cost them much dredging time. They kept track of the tidal currents in New York Harbor and, if possible, they went to and from Fulton Market with favorable currents ("saving the tides"), because their boat had little power. They raised its sail if a breeze blew to help their speed. In exceptionally cold winters, the crab boats had to avoid flows of ice cakes in the Hudson River (Interview, 5 November 1987).

In some winters, several New Jersey fishermen dredged for blue crabs in the Hudson River near the Statue of Liberty. At night, they tied their boats at Fulton Market and slept there. On weekends, they came home by train. When they left their boats in another port, however, they had to be wary of robbery. Once, in the 1930s, Kittle Thompsen and two other men from Belford had tied their three sloops at Fulton Market. The three went home to New Jersey by train on the first weekend. To guard the sloops against robbery, two of them simply locked their cabin doors. But Thompsen, believing that locks would not be sufficient, decided to make it appear that someone was aboard his sloop. He lit his coal stove to have smoke coming out of his chimney, and he did not lock the cabin door. When the three returned on Monday, Thompsen's sloop was the only one that had not been robbed (Interview, Louie Egnatovich, 14 February 1986).

In the late 1930s and thereafter, the New Jersey fishermen landed their crabs in Belford, where they were picked up by buyers' trucks. The buyers paid fishermen at the end of each week. To supplement their earnings, some crabbers saved the two or three dozen rock crabs with soft shells they found while picking the blue crabs on their decks and sold them to people at the docks for ten cents apiece. This could be done only in January and early February, the months when the rock crabs molt and grow in Raritan Bay and other estuaries.

One of the colorful "landmarks" in Red Bank in this period were the vendors of soft-shelled blue crabs. Many people believe that soft-shelled

47. Girls catching blue crabs in the shallows of Raritan Bay, circa 1904. Courtesy of Moe Coucci.

crabs are the most delicious of seafoods, and the sale of these crabs in Red Bank had begun at least as early as the 1890s (*Red Bank Register,* 18 August 1947, 22 July 1948). Two or three vendors usually appeared on Broad Street, Red Bank's main street, in late July and August. They had caught the crabs themselves and sold them in shoe boxes lined with sea lettuce.

The best-known vendor was "Chum" Chandler, a tall scruffy-looking man. For at least thirty years, from 1919 to 1948, he sold soft crabs in front of the Second National Bank and Trust Company. Usually he had six to eight boxes of the crabs lined up on the sidewalk. The boxes contained either six or twelve crabs, which sold for ten cents each. In the summer, Chandler also rented rowboats on the Navesink River beside a houseboat on which he lived. In the winter, he speared eels.

Fishermen as Rumrunners

During the Prohibition Era, large quantities of liquor were landed illegally by fishermen and others in the fishing ports of Raritan Bay. The ports of Great Kills Harbor, Perth Amboy, Matawan, Keyport, Union Beach, Keansburg, Belford, Atlantic Highlands, and Highlands were all entry points for liquor. In the ocean, outside the mouth of Raritan Bay, ten to fifteen old tramp steamers and large schooners laden with rum from the Caribbean islands lay at anchor at all times. They remained in international waters and could not be apprehended. At first, the international line was three miles offshore, but it was later extended to twelve miles. Sometimes individual ships lay offshore for a few months at a time.

The liquor was brought ashore by men who had boats large enough to carry substantial loads. The boats included some of the fishing sloops and skiffs used in the bay, but most were specially constructed boats with high-speed engines. Some were powered with three airplane engines. A trip to a port in the bay took the fishing boats about two hours.

Perhaps twenty-five bayshore fishermen were enticed into becoming rumrunners by the syndicates running the illegal operation. Some made runs fairly regularly and some only occasionally when fishing was poor and they were short of cash. They were paid one hundred dollars for each load brought in, much more money than they were earning from fishing. The remaining fishermen refused to take part in rumrunning, however, because the work was illegal and dangerous.

When a boat crew went out for a load of liquor, its contact was a supercargo (superintendent of the cargo) on board the ship; the crew on the ship had nothing to do with the liquor. The man who arranged the deal on shore gave the captain of the crew a torn half of a dollar bill or playing card. The captain had to have it when he went out to the ship. The supercargo had the other half, and he put the two halves together to see whether they matched. If they did, he gave the captain the liquor. The most successful runs were made at night.

Rumrunners coming into the bay had to dodge and match wits with the Coast Guard almost constantly. The Coast Guard's boats were seaworthy, but slow, and the rumrunners could usually outrun them. If, during a chase, a Coast Guard boat happened to get close to a rumrunner, the crew usually threw a rope in its path. The rope, whose diameter was three inches and whose length was about twenty feet, wound up in its propeller and stopped its progress, enabling the rumrunner to escape. If they could not outdistance a Coast Guard boat, however, the rumrunners had to dump the liquor overboard in order to come ashore without being apprehended. They would not be paid by the syndicate if this were done.

After a dumping, the fishermen usually went out with clam rakes within a day or two to recover some of the bottles and sell them to speakeasies. They called this practice "bottle fishing" (Interview, Stockton Hopkins, 19 November 1988). By the late 1920s, the bottom of Raritan Bay was strewn with many thousands of liquor bottles, some in cases and some loose. One of the blue-crab fishermen of Belford enlarged the opening of one of his dredges enough to hold cases of liquor, and he dredged up some of the liquor bottles to sell.

The liquor in bottles lying on the bay bottom remained fit to drink as long as the necks were in mud; otherwise, seawater got in and spoiled it. If the neck of the bottle had an air space, the liquor was good. The hard clammers, using hand rakes, sail dredges, and rocking chair dredges, picked up full bottles regularly. Many drank it immediately and "some of the clammers used to get drunk as hell out there" (Interview, Louis Egnatovich, 14 February 1986). The liquor bottles were found as late as the 1950s.

Any person arrested and convicted of running liquor had to pay a fine of about $275. Moreover, the Coast Guard sometimes shot at rumrunners who would not stop during a chase, injuring a few and killing one occasionally.

Besides the Coast Guard, the rumrunners were preyed upon by hijackers, who tried to take the liquor away from them forcibly. Coming into ports at night to avoid being seen by government enforcement officials, the rumrunners were vulnerable and were frequently held up at gunpoint by the hijackers. The bayshore ports became similar to the Wild West; the rumrunners carried guns in their back pockets, and there were many gunfights and killings. Gunshots in the night were a familiar sound to bayshore residents.

Henry Pulsch of Port Monmouth described the rumrunning era vividly:

> Gangs of guys used to hide in the meadows along the creeks waiting to hijack the rumrunners. There were no lights; it was usually dark. I know of a lobsterman and a hard clammer who worked together running liquor. One night, they came up Compton's Creek and got to a place to unload some liquor off their boat. One said to the other, "I don't like the looks of things. I have a feeling that something is wrong, so let's watch it." When they tied up, a gang of five appeared to hold them up. The two pulled their guns and shot, and they ran. The lobsterman said to the clammer, "I'm sure that we shot somebody." The clammer said, "Aw, we didn't, I shot into the air." The lobsterman said, "Darned if I did." Early the next morning, they went down to the creek to see if anyone was lying there. No one was, so they were satisfied they did not kill anyone, but the liquor was gone.
>
> A few months later, the lobsterman was at a dance at a local speakeasy. A guy from the band came limping over to the bar for a drink. The lobsterman said, "What happened to you?" The guy said, "I got shot. Like a damn fool, I was with a gang of friends. They talked me into going down to the creek to hijack a load of liquor." He told him where and when it happened. The lobsterman said, "You know something, buddy? I'm the guy

who shot you!" The guy was dumbstruck. He met the man who shot him. Wasn't there some goings on at that speakeasy during the rest of the evening!

One time the lobsterman in the first story came over to my house and said, "Do you want to go off with me tonight? I need someone to run my motors while I steer, because my regular man can't come." I said, "Okay." But just before we were to leave, the engine man showed up. I didn't go. He went.

When they came in with the liquor, the Coast Guard was waiting for them. They maneuvered back out of the creek and there was a chase. The Coast Guard turned a machine gun on them and hit the engine man with seven bullets down one side of his body. They came in and brought the guy to Long Branch Hospital. Darned if he didn't live. The bullets went right through him. See, if I had gone, that would have been me. I said to hell with that rumrunning! (Interview, 15 June 1988)

9

Fin Fishing After World War II

Prior to the 1940s, some trends had been developing which were to have profound effect on Raritan Bay fisheries. One was the development of improved commercial fishing gear. In the 1600s and 1700s, the only available gear besides eel pots and hand lines were the haul seines and fyke nets used to catch fish along the shores. In the 1800s, pound nets, gill nets, and purse seines were developed to catch fish in the main areas of the bay. By the early 1900s fishing boats became substantially more effective when engines were installed to replace sail power.

Prior to the 1940s, fishermen everywhere had felt that there were plenty of fish at times, but their gear was inadequate to catch them. As time passed, however, their gear kept improving and eventually became, paradoxically, too efficient. For example, in the 1940s, otter trawls, the most efficient gear for bottom fishing, were brought into the bay. And beginning in the 1940s, fishing with otter trawls expanded on the continental shelf off the coast of the United States. In the 1950s foreign fleets in large numbers fished in the continental shelf. Off Long Island and New Jersey, the ocean pound nets declined in numbers in the 1950s, in large part because of hurricane damage, and by the 1970s they disappeared. To catch the fish in ocean waters, New Jersey fishermen, including increasing numbers from Belford, joined the offshore fleets by purchasing oceangoing vessels and otter trawls. As will be seen, the fishing effort by the vessels on the continental shelf became so intense that the numbers of fish declined substantially.

The 1940s can be considered the beginning of the modern era, when people began migrating from farms and fishing villages in large numbers to work in manufacturing. An outgrowth of this shift was an increase in leisure time. Sport fishing had existed in Raritan Bay from early times and had been increasing, but it expanded substantially as leisure time and discretionary income increased. The increase in fishing power by commercial fishermen brought them into conflict with the sport fishermen. The sport fishermen, using chumming methods learned from the commercial fishermen, caught large numbers of bluefish and mackerel, sold many, and undercut the commercial market. Currently, with the proliferation of private boats and head boats, more food fish are taken in the bay by sport fishermen than by commercial fishermen.

Since about 1900 water pollution had been increasing in the bay. By 1925, domestic pollution had forced the curtailment of the oyster fishery. In the 1930s and 1940s, it threatened the New Jersey clam beds and eventually closed them. Industrial pollution began in the 1940s and increased to such alarming levels by the 1970s that health advisories were posted for eels, striped bass, and bluefish.

The 1940s were a pivotal decade in the history of Raritan Bay because four fisheries—haul seining, gill netting, fyke netting, and soft clamming—ended then or soon thereafter, while considerable development occurred in others. The most important innovations were synthetic fibers for nets and ropes; airplanes to spot bunkers for purse-seining boats; otter trawls to catch porgies; depth recorders to find porgies and other fish; small, inexpensive outboard motors for eeling, sport-fishing, and hard-clamming boats; rocking-chair dredges for hard clams; and Nova Scotia-style boats for lobstering. There were further developments: the prices of fish, in contrast to their being extremely low during the 1930s, rose to their highest levels ever and remained high thereafter; substantial numbers of New Jersey fishermen raked hard clams illegally in New York waters; and industrial plants in and around Greater New York City and along the Raritan River were constructed to manufacture goods for the war effort. The plants emphasized production and, not being concerned about water pollution, discharged their wastes into Raritan Bay.

During World War II, Raritan Bay fishermen, who had been struggling economically during the 1930s, began to make more money, and many fishermen and farmers applied for and received exemptions from the draft because they were primary producers. Some draft-age men switched from nonessential jobs to fishing and farming to obtain such exemptions. Commercial fishermen had to carry photo identification cards and fill out forms for the federal government, stating what species they caught in the bay and ocean. The U.S. Coast Guard encouraged these fishermen, especially lobstermen, to work in the ocean because they could serve as spotters of German submarines. The Coast Guard anchored one of its vessels just inside the bay mouth and required each fishing crew going to or from the ocean to hold up a sign showing a number it had been assigned. As noted, however, the government forbade head boats from operating.

After World War II, the passage of the G.I. Bill enabled war veterans to attend colleges and trade schools with financial assistance from the federal government. The war stimulated construction of factories and other businesses in the area and invigorated the local economy. As a result, after the war many young men were not interested in farming and commercial fishing, and the result was a shortage of help for farmers and pound-net fishermen, and fewer fishermen overall.

Pound Netting

The number of pound nets in the bay increased from about 25 in the 1930s to 128, and the number of boat crews operating them increased from 10 to 30. New Jersey had 63 of the pound nets. They were installed in several rows of 4 each; the rows were at right angles to the shore, between Union Beach and Belford and off the west coast of Sandy Hook.

The government had installed a submarine net between Staten Island and Long Island to prevent German submarines from approaching New York City. Fishermen supposed that shad on their spring spawning run up the Hudson River might be deflected by the net toward the Staten Island shore and be held in the area longer. They installed a few pound nets there and indeed caught large quantities of shad. Within a year or two, fishermen installed about sixty-five pound nets from Great Kills to South Beach, Staten Island (Interview, Cris Anthropolis, 27 March 1988). The state of New York modified an earlier law and allowed the installation of pound nets in its waters on the condition that fishermen remove them by 15 May each year to avoid taking any "good" fish, such as bluefish, striped bass, and weakfish; they could take only alewives, shad, and bunkers. New York fishermen owned only two of the nets. At first, New Jersey fishermen could not obtain licenses for the nets, and someone suggested that the commission merchants in Fulton Market obtain them and the New Jersey fishermen could fish in their names. Then, state authorities, realizing that New Jersey fishermen were selling nearly all the fish to New York, decided to sell them licenses. The license for each pound net cost twenty dollars (Interview, John Fisler, 4 December 1987).

In the early 1950s, however, fishermen had to abandon the practice of putting pound nets for shad off Staten Island because catches had

48. Crewmen applying copper paint to preserve pound-net poles, circa 1950s. Courtesy of Spy House Museum, Port Monmouth, New Jersey.

fallen considerably after the submarine net was removed. Moreover, the demand for local shad had fallen sharply and the price was low. Consumers wanted to purchase only the roe of female shad (Interview, Ray Richardson, 20 November 1986).

The development of synthetic fibers during the war meant that nets could be made of them instead of cotton. They required little or no maintenance, were stronger, and lasted several years. Pound-net fishermen tarred them only once a year in the spring, and perhaps even that was unnecessary. The first fiber was Nyack, which was replaced after a few years by nylon. Nylon decays slowly from the ultraviolet rays of sunlight (shades of yellow and orange decay faster than black nylon), however, and some rotting occurred where the upper parts of pound nets extended out of water. Immediately after the war, inexpensive portable pumps also became available. Pound-net fishermen purchased them to wash the mud off the dirty sections of their nets when they changed them. Previously, they had to tow the nets through the water to remove the mud.

In the years following World War II, several pound-net owners left this fishery because good men were not as available for the work. They had found more lucrative occupations ashore. Owners sold their boat,

49. *Boats and docks in Compton's Creek, Belford. Note bundle of pound-net poles in water ready to be towed to site where pound net will be installed. Photograph by author.*

nets, and poles for about one thousand dollars. Bill Braun, a former owner, described his experiences with poor help at that time:

> The trouble with fishing is that you don't fish all year around. You have to lay guys off in the fall. The next season, they might have a job somewhere else. So, you have to hire new guys. Well, there's a lot to know. You get guys who don't know how to mend, tie a line, or handle a boat, so you are almost on your own. My crew was putting all the work on me. One guy used to get drunk a lot and I didn't know whether he'd show up the next day. So, I got fed up and got rid of the gear. (Interview, 17 December 1986)

In seasons when bunkers were abundant, the pound-net crews could not carry the total quantity trapped in their pound nets in late April and May; one boat sank because its crew had overloaded it with bunkers. In the early 1950s, when there were about ninety pound nets in the bay, the pound-net crews hired three sloops and two fishing draggers to help them lug the bunkers. The sloop owners put boards around their decks, making bins that held about seven hundred bushels. After the pockets of the pound nets were drawn up by the pound-net crews, the hired boats tied up alongside them, and their crews, using brail nets, transferred the bunkers over to them. When the pound boat and hired boat were loaded, the two boats went to the factory together. To unload their boats, the crews, with help from the pound-net crew, pushed the bunkers into a hopper on the deck. A bucket conveyor placed inside the hopper transferred the bunkers to the factory. The hired boats went from one pound-net crew to another lugging them; each carried up to five loads a day. Hired boat owners were paid forty dollars a load for lugging bunkers from pound nets near Belford and fifty dollars a load for lugging them from those at a longer distance near Sandy Hook. At times, individual pound-net owners sold as many as two thousand bushels of bunkers a day from their three pound nets. This practice of hiring boats to lug for them continued until the factory closed in 1981 (Interview, Art Thorstensen, 9 April 1991).

The number of pound nets continued to fall. In the 1980s, the bay had ten to thirteen pound nets and four to five pound boats. In 1991 the bay had only nine of them and four pound net boats; only sixteen men worked in the pound-net fishery. In the 1980s, the demand for food fish remained high, but demand for bunkers was limited to bait for local sport fishermen and lobstermen and Chesapeake Bay and North Carolina blue-crab fishermen. At times, fishermen could have landed about twice the quantity of bunkers, and they often removed only a portion of them from their pound nets, because that was all they could sell. Pound-net crews earned $300 to $350 a week, or about $10,000 a season. The pound-net fishermen continue to represent a wide span of ages, and experienced men should be available to continue the fishery when the oldest men retire.

Gill Netting

In the late 1940s, gill netting ended. During the 1940s, the pound-net fishermen had become increasingly hostile toward the gill netters, whom they believed were taking too many food fish away from them. Pound netters believed that they were at a disadvantage with fixed gear, whereas drift gill netters could move their gear around. Moreover, drift gill netters often set their nets near the pound nets, supposedly taking some fish which might have gone into the pound nets (Interview, Jigs Apel, 11 March 1986). Belford fishermen argued about it frequently, and in 1948 the pound netters were able to convince New Jersey legislators to pass a

50. *Crew removing fish, which appear to be mackerel caught in Atlantic Ocean, from gill net in Compton's Creek, Belford, circa 1960. Courtesy of John Seminski.*

bill outlawing the use of drift gill nets and staked or anchored gill nets in the bay (Interview, Elmer Layton, 15 December 1985). In 1981, however, New Jersey passed a bill permitting fishermen to use staked or anchored gill nets, but only for catching shad in the spring. Four fishing crews began using anchored gill nets made of monofilament to catch shad in 1981, but their numbers declined to only one by 1991.

Purse Seining

During and after the 1940s, the seining procedures of boats belonging to the J. Howard Smith fish factory developed considerably. Crews had not been able to find bunker schools swimming below the water surface, where they spend most of their time, and distinguishing whether schools were large or small had always been a major problem. Sets on the small schools were scarcely profitable. Crews could not see the schools when it rained either, because the drops hitting the water masked the whips of bunker fins normally visible at the surface. In 1947 the factory bought three airplanes to find schools for its ten seine boats. Pilots could not only spot schools swimming as deeply as twenty feet below the surface, but could also see them in light rain and choppy seas. Heavy rains and low cloud ceilings made such spotting impossible, however.

The planes flew from an airstrip that the factory constructed in Belford. Each pilot flew for eight to ten hours a day, and, by working in shifts, at least one plane was in the air from dawn to dusk. The planes normally flew at an altitude of about twelve hundred feet, but if two planes flew together, one dropped down to nine hundred feet for safety reasons. The first planes were Piper Pacers; after that they were Cessnas.

During the first couple of years, when a pilot spotted a school, which appeared as a black or purple mass whether at the surface or below, he landed and telephoned its location to one of the boats. The time lag was too long, however, and many schools were lost. The factory then equipped the planes with bullhorns, which flew over the seine boats and yelled, and finally with radios to communicate directly with the boats. Using radios, planes could direct the purse boats precisely around schools even those below the surface.

At first, the seine-boat captains resented the planes, believing they did not need any help. To gain their cooperation, the pilots took them in the air to show them what they were seeing, and they took photographic slides of what they saw and showed them to the captains during days of bad weather. Catches were better when the planes were used, and since captains and crews were paid on the basis of their catches, they came to welcome the assistance and the teamwork became smooth. The pilot's wages, too, were prorated on the catches (interview, Dave Timadowski, 7 January 1988).

The factory's seining boats also became more efficient and modernized when oil-powered steam engines replaced coal-powered engines, and power blocks in purse boats replaced men's muscles to haul in the nets. In the 1950s and 1960s, some of the wooden boats were replaced by larger, steel-hulled boats with refrigerated holds to preserve the bunkers. Each could carry about two million bunkers, and they ranged from Belford to Connecticut, Massachusetts, and Maine to seine them. The seines the boats used were made of nylon instead of cotton and required much less care than the cotton nets. The only drawback was that they decayed if left in sunlight, so they had to be covered when not in use.

By 1950 the factory had installed ten-inch diameter suction pumps powered by 671 diesel engines in some of the larger seine boats to transfer the bunkers from the drawn-up seines to the boat holds. The pumps had been constructed for dredging sand from shipping channels, but they pumped the bunkers efficiently. Later, twelve-inch pumps, powered by V-8 diesel engines, were installed; they could transfer as many as nine hundred thousand bunkers a hour. The factory also installed pumps at its Belford dock to pump bunkers from the boat holds. The pound-net boats were emptied by ten-bushel tubs.

In the 1940s and 1950s, during June, a peak month, perhaps three of ten factory boats were making a set on bunker schools in the bay at any one time. Their crews chanted songs as they drew in the nets. Cris Anthropolis, a former crewman on a seine boat, recalled warmly, "It was just like going to church. What beautiful listening" (Interview, 21 July 1990).

The various members of the seining crews received different percentages of the take, according to their jobs. Captains earned the most, $1.00 per thousand fish; crewmen the least, 12.5 cents per thousand fish. During the 1950s, in weeks of exceptionally large catches, captains earned as much as $1,000 and crewmen earned $125.

The last good year for the factory was 1964; after that catches declined sharply. Under heavy fishing pressure, the bunkers had become relatively scarce. Several interviewed fishermen believe the planes ruined the bunker business because they were too efficient in finding schools, resulting in overfishing (Interview, Jigs Apel, 18 April 1980). Catches of bunkers also fell sharply in the pound nets. Rather than each pound net being emptied as often as four times a day in May, each was emptied only once a day, and the total bunker catch for a crew from three nets was often as small as one hundred bushels.

During the 1970s, state laws pertaining to seining bunkers became restrictive, posing a large problem for the factory boats. The strongest opponents of the fishery were sport fishermen, who claimed that the bunker boats took many sport fish. Subsequent impartial studies, however, showed that each boat usually caught no food fish, or, at most, only about five per set. Sport fishermen countered that removal of bunkers eliminated a supply of food for sport fish, which then migrated. New York and Connecticut authorities placed limits on where boats could seine and declared some inshore waters off-limits. For instance, beginning in 1979, authorities of Richmond County, the political entity for Staten Island, declared that bunkers could not be seined within three miles of Staten Island shores. This time, the argument against the seining was that the water being discharged back overboard from pumping bunkers from the nets contained so much fish blood and slime that it fertilized the water and produced damaging algal blooms. This was never proven, but many sport fishermen agreed.

In 1974, Hanson Limited Trust of London bought the J. Howard Smith factory. In the late 1970s, the bunker fishery of Belford employed from 70 to 120 fishermen and up to 100 processing personnel (Caruso 1982). But in 1981 the factory closed permanently, because bunkers had become too scarce, demand for fish oil had declined when soybean oil was produced in large quantity and sold at a lower price, and seining and processing operations for bunkers were more cost-effective in the Gulf of Mexico (Ahrenholz, Nelson, and Epperly 1987).

Porgies

In 1946 the porgy fishery, which became substantial in size and highly profitable, was founded in the bay. Before World War II, landings of porgies had been small because demand for them was weak: often, they brought pound netters only fifty cents a bushel or a cent a pound, and they were considered a poor man's fish. During and after the war, however, the price of porgies rose to an average of six dollars a box (six cents a pound). The principal type of net used to catch them was the otter trawl, a wide bag-shaped net that is towed along the bottom and catches fish more efficiently than other gear.

Fishermen had introduced the otter trawl to the East Coast from Europe in the early part of the twentieth century. It replaced the awkward beam trawl which had been in use mostly in New England; the beam trawl was so named because a long, stout beam held the net open. The otter trawl was actually the "auto" trawl, so named because it remained open without the beam: only two small doors, towed at an angle through the water, one on each side of the net, a chain along its bottom, and floats holding up its headrope, held it open. Unfamiliar with the term *auto*, the fishermen thought the word being used for the net was *otter*, a common animal in those days. The otter trawl used in the bay had a spread of twenty-eight feet along its top and thirty-five feet along its bottom, and it measured about fifty feet long. Its doors were two feet high and four feet long; the length of rope between the doors and the net measured about thirty feet.

In 1920 the New Jersey legislature had made a ruling forbidding otter trawling and purse seining for food fish in Raritan Bay (McCay 1984). Thus, porgy fishing with these gears was illegal. In 1946 the fishermen asked New Jersey authorities to make them legal, while establishing a limit for each boat on its daily catch of porgies, but the authorities would not change the law. About this time, the state of New Jersey assigned five Coastal Patrol wardens to Raritan Bay to enforce its laws. Two or three Coastal Patrol boats were on the bay during daylight hours. Their specific assignment was to prevent the otter trawling, purse seining, and gill netting of porgies and the landings of striped bass by pound-net fishermen and short lobsters by lobstermen. The Coastal Patrol was encouraged to act by the sport fishermen, who complained to New Jersey authorities and politicians about the commercial fishermen.

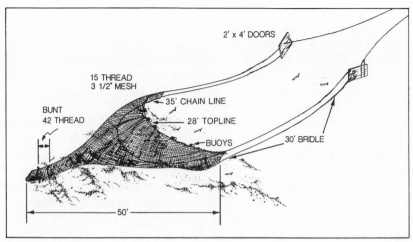

51. Design of otter trawl used to catch porgies in Raritan Bay, 1946 to 1963. Author's collection.

The Coastal Patrol wardens had some sympathy for the commercial porgy fishermen, however, and generally just showed a presence on the water to calm the sport fishermen (Interview, Bill Jenks, 1 March 1991).

In 1946, the first otter trawl was brought to the bay by Willie Alexander, a fisherman from Belford, to catch porgies. Many others soon joined him with otter trawls, purse seines, and gill nets, catching porgies all over the bay. This fishery peaked during the 1950s and lasted through 1962. B. J. McCay, an anthropology professor at Rutgers University who specializes in fisheries, called this the Golden Age of Belford, because the porgy fishery was the most profitable fishery for individual fishermen in the history of the bay (1984). McCay also said that large landings of porgies helped the fishermen's cooperative, founded in 1953, become a success and achieve the independence fishermen had desired from the fish merchants in Fulton Market. During the winter, many of the porgy fishermen worked in the rocking-chair clam fishery.

Each year, the porgies arrived in the bay around the Fourth of July and remained for four to four and a half months; however, a September hurricane could drive them back out to sea earlier. Most weighed a pound and a half to two pounds. They were so abundant that the fishermen called Raritan Bay the porgy capital of the world. Even though many boats were catching them, they said, "We never put a dent in 'em" (Interview, Louie Egnatovich, 14 February 1986).

Fishermen used "Maycraft" boats, from twenty-two to twenty-eight feet long, to tow their otter trawls. The boats were made of plywood, had a broad beam, and had been designed for sport fishing. Fishermen purchased them cheaply and installed automobile engines with marine conversions in them for the speed they would need to escape arrest by the Coastal Patrol wardens: they had a maximum speed of about forty knots. Fishermen painted all of them white, so they looked alike on the water. Each boat had a crew of four and could carry as many as sixty boxes of porgies. There were about twenty-three such boats, all docked in Belford (Interview, Bill Jenks, 1 March 1991).

Fishermen towed the otter trawls for ten to forty minutes and hauled them in and emptied them by hand. "The porgies were jumping when they poured out of the nets onto the decks," said one. In ten-minute tows, a crew could catch as many as thirty boxes; longer tows sometimes caught fifty boxes (Interview, Louie Egnatovich, 14 February 1986). A crew once caught one thousand boxes of porgies in one week. Few fish other than porgies were caught except for roughtail stingrays, which weighed as much as three hundred to four hundred pounds apiece. Crews usually had to make only one or two tows for a substantial catch. Then they returned to Belford with the porgies piled loosely on the decks of their boats. After crews hosed them down, shoveled them into boxes, and lifted them onto the docks, their boat decks were often covered with one or two inches of duck clams and juvenile blue mussels, about half an inch long, that the porgies had regurgitated (Interview, Jigs Apel, 21 October 1987).

The otter trawl fishermen were able to pursue their fishery and land the porgies almost unhindered because the Coastal Patrol boats had a maximum speed of only ten knots. To arrest a fishing crew and have the conviction stand in court, the wardens had to see the otter trawl in the water being towed or being retrieved with fish in it, and to identify the crewmen. If the wardens approached a boat in the bay and it had finished trawling and had a load of porgies and an otter trawl aboard, the fishermen could say they had caught the fish in the ocean beyond three miles from land where trawling was legal, and they would not be arrested.

The fishermen carefully managed their trawling procedures to elude arrests. First, they trawled in groups of seven or eight. Second, at least one boat of each group had a warden spotter, usually a youth, aboard. Third, if they saw a Coastal Patrol boat coming at a distance toward them, they all hauled in their nets quickly, or, if they did not have time to retrieve them, they let them go and sped away. They retrieved the nets later, sometimes the next day. A patrol boat rarely got closer than two miles from them. During weekends, when the wardens were off duty, fishermen were unhindered.

A fishing crew once had a large quantity of porgies in its net and did not feel like letting the net go when a Coastal Patrol boat approached them from a distance. They anchored their boat, tied a fishing line onto one of the trawl lines, and let it fall to the bottom. The captain tied the other end of the fishing line onto his big toe and lay back in the boat, pretending he was sport fishing. The patrol boat came up to him, the two crews made small talk, and then it left. Afterward the crew hauled up the lines and net and loaded the porgies into the boat (Letter, Bill Jenks to author, 20 February 1991).

This incident notwithstanding, many arrests were made, and the courts had to deal with them. The fishermen were hoping that the judges would tire of handling the cases and urge state authorities make the commercial fishing legal. Fishermen felt that the law had been initiated by sport fishermen and written by politicians who passed it to obtain the sport fishermen's many votes. Commercial fishing had a long history in the bay. Why should the commercial fishermen allow the sport fishermen to stop them from fishing? If the commercial fishermen abided by all the state laws, there would not be any commercial fishing except for pound-net fishing.

Because of their lawbreaking, the Belford fishermen were commonly referred to as pirates. From their point of view, however, they were just trying to carry on with their fishing tradition while earning a living doing it. Pirates are not usually thought of as hard-working, ambitious, and good family men, but most of the Belford fishermen combined all three traits.

The fishermen also did some trawling at night when the moon was full to avoid the Coastal Patrol. Each boat had a deck light shining so the crew could see what they were doing; the light had a rheostat so they could dim it enough to make it hard for Coastal Patrol wardens to see them from a distance. Porgies swim close to the bottom during daylight and on clear nights when the moon is full or nearly so. They rise above bottom on dark nights, however, and could not be caught with the otter trawls. Fishermen found that the porgies were down only on clear nights when the full moon was brightest, and that was an hour later each night. A tow made when the fish were down often had fifty to sixty boxes, but a tow made in the same area half an hour before they descended might have only one box. One fisherman recalled, "You had so many guys working at night that you always had someone going out or coming in, so there were always some trying to see when they were down" (Interview, Jigs Apel, 11 March 1986).

When they fished at night, the fishermen tried to sleep during the day, but it was usually too hot during the days of July and August to sleep. Thus the fishermen bought air conditioners for their bedrooms for the first time. They were proud of them and boasted about the comfort they provided.

The Maycraft boats took a severe pounding during the many chases by the Coastal Patrol, and they all leaked badly. To slow the leaks, the fishermen "dusted" their boats in Compton's Creek. This involved nailing a can on a stick, filling it with dry sawdust, and putting it under their boats where the bad leaks were. The sawdust floated out of the can and was drawn into the leaks, filling them enough that the pumps of the boats could keep their bilges dry (Letter, Bill Jenks to author, 20 February 1991).

Fishermen also caught the porgies with purse seines, gill nets, and pound nets. Fifteen to eighteen boats used purse seines. One type was a dragger, sixty to seventy feet long, with a seven-man crew. A smaller type was the pound boat, about thirty-six feet long. Purse boats carrying the nets used with both types were pound boats. The seines ranged from five hundred to one thousand feet long and were from thirty-two to forty feet deep. Porgy fishermen had obtained them secondhand from the bunker-seine crews and cut them down to size. Fishermen seined porgies mostly in the ocean but also in the bay.

The captains of the larger boats found concentrations of porgies by using depth recorders, which fishermen first used on their boats in 1949. (Fishermen came to rely heavily on depth recorders to find fish. A common saying was "Without a scope, there ain't no hope.") After finding porgies, they ran their seine around them. Next, they pursed the bottom of the net, drew it in, and brailed out the porgies. A single operation took about an hour. The seiners actually fished about two hours a day, five days a week.

A purse-seine captain described how he once made a set on a huge school of porgies, but lost most of them:

> One night off Coney Island, we made a set with a purse seine which must have had three or four thousand boxes of porgies in it, but we lost them. What happened was, we couldn't get help quick enough. Whenever we got a big set we'd double up and triple up with crews because we were pulling everything by hand. These fish sanded. That is to say, there were so many in there, they got to boiling the sand, and the lead line and some of the net sank in the sand and got stuck in the bottom. We tore the net when we retrieved and they escaped. I think we saved thirty or forty boxes of porgies. Those big rubber-nose porgies ran about two pounds apiece!

Each seine boat had a daily quota of one hundred boxes, each holding one hundred pounds, arranged through the fishermen's cooperative, because the Belford dock could handle only twenty-five hundred boxes of porgies a day. Frequently a seine boat got from two hundred to one thousand boxes of porgies in a set, so the boat making such sets got the quota for itself and up to nine additional boats. Its crew telephoned the other crews not to set, since it had enough for all. The boats came into Belford together, their crews unloaded the boat with the porgies, and they divided up the money from their sale equally. The next day, another boat might get its quota first as well as that for some other boats in their fleet (Interview, Jigs Apel, 18 April 1989).

The purse seiners caught porgies under the guise of seining bunkers, and many did return to the bay to seine bunkers after they unloaded their limit of porgies. If a Coastal Patrol warden caught a purse-seine crew with porgies in its net, the crew said that it thought that the fish were bunkers when they put out the seine, and they released them. One fisherman had to release an enormous quantity of porgies. He related, "We had our net around five thousand boxes of porgies and had five boats there ready to load them. But the 'law' came and we had to let them go."

The sport fishermen complained to New Jersey authorities about the porgy fishermen because they felt they were hurting sport fishing by taking too many porgies. Once, a head-boat captain told a Coastal Patrol warden that he would take him right up to a trawling boat on his head boat; if the warden hid from view until they got there, he could catch the crew with the net in the water and arrest them. He did that, the conviction held, and the court fined the trawling captain two hundred dollars. The porgy fishermen did not want that to happen again, and so one night they got a fellow who hung around Compton's Creek drunk, gave him a gallon of creosote, and then got him to spread it all over the varnished decks and rails of the head boat. It took several days to remove it. After that, no head boat ever dared to take out a warden on such a venture (Interview, Bill Jenks, 12 February 1991).

About twelve crews in skiffs employed drift gill nets to catch porgies. The porgies would not gill themselves in a net by day, so the fishermen had to operate at night. Crews left their nets out for about fifteen minutes and sometimes caught large quantities of porgies. They pulled their nets aboard, shook out as many porgies as they could—about two-thirds of them—and then had to pick out the remainder. Catches ranged from five to fifty boxes per crew each night.

Bud Thompson, of Port Monmouth, remembered that a gill-netting crew frequently brought porgies into Compton's Creek and asked for his help getting them out of their net:

> They'd come over to my house and get me at all hours of
> the night. Somebody'd bang at the door and ask me to give

them a hand. I'd get dressed and go down there. The net was so damn full of fish that they didn't even bother with it in the bay. They just pulled the net and fish into their boat and came into the creek. I'd get fifteen to twenty dollars for only a couple of hours of work. (Interview, 14 December 1987)

The fishermen landed the daily limit of twenty-five hundred boxes of porgies a day as set by the fishermen's cooperative in Belford regularly. The dock remained open all night to handle them. Like the bay, it was usually a beehive of activity, day and night. The porgies were either loaded directly onto trailer trucks or put temporarily into a cooler if a truck was not there. They were taken to New York City, Philadelphia, Baltimore, and Hampton, Virginia, for sale.

Jigs Apel related:

We never made real good money on porgies, because there was such a supply coming in. The guys in the market, they knew they had you. You were catching them and you had to sell them. We packed many a porgy for four and five dollars a box. I mean thousands of boxes for that money. It got so bad sometimes it wouldn't pay to fish, so everybody'd just tie up. Guys would stop if they figured they couldn't go out there and make a day's work. They stopped till the market got better, sometimes for a week. They let the guys get hungry in the markets, the price would go up and the guys went back to work. If they had kept on working, they'd have probably got nothing for their work. There was a lot of gypsy trucking of the fish. A guy would gypsy-fish [drive to a market without a prior arrangement to sell a product and try to peddle it when he got there] all the way down to Hampton. (Interview, 11 March 1986)

The fishery ended for good in the summer of 1963, seventeen years after it began, because the porgies became scarce in the bay and along the entire northeast coast of the United States. From 1960 to 1966, landings of porgies fell by 54 percent in the region. Intense fishing by the European fleets on the porgies' overwintering grounds near the edge of the continental shelf was held responsible (Smith and Norcross 1968). Those fleets took many thousands of tons of porgies every winter. The porgy population has never recovered; landings remain relatively low and available porgies are small, most weighing less than a pound. Many porgy fishermen in Belford reverted to lobster fishing when the porgy fishery ended.

Marketing Food Fish

The Belford Fishermen's Cooperative

In 1953 the fishermen of Belford founded a cooperative, with twenty-five charter members, to sell their fish. The main species for the first ten years was porgies. It will be recalled that fishermen had been shipping about 90 percent of their fish to commission merchants at Fulton Market on consignment. They never knew what prices they would get and they believed they were being cheated. Walt DeGrote, a seventy-two-year-old Belford fisherman, related his thoughts, which were typical:

> They could tell us anything they wanted about price. For instance, they could sell the fish for ten cents a pound and tell us they sold them for three cents. We would never know the difference. One time, the father of one of us took some lobsters to the market and he was right there when the lobsters were sold. They were all alive. When he got the returns, the commission merchant paid for only half of them, because he said that the other half were dead. Another time, we sent five hundred pounds of bluefish there and they sent us back a bill for the freight, saying that the fish were rotten and had to be dumped into the river. We know they weren't. That's how they cheated us, but they had us over a barrel, as we had no place else to sell fish. (Interview, 4 August 1989)

Sentiment against the Fulton Market merchants deepened, especially when the story about the "dead" lobsters spread around Belford. The fishermen were eager to establish the cooperative with the goal of gaining independence from Fulton Market. They also wanted to improve Belford's fish unloading facilities, which had been inadequate during the 1940s when the bay had 128 pound nets.

The cooperative leased land alongside Compton's Creek from the J. Howard Smith Fish Factory, then installed a freezer for bunkers, an ice machine, and motorized lifts to remove fish from boats; it also built a retail market. Forklifts were purchased to transfer boxes and barrels of fish from the dock to waiting trucks.

The cooperative insisted that wholesale buyers confirm the price of fish before any shipment was made, and it recorded the weight of fish before they were shipped. The principal markets were Fulton Market in New York City; Philadelphia; Baltimore; and Washington; fish were sent wherever prices were highest. Thus fishermen obtained generally higher

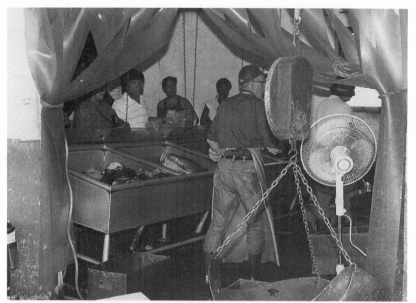

52. Fish market at Belford fishermen's cooperative. Photograph by author.

prices for their fish, and cheating ended. Another advantage gained was that fishermen could purchase supplies in bulk, at cheaper rates. Members paid the cooperative 15 percent of the sale price of their fish to cover operating expenses, which included the salary of a manager. They also paid for fish boxes and ice. In the 1980s, the cooperative seemed to be functioning well, but several fishermen interviewed in Belford said that it had financial problems whenever fish landings were small.

The cooperative's retail market sold only whole fish. It sold about 25 percent of the food fish landed by the cooperative fishermen. It became popular and was usually crowded with customers, especially on weekends, because its fish and shellfish, representing from fifteen to twenty-five species in any one day, were the freshest available anywhere and sold for reasonable prices. A large portion of the customers were Asians who ate uncooked fish, which must be fresh to be palatable. People from relatively distant points, such as Newark and Paterson, often bought three or four fifty-pound cartons of fish; more local people purchased smaller quantities. Customers took the cartons of fish home in the trunks of their automobiles.

Caviar

In April and May each year, from the late 1800s through the 1960s, one or two fishermen prepared caviar from the roe of Atlantic sturgeon caught in pound nets. Fishermen caught about four roe sturgeon per week, thirty to forty during the season, yielding about three hundred pounds of caviar. Fishermen shipped carcasses of the sturgeon to Fulton Market, where they were cut into steaks.

From the 1940s through the 1960s, Joe Adubato, a pound-net fisherman, and his wife, Bea, of Belford, processed all the caviar. Joe caught some sturgeon and obtained the rest from other fishermen; he split the profits fifty-fifty with them when the caviar was sold.

The roe had to be processed within an hour after they were removed from the fish. Joe brought the roe home to Bea, who did not refrigerate them because that would harden the fat surrounding the eggs. First, she pushed the eggs through a screen that had quarter-inch openings; the eggs retained much fat on their surface. Next, she mixed in kosher salt at a rate of one pound of salt to seven pounds of eggs. The salt cleaned the exterior fat and drew out moisture from the eggs, hardening them. Then she put the eggs on a fine screen to drain for about an hour. In the final step, she scooped the eggs, now considered caviar, into tin cans. When the Adubatos had between fifty and one hundred pounds of caviar, they delivered it in their automobile to the Romanoff Caviar Company in New York City, which paid $7.50 a pound for it in the 1960s. The company requested that the eggs from different fish be kept separate because they were in different stages of development. It did not process the caviar further, but put it directly into small jars for consumer sale. Marketing of caviar from bay sturgeon ended about 1970, when this species became scarce in the bay (Interview, Joe and Bea Adubato, 1 May 1987).

Eel Market, Methods, and Decline

After the late 1940s, the eel market in the U.S. slowed and remained weak. The demand was good only during the December holidays when people of Dutch, German, Italian, and Portuguese origin ate them. As a result, many fishermen had to abandon eeling. Beginning in the mid-1960s, however, wholesale buyers found markets in Europe and Japan for U.S. eels, and since then most eels have been shipped abroad live by air freight. In the 1980s, the East Coast had five large eel buyers. They shipped six to seven million pounds of eels to Europe a year and sold only three hundred thousand pounds in the U.S. Most of the eels went to Holland, where they were sold locally and redistributed to other European countries. The U.S. eel market was good only at the beginning and end of the season—March to April, and October to December. Other than that it was glutted.

In the 1950s and 1960s, fishermen used fourteen- to sixteen-foot

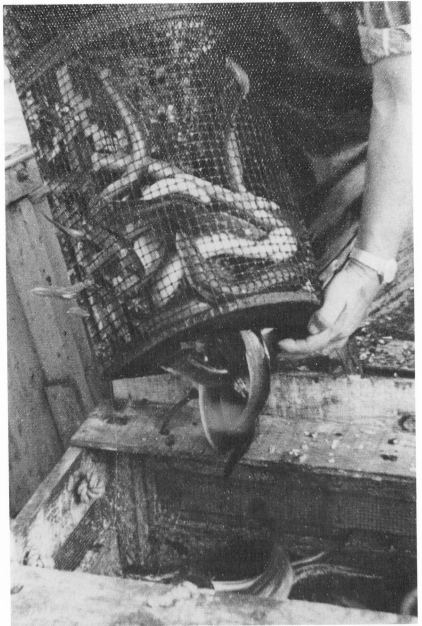

53. Emptying potful of eels into a live car, circa 1963. Courtesy of John Seminski.

bateaux, fitted with outboard motors, to tend their eel pots in Raritan Bay. They lifted the pots every day, except at the end of the season, when they usually lifted every other day because catches had fallen. By the 1960s, fishermen purchased larger, forty- to eighty-horsepower outboard motors. Eel fishermen then purchased boats eighteen to twenty-two feet long along with these motors and used them for eeling. They began using hydraulic hoists to lift their pot lines in the early 1970s.

Fishermen held their eels in floating wooden cars tied to poles near their boat docks for as long as two weeks before selling them. The cars measured about thirty-two inches long, twenty-one inches wide, and twelve inches deep; their bottoms and sides consisted of plastic-coated wire screen. Openings in the mesh were one inch by four-tenths of an inch. Fishermen chose this size mesh because it retained the salable larger eels and permitted the smaller eels to escape. The cars were thus self-culling, saving the fishermen from doing that task. The market for small eels had always been poor, and fishermen liked to return them to the water for conservation purposes.

Fishermen did not feed eels in the cars because their guts had to be empty when they were sold live. If eels excreted feces in the tanks in which they were held while being transported to markets the water would become "sour" and adversely affect the quality of their flesh. Fishermen had not found it profitable to hold eels in cars for extended periods while waiting for a higher market price, because they lost too much weight (Interview, Jim Kaplinger, 1 November 1985).

The Delaware Valley Line Fish Company of Philadelphia bought eels from bay fishermen in the 1980s and earlier. Its collection truck had a large tank divided into four compartments, each measuring six feet long, thirty inches wide, and three feet high. The compartments, which were painted white inside, had walls four inches thick. They were filled with refrigerated and highly aerated salt water. Each compartment could hold 1,500 pounds of eels when full, for a total of 6,000 pounds on the truck.

Jim Kaplinger of Highlands was one of the eelers who sold to this company. When ready to sell, he had about 2,000 pounds of eels in fifteen floating cars, each holding about 140 pounds. Eels filled the cars four-fifths of the way to the top when taken out of water. This total was caught about every two weeks by Jim, his father, and his son, each of whom had his own boat and pots. Jim lifted the floats onto the dock with an electric hoist and the driver of the fish company's truck and his helper emptied them into a perforated barrel, a float-full at a time. Then they lifted the barrel onto a scale attached to the back of the truck and tallied each weight in a notebook. Finally, they dumped the eels into the compartments. In Philadelphia, the eels were packed live in boxes of waxed cardboard, without water but with clean ice to keep them at about 30° F, and then air-shipped to Holland.

In 1980 there were ten eel fishermen in the bay. In the mid-1980s one fisherman had 300 pots and caught 200 to 250 pounds of eels on good days; his rare largest catches ranged from 700 to 1,000 pounds a day. However, by 1989, the number of eel fishermen had fallen to four, and, by 1991, to only two.

Eel Spearing

Eel spearing continued in the winters of the 1940s and 1950s, and the Navesink and Shrewsbury rivers had a few hundred spearing holes chopped through their ice every cold winter. During the 1940s, a local ordinance was put into effect requiring that the holes on the Navesink River not be more than ten inches in diameter; they had to be at least fifteen feet apart. In addition, all particles of ice and sticks had to be pushed into the holes when the eeler was finished spearing. These measures were to prevent injuries to the many skaters and iceboat enthusiasts who used the river (*Red Bank Register,* 22 January 1948). Spearing declined after the 1950s, however, and was practiced only rarely after the early 1970s.

Market Conflict with Sport Fishermen Ends
Commercial Bluefish Hand Lining

In the early 1950s, about six boat crews from Belford were still hand lining for bluefish. The fishery ended in the late 1950s, however, because sport fishermen had become numerous, and many learned from the commercial fishermen how to catch bluefish in large quantities by chumming. They sold them and glutted the market. Prices fell so low that the commercial fishermen had to abandon the fishery. Hand lining for mackerel disappeared for the same reason: an increasing number of head boats sought mackerel and sold them, reducing the landed prices too low for commercial fishermen to earn an adequate day's pay catching them (Interview, Walt DeGrote, 4 August 1989).

Sport Fishing

Immediately after World War II, sport fishing in the bay increased sharply, both because people had more leisure time and because equipment improved. For example, lightweight aluminum and fiberglass boats replaced wooden boats; six- and seven-horsepower outboard motors became available to power them, replacing oars and muscle power (when the motors started!), fishing reels made of lightweight synthetic materials replaced metal ones whose weight had contributed to numerous back-lashes; rods were made of fiberglass instead of wood; and durable synthetic lines replaced cotton and linen lines. Local sport shops sprang up to sell equipment and bait. These shops purchased the bait from local fishermen, especially those from Staten Island and Highlands, and from dealers in New England. In addition, the number of head boats increased to meet the demand. Jimmy White, a clammer and former schoolteacher and mayor of Highlands, ascribed the increase in sport fishing to the loss of the two major league baseball teams in New York City in the late 1950s:

> When the Dodgers and Giants left New York, sport fishing around here at least trebled. For something to do on a weekend, people in New York City came down here to go fishing. They rented tackle, boats, and outboard motors. Every year, there are more boats and more people. There's got to be over a thousand people fishing for flounders and fluke on weekends beginning in March and April and continuing all summer. The people are on beaches, bulkheads, and boats, wherever they can get a line overboard. (Interview, 16 May 1986)

In the 1940s, the *Red Bank Register* began carrying a weekly column about sport fishing, evidence of its growing popularity. Called "Surf, Field and Stream" and written by Stew Van Vliet, the column featured news about fish catches at various sites and by individual party boats, recreational eel fishing, meetings of rod and gun clubs, and the progress of any fishing bills in the state legislature. The first bill it followed was intended to prohibit the sale of striped bass caught in pound nets. From the 1850s through the 1930s, almost weekly during the warmer months, the *Register* had printed a column relating to commercial fishing and shell fishing in Raritan Bay. Sport fishing, being relatively minor then, was rarely mentioned. By the 1950s, other newspapers, striving to attract readers, carried similar weekly columns about sport fishing. Eventually, the columns in each newspaper appeared as often as four times a week.

During the late 1940s, bait fishermen used garden forks and also motors to obtain worms to sell for sport fishing. The bait fishermen had observed that when they anchored boats in shallow water with their inboard motors running in neutral, tapeworms emerged from the bottom; the motors' vibrations agitated the worms and forced many to leave the sediment. To gather tapeworms in commercial quantities, fishermen loosened the motor bolts from the hull of their boats, twisted the distributor of their motors, and started them; this made the boats vibrate vigorously. The fishermen caught the worms as they drifted in the current away from the boat in a fine seine or in their hands. Tapeworms obtained by using the motors were in good condition because they were whole, whereas forking broke each one into several pieces. A fishermen could obtain one to two gallons of tapeworms every low tide. In the 1940s, bait fishermen sold sand worms and bloodworms for 1.5 cents each, and tapeworms for six to eight dollars a gallon to sport shops and to the Keansburg Pier, a popular fishing spot (Interview, John Seminski, 7 June 1991).

Sport shops also sold killifish and shrimp. Fishermen caught the killifish in pots similar to eel pots that they baited with broken soft clams and placed in marsh creeks. They seined the shrimp.

Commercial worm digging came to an end during the 1950s because worms became scarce in the bay then and thereafter. No one has investigated the reasons for the scarcity, but possibly it was caused by overdigging; increased erosion of shorelines after the disappearance of eelgrass; pollution of sediments and water by oil spills and other industrial wastes, which spoiled the worms' habitat; and perhaps the vibrations from the increased multitude of motorboats traversing the bay. Former diggers say, "The worms disappeared with progress" (Interview, Johnny Mount, 19 July 1989). As sport fishing increased after the 1940s and the demand for worms increased, the digging areas moved northeastward from Raritan Bay, to Massachusetts, Maine, and Canada's maritime provinces, where they have since become scarcer.

In the 1950s, head boats, about sixty-five feet long and eighteen feet wide, began to appear in the bay. Typically, a waist-high rail on the main deck ran along their sides from bow to stern for fishermen to lean on while holding their poles. About every four feet along the rails, vertical tubes were fastened for holding fishing rods when fishermen wanted to take a break. The main deck had a large heated cabin, offering fishermen protection from the weather if they desired it, and continuous benches for sitting both inside and outside the cabin. The wheelhouse was on the upper deck. Early every morning, fishermen gathered at docks to board them and were taken out for a half day or full day. When the fishing and weather were good, more fishermen came than the head boats could carry, and some had to remain behind. Head boats were popular because they took fishermen to areas that provided good fishing.

In the early 1980s the bay had about seventeen head boats sailing from its ports. In the early 1980s, Staten Island had six to eight (one in Tomkinsville, four to six in Great Kills Harbor, and one in Tottenville), but by the mid-1980s they had all left for other ports in New Jersey or

Sheepshead Bay, New York. In 1989 the numbers in various New Jersey ports were: one in Perth Amboy, one in Keyport, two in Leonardo, nine in Atlantic Highlands, and two in Highlands. In summer, the fishermen who went on head boats consisted mostly of men, some women and children, and, increasingly, senior citizens. During the remainder of the year, most fishermen consisted of seniors and men who had days off. Head boats charged twenty to twenty-two dollars per fisherman for a full day; some charged the seniors half price. When the fishing was poor, head-boat captains required that at least eight fishermen be on board to fish in the bay and ten to fish in the ocean, or else they did not go out. Most fish were caught in July and August, followed by September and October; January and February were the least productive months (Smith, Lipton, and Norton 1983).

The five fishes that head boats concentrated on were fluke and winter flounder in the bay and blackfish, ling, and whiting in the ocean, but other species were caught also.

Fluke

Fluke were the most popular fish from the warmer months to mid-October. They were not numerous during the 1960s and early 1970s, but during the late 1970s, catches improved substantially and were abundant through 1988; then they were scarcer.

Killifish, shiners (silversides), sand eels, strips of squid, or strips cut from fish bellies were used as bait. Bait must move over the bottom to catch fluke because their natural foods—small fish and crustaceans—are motile, so the boat had to drift. During most of the summer, fishermen caught this species all over the bay, but the best areas were along the banks of dredged channels and dredge holes.

Winter Flounder

Fishermen caught this species from March to May, but in less quantity than fluke. The natural foods of winter flounder are sedentary, bottom-living invertebrates. The most common bait was cut-up pieces of surf clams. Head boats did not drift; they anchored and often chummed to catch winter flounder. They put over one to two bushels of crushed surf clams or mussels and even canned corn for chum on the bottom around the boat. The chum usually helped, but not if the boat happened to anchor over a concentration of fish. The grounds were about the same as for fluke, except that the winter flounder never inhabit the dredged channels in the bay. When the fishing began in March, winter flounder inhabited near-shore areas in eight to ten feet of water. Because the water

54. *Sport-fishing boats after winter flounder in Shrewsbury River, a southeastern arm of Raritan Bay, in March 1988. Photograph by author.*

was warmer in the Navesink and Shrewsbury rivers, they began to bite there before they bit in the bay.

Blackfish

This species was caught on the Romer Shoal mussel bed off the tip of Sandy Hook and in the ocean two to five miles from shore over wrecks and rocks. The best baits were whole fiddler crabs and cut-up pieces of green crabs; pieces of surf clams were also used. Crabs were expensive bait, because they had to be imported from Massachusetts. Fishermen had to be alert and reel up the blackfish as soon as they bit; if they hesitated the fish could swim under the wreck or rock and could not be dislodged. Fishermen lost considerable tackle when fishing for blackfish.

Ling

The best bait for this species was strips of fresh herring, cut about three-fourths of an inch wide. Fresh herring and frozen herring, also used, were available in bait shops.

Bluefish

Many boats used to go for bluefish, but in the 1980s people developed a distaste for bluefish, preferring the less oily fluke and winter flounder. To catch bluefish, head boats anchored and chummed with minced bunkers, using the same method that commercial fishermen used to lure this species to their boats. When fluke were scarce in 1989 and 1990, the principal fish available in summer were bluefish. Head-boat captains found that their business fell off considerably when that happened.

Charter Boats

Another type of sport fishing boat was the charter boat. The boats were thirty to thirty-five feet long, with fiberglass or wood hulls. They had two seats for fishermen to sit in while holding their poles. Most boats had gasoline engines, but some were diesel. They were operated by a captain and sometimes a mate. Parties of four to six people hired them to go trolling in the bay and ocean for bluefish and striped bass. In 1980, Great Kills Harbor had four such boats; in 1991, it had none, while Atlantic Highlands had six that year.

Private Boats

Fiberglass boats owned by individual fishermen have become increasingly popular in the bay since World War II. They are generally eighteen to twenty feet long. Fishermen keep them at their homes and bring them to launching ramps around the bayshore on trailers towed by cars or pickup trucks; some keep them at marinas, either tied at docks or stored on trailers. On summer weekends in the 1980s, when fluke were abundant in the bay, at least one hundred fiberglass fishing boats were on the water at any time, carrying from one to four fishermen each.

I estimate that from 1963 onward, when the major commercial fishery for porgies was no longer practiced in the bay, sport fishing became so popular that it was larger in terms of participants and in catches of food fish than commercial fishing was. Moreover, Raritan Bay was probably the most popular fishing area in the northeastern United States (Smith, Lipton, and Norton 1983). A survey of all the bay and ocean waters of New York and New Jersey in the 1980s revealed that sport fishermen caught more bluefish and winter flounder, about the same quantities of fluke and weakfish, and fewer porgies, than commercial fishermen (McHugh 1990).

10

Shell Fishing After World War II

The beginning of the post–World War II period was marked by the illegal digging of hard clams by New Jersey fishermen in Staten Island waters and the use of the rocking-chair dredge for hard clams; later the hard-clam fishery was sharply curtailed because the beds became polluted. The soft-clam fishery continued to be active, but then declined and ended when the clams became scarce and the beds became polluted. The lobster fishery was enhanced substantially by developments in gear, and the blue-crab fishery remained about the same except that catches were smaller than they had been during the 1920s and 1930s.

Hard Clamming

By the late 1930s, the daily catches of the hand rakers in New Jersey were eight to ten bushels per man, the clams being mostly cherrystones and chowders. In 1939 some fishermen from Keyport discovered that the clams were much more abundant in Prince's Bay, off Staten Island, and they began to dig clams there. They had to do their raking under cover of night to avoid being seen by the New York warden, since it was illegal for nonresidents to clam there. Bill Richardson, a Keyport fisherman, related:

> I had been pound-net fishing, earning twenty-five dollars a week. When we pulled out the pounds, I didn't have a job, so I

bought a twenty-four-foot boat with a seventy-five-horse-power Chrysler automobile engine for clamming in Prince's Bay. My partner and I left Keyport in the boat just before dark and reached Prince's Bay just after dark. The clams were as thick as coal in a coal bin. The worst job was getting a hole started with the rake. We gave our rakes only twelve or fourteen jerks and they were full, about half a bushel. We didn't sort the clams by size, rather we dumped them in half-bushel baskets and then into a sack; a bushel in a sack. The two of us got as many as fifty bushels a night. We came home, washed up, and went to bed. Then, we got up around 9 A.M., had a good breakfast, sorted the clams by size, and sold them for a dollar a bushel. [Over] the first four days of doing this, we made one hundred dollars apiece. After that, the money was still good, but a little less. (Interview, 5 October 1985)

The remaining clammers in New Jersey could see the Keyport fishermen going over to Prince's Bay, and they heard that each was getting around twenty bushels of clams apiece every night. Soon, New Jersey diggers from Keansburg, Belford, and Highlands as well as Keyport went there in their boats. Perhaps half the New Jersey hard-clam rakers went there when the weather was suitable. One minor problem with the nighttime digging was that a breeze rarely blew to keep the boat moving in the direction a man was raking. The clammers had to depend on tidal currents for this.

The Staten Island fish warden soon discovered the clammers, and he attempted to chase them away from the beds in his boat. To avoid being arrested, the clammers kept their outboard motors in such good condition that they started with the first pull of their starter cords. As soon as the clammers spotted the light of the warden's boat coming out of Lemon Creek at Prince's Bay toward them, they quit raking and headed for home waters at high speeds. If the warden followed them across the bay, they found safety when they arrived near shore because the water was shallow and the warden's boat, which was larger, could not follow them there.

One summer in the 1950s, the warden went out to the clam grounds just before dark one or two nights a week instead of doing so after the rakers were there. This presented a major problem, because when they saw him they had to return home without a night's pay. The Keyport men were not to be denied completely, however. One of them had a friend living in Prince's Bay, and he got him to go down to the warden's boat every evening to determine whether it was gone. Then the friend telephoned the information to the raker in Keyport. If the warden was out, the rakers stayed home; if he was in, they went to Prince's Bay (Interview, Johnny Wallace, 8 December 1985).

The Staten Island fish warden confronted New Jersey hand rakers only rarely in midsummer, because he did not wish to harm sport fishermen in the area. Often, on summer nights, from twenty-five to fifty people in small boats were angling for weakfish in the clamming area. The warden believed that if he chased the clammers, they would race through the sport fishermen, perhaps killing someone. On one occasion, however, he dressed like a clam fisherman, got into a clam boat with a rake, drifted into the fleet of clam boats unnoticed, and arrested a New Jersey clammer.

Bill Braun, a Keansburg fisherman, described some of the New Jersey clammers' experiences with the warden in Prince's Bay:

> The warden shot somebody in the knee once. One time, he fired at my brother, but his bullet hit our engine. If it had gone three or four inches higher, it would have gone into the middle of his back. One day, the warden shot alongside my elbow and I saw the water splash. But I was acting as though it was a big joke; you know, when you're young, you're nutty. We worried my mother and father to death going over there at night.
>
> I was caught by wardens three times in Prince's Bay. The first two times, the fine was twenty-five dollars, but that didn't mean too much because I could make about that in one night. The third time, the warden took me into Great Kills Harbor as usual. I didn't have any money with me so I had to call my brother over from New Jersey to bring some money. He brought along a friend of ours, who was a clammer and a big-mouth guy. The conservation office had two rooms: one was a receiving room and the other was an office. The warden and I were sitting in the receiving room when my brother and the friend arrived. Our friend told the warden in a joking manner about how many times he got away from him and about the time when it was snowing and the warden went right close by and didn't see him. The door was partly open to the office. I was hoping that he'd shut up, but he wouldn't. After about twenty minutes, somebody came over to the door and motioned the warden and me into the office. Two guys were sitting behind a desk. One of them says: "We heard all that went on out there. You fellas think this is just a big joke, don't you? Now I'm going to tell you that we had in mind to fine you twenty-five dollars, but we're going to have this trouble continually unless we

increase it. So, we're going to raise your fine to seventy-five dollars. Maybe that'll make you think it over! (Interview, 12 December 1986)

The New Jersey fishermen believed that they should be able to dig wherever they wished. If Staten Island fishermen had a right to dig in New York waters, so did everyone else. No one put the clams there, so they did not feel that they were stealing from anyone. In fact, the state of New York was stealing their right to get the clams (Interview, Bill Braun, 12 December 1986).

During 1939 and the early 1940s, about twenty regular clammers and seventy-five part-timers living on Staten Island were licensed to dig hard clams. On good-weather days, thirty to forty were actually digging. After that, the number of Staten Islanders raking clams bore an inverse relationship to the job market on shore, as was typical of many fisheries. For instance, when servicemen returned home after World War II, many went clamming because they could not find other jobs. In 1947, the S. S. White Factory, manufacturers of dental supplies in Prince's Bay, had a large layoff, and many men put out of work went into hard clamming; the number of hand rakers on Staten Island rose to about one hundred. In 1950, the Korean War began and many war-related jobs became available around the island, so the number of rakers declined to about thirty-five.

Rocking-Chair Dredging

Willie Alexander of Belford introduced the rocking-chair dredge for hard clams to the bay in 1946. Fishermen had been aware that hard clams were abundant in the central area of the bay, which had mostly a mud-sand bottom lying under twenty to twenty-five feet of water, but they did not possess any gear to gather them. Alexander purchased his dredge in Rhode Island, where rocking-chair dredges had been in use for some time, and began gathering clams with it in that central area, using his motorized sloop. The dredge consisted of a tooth bar about two feet wide with teeth about seven inches long, a metal sheet measuring about sixteen by twenty-four inches placed on top of the dredge and angled slightly from vertical to hold the dredge down, and a chain bag that could hold about eight bushels. When towed, the teeth and sheet worked opposite one another and rocked the dredge fore and aft; hence the name.

Within a few months, most of the fishermen who had been sail dredging for hard clams (and some other fishermen) obtained rocking-chair dredges. By the late 1940s, twenty boats were gathering clams

55. Rocking-chair dredge used for gathering hard clams in Raritan Bay from 1946 to 1961. Photograph by author.

with them regularly in the bay; seventeen were from Belford and three from Great Kills Harbor. A captain and two deckhands manned each boat. The sixty or so men who worked in the fishery liked rocking-chair dredging because the work was much easier than sail dredging. It did not involve hand pulling dredges, and they could gather clams rapidly and make good wages; each boat crew grossed about sixty-five dollars a day.

Crews towed their dredges for about ten minutes before retrieving them. It took about three minutes to wind them aboard, release the drawstring at the bottom of their chain bag to empty out the clams on decks, and return them to the bottom. Each tow yielded two and a half to four bushels of clams, almost entirely cherrystones and chowders with few littlenecks. About five tows were made per hour. Usually the deckhands worked steadily, picking clams off the decks and bagging them, but if they were dredging at night, as they commonly did to avoid wardens, the crews bagged the clams the next day in port. Boats could gather about 50 bushels of clams a trip; the highest reported catch was 115 bushels. To conserve the clam resource, however, fishermen agreed among themselves to limit their daily catches to about 40 bushels. If dredging by day, boats were back at their docks by 9:00 A.M.: "We were young and wanted to finish early so we could live a little bit, too" (Interview, Jigs Apel, 11 March 1986).

Beginning in the late 1930s, trucks gradually took over the transport of shellfish from Belford and the overwater transport ended. Truckers who bought hard clams arrived at the docks about 4 P.M. each day. The fishermen lifted the clams out of their boats by hand and put them on the truck while the driver kept track of the number of bushels loaded. From the 1930s to the late 1950s, one of the most prominent buyers was Marty Feldman of Locust, New Jersey. He operated entirely out of his truck and did not have a storehouse. Feldman had customers in several New Jersey cities. Through the years, he had built up a trust with his customers by being reliable, and his customers would not purchase from other clam buyers.

Many of the chowder clams being gathered in the bay were sold to canning companies. They ground their meats, added them to a soup base, and sold them as Manhattan and New England clam chowders to grocery chains.

Fishermen could use their rocking-chair dredges only from November through February, when the clams were dormant and closed. During the other months, when the clams were open for feeding and respiring, the dredges would force mud into them and they could not be sold. Nearly all the fishermen trawled for porgies in the summer.

After a few years, New Jersey and New York declared that clamming with rocking-chair dredges was illegal. Nevertheless, fishermen persisted in using the dredges, because they were making relatively large wages and believed that they should be able to use them since they were legal in other states, such as Connecticut and Rhode Island. At times, they resorted to clamming at night to avoid wardens, successfully most of the time. If wardens did approach a dredging boat, the crew let the dredge and its four-hundred-foot dredge cable run off its winch so it could not be confiscated, gunned the engine, and outran the warden. Later, they retrieved their gear with a grapnel. When fishermen tied their boats to the dock, they left their dredges aboard and did not try to conceal them. If wardens asked what they used the dredges for, fishermen told them they dredged mahogany quahogs in the ocean.

Bill Jenks, a former warden with the New Jersey Coastal Patrol, recalled:

> I was the "clam cop" out of Leonardo State Basin. I enjoyed the game of "hide and seek" with the resourceful clammers of Belford. Actually, it was no contest: their boats were faster and they had a spotter with a radio at the entrance to the

basin. They were the most organized bunch of fishermen I have ever seen!

One afternoon, I saw the spotter car with the long aerial at the entrance to the basin. I knew that if I got in the patrol boat, it would go out over the radio and it would be wasted gas and effort. I drove the state car down to the spotter car and there was a clammer's son sitting there with the mike in his hand. I said: "Say hello to your father for me." He laughed and did just that.

One time, I was on from midnight to 8:00 A.M. I rode around in the state car most of the night checking for illegal activity. At 4:00 A.M., I went past the house of a suspected "pirate" and saw the lights on. I knocked on the door and was invited in for breakfast. He had just returned from a night of dredging on the water!

The clammers had high horsepower engines which they got from wreck cars in junk yards, so they could outrun us. If we gave one of them a chase, they would run into Belford minutes ahead of us, tie up, drive home fast, and then telephone our office that their boat had been stolen. (Letter to the author, 20 February 1991)

Some of the hand rakers resented the rocking-chair clammers because of their superior equipment. A former dredge-boat captain described a conflict he had with Staten Island hand rakers in the 1950s:

One time, when I was rocking chairing, some hand rakers from Staten Island came by and said they wanted a dredgeful of my clams, or else they'd complain to the warden. So, I gave each a dredgeful. But one guy came by and said he wanted a second dredgeful, and after that a third. So, I filled my dredge with sand and mud, dropped it in his bateau, and nearly sank it. He didn't ask for any more clams!

During the 1940s, hard clams sold for $1.25 to $2.00 a bushel; during the late 1950s, cherrystones sold for $3.50 and chowders for $1.50 to $2.00. Some clams were marketed locally in fish markets. Most of those were taken home for eating, but some were eaten on the half shell at bars in the markets.

In some years, for periods of several weeks, hard clams in the bay got a green color on their gills, caused by the bloom of an alga on which they fed. Though the clams could be eaten without harm to one's health, people resisted eating them and demand slumped. The owner of one Keansburg fish market knew that a yellow light will mask a pale green color when shined on it. He installed a bright yellow light over his raw clam bar, and his sales returned to normal (Interview, Louie Egnatovich, 14 February 1986).

The End of the Era

Before World War II, there had not been any contamination problem with hard clams. But in 1942 and thereafter, areas of the bay were closed to hard clamming because the waters were polluted by sewage. In 1942 the U.S. Health Service closed 30 percent of New York waters and 40 percent of New Jersey waters in the bay. The immediate feeling of the bayshore families was one of animosity toward federal and state enforcement agencies. They felt that they were surely worse than Hitler in their assumption of dictatorial powers (Long Branch *Daily Record,* 15 April 1942).

In June 1961, the entire bay was condemned when a number of people contracted infectious hepatitis from eating hard clams dug in the bay. The state of New Jersey increased the number of wardens from three to fifteen and put them on twenty-four-hour patrols to make sure that no clams were dug in the bay. Thus hard clamming with all types of gear ended in the bay. Rocking-chair dredging was never practiced again; it had lasted only fifteen years.

In the 1960s and 1970s Sandy Hook Bay was open for brief periods to the direct marketing of hard clams. In 1962 Raritan Bay remained closed, but in 1963 a small area was reopened for clam digging in Sandy Hook Bay. By this time, the clamming fleet in the bay consisted of only a few part-time sail-dredging boats and ten to fifteen hand rakers. Sandy Hook Bay remained open until 1974; since then, the entire bay has been closed to the direct marketing of hard clams. Sail dredging, which had lasted about a century, ended for good with this closure.

Like the closing of the oyster industry some years earlier, the end of direct marketing of hard clams caused both unemployment and chagrin around the bayshore. Bill Kendrick, a fisherman of Highlands, related that he had just bought two rakes the week before the announcement of the closure. He broke down and cried when he heard it. Closures were particularly stressful to those clammers who had done this work all of their working lives. Kendrick went on to say, "It was rough when they said that you couldn't do it anymore. It was as if they took away your life" (Interview, 8 October 1985). The clammers had anticipated that each closure would be temporary—a few months at most.

Hard-clam beds off Staten Island and in Sandy Hook Bay were

56. *Sail dredging for hard clams in Raritan Bay (note four ropes towing dredges), circa 1950. Courtesy of the Monmouth County Historical Association.*

reopened when plants for depurating hard clams were constructed. In 1979 the first depuration plant for hard clams in Raritan Bay opened in Great Kills Harbor. Its owner was William Ryan, who had received approval from the state of New York to operate it. Depuration involves placing clams in tanks of water that is continuously pumped past ultra-violet lights and thus sterilized. As the clams excrete digested algae and any sewage bacteria from their digestive tracts into the water, the lights kill the bacteria. When the clams are removed from the tanks forty-eight hours later, they do not contain enough bacteria to harm humans. About seventy men bought licenses to dig clams in New York waters for this plant, and about twenty dug each day in the warmer months. The clamming area was from south of Great Kills Harbor to Prince's Bay; in winters when ice formed, they also dug in Great Kills Harbor itself. The clam digging did not last long, however. The depuration plant closed at Christmas, 1983, because it was not making a profit.

In 1983 a depuration plant for hard clams opened in Highlands, New Jersey. The state of New Jersey allowed only hand rakers to sell to the plant, and they were restricted to southeastern Raritan Bay and the Navesink River. The hand rakers could dig six days a week, from sunup to sundown each day.

The idea of relaying clams for depuration from Raritan Bay to Barnegat Bay was conceived by Bill Jenks, a former Raritan Bay clam warden from Bricktown, New Jersey; Chuck Steidle, a clam wholesaler from Southhampton, Long Island, suggested the relay from Raritan Bay to Peconic Bay. They had to convince other fishermen that the idea was sound. Eventually, they found support from state officials who helped to formalize the plans.

When the depuration plant opened, the state established a system for relaying clams from Sandy Hook Bay to two nonpolluted areas in Barnegat Bay for depuration. In Barnegat Bay, each digger could have three half-acre leases on which to depurate their clams; the clams had to remain on them for thirty days at temperatures 52° F and above before they could be marketed. The state program was open to all clammers in the state. Those in Highlands and Belford felt that the clams belonged to them, however, and they were strongly opposed to the clammers from Barnegat Bay digging them and relaying them there. When the state proclaimed that Barnegat Bay men had the right to dig the clams, the northerners had bumper stickers made that said, "Keep the clams in Raritan Bay." In addition, they warned, "We are sharpening our axes to destroy any southern boats which appear." As an appeasement, the state authorities decided to restrict the southerners to two days a week, Monday and Wednesday, and from sunup until only noon. When the southerners did come up to rake, there was no violence (Interview, BIll Jenks, 20 June 1991).

In 1988 the state of New Jersey forcibly closed the depuration plant, however, because it did not follow proper procedures for depurating the clams. At that point, the state modified its ruling and allowed the relaying of Raritan Bay clams to Barnegat Bay to operate five days a week, Monday through Friday. Some of the Belford and Highlands diggers obtained Barnegat Bay leases to depurate their clams. The diggers had to land their clams at Brooks Marina in Sea Bright by noon each day, put them on a truck to be sealed by a state conservation officer, travel by one designated route to either Swan Point or Tuckerton, Barnegat Bay, and arrive there at 2 P.M. and 2:15 P.M., respectively. At those sites, the same conservation officer removed the seals and watched the diggers load the clams into their boats and run out to their beds. The clammers' trucks had to have a cap on them and any windows had to be glued shut; the cap and seal prevented the clammers from selling the clams illegally en route. By the late 1980s, the northern clammers had become used to the southerners digging in Raritan Bay and did not oppose them. When the depuration plant closed, the northerners were glad that the relay to Barnegat Bay had been established, because it meant they could continue clamming.

In 1990, about fifteen New Jersey clammers were digging every day in southeastern Raritan Bay. They found a large quantity of littlenecks and smaller numbers of larger clams distributed over a substantial area. In 1991 the number of clammers increased to about thirty; each gathered about eight bushels of clams (80 percent littlenecks) a day for relaying to their leases in Barnegat Bay.

In the 1980s, some fishermen tried to persuade the New Jersey legislature to allow sail dredging in Raritan Bay again. Under one plan the clams would be sold to Barnegat Bay leaseholders, who would hold them on their beds for depuration. After being landed in Belford, the clams would be put in sealed trucks for transport to Barnegat Bay. Walter Thompsen, a sixty-five-year-old semiretired fisherman who had sail-dredged for twenty-one years, wanted to do it again, but with few restrictions. He had this to say:

> To go clamming again, I'd have to rig up my boat and then break into the work physically. This would be possible, yet difficult at my age because sail dredging is hard work. We would have the wind and currents to worry about as always. Then, they'll tell us where we can dredge. We can't go west of the Navy Pier at Leonardo as we used to when the wind and tide were not right for sail dredging in the eastern part of the bay. Then, we all have to land the clams at one designated site in Belford and at a specified time, and the clams have to be shipped in a sealed truck. All this is too much. I'd rather keep out of it. (Interview, 6 January 1985)

His wife said to me privately, "These elderly men have it rough, because they have had little to do since they closed the beds."

In 1989, the New York Department of Environmental Conservation developed a plan to allow hand rakers to dig hard clams from the New York waters of Raritan Bay and relay them to clean beds on Long Island for depuration. The clams could be dug only from May to mid-October, when they were feeding. They were taken to beds mainly in Peconic Bay, and held in them for at least twenty-one days before being sold. Nearly all the rakers lived on Long Island.

The New York relay plan went ahead with fewer territorial problems than had occurred in New Jersey. The Staten Islanders believed that the clams belonged to them rather than to all New Yorkers, and they grumbled about the relay to themselves, but they did not take the issue to state authorities. The clammers landed their clams in Prince's Bay and Tottenville and trucked them to eastern Long Island. In 1989 eighty clam boats with rakers landed 55,639 bushels of clams. In 1990 the number fell to twenty-five boats, but by working longer hours each day they landed 47,909 bushels of clams. The clams landed were largely littlenecks (Letter, Debra Barnes, New York State Department of Environmental Conservation, to author, 29 July 1991). Each boat had two men—a raker and a helper, who pulled up the rake with a rope and sorted the clams. In 1991 the best pairs dug as many as thirty bushels of clams a day. The high catches are evidence of Raritan Bay's great capacity to produce hard clams. During the same years, good rakers in Long Island's Great South Bay were digging about three bushels a day, while those in Barnegat Bay were digging only two bushels a day.

In the 1970s and 1980s, the clammers used rakes that were designed better and had aluminum handles. The new rakes caught more clams per unit of time than the old ones did. The handles were also superior to those made of wood, because they were lighter, it was easier to adjust their length, they did not require any care, and there was no danger of splinters. The handles came in twelve-foot sections; handle length was adjusted by moving the sections inside one another, their positions being held by hose clamps. The crossheads the diggers held were fourteen inches wide. In 1988, a rake cost $85 to $100 and a handle $125.

Soft Clamming

During World War II, about twenty-five fishermen from Highlands revived the practice of gathering soft clams with motor-driven propellers. Between them, they had ten boats, fourteen to sixteen feet long, which had outboard motors of about six horsepower. They worked in the Navesink and Shrewsbury rivers, anchoring the boats by their sterns over clam beds when the tide fell to about two and a half feet deep. They would start the motors, and by swinging the boats back and forth, wash the clams onto the bottom surface. Then they scooped them into their boats, getting as many as twenty bushels per man every day—a real bonanza for these them.

During this period, one fisherman found a clam bed about two acres in size in the Shrewsbury River. The bottom was not sand, but a tight mixture of clay and sand, and when he attempted to churn the clams they all broke. He found he could wash them out unbroken with his outboard motor, however. After he did this for a couple of years, the bottom became softer and fishermen could churn the clams in the bed thereafter.

Authorities did not permit the propeller digging of soft clams, because fishermen dug them too fast and depletion would result. Nevertheless, the fishermen dug them illegally by this method for several years, evading wardens, while the majority of clammers gathered them with churning hoes, scap nets, and rakes. When servicemen returned from duty at the end of World War II and found the clams much scarcer as a

57. A churning hoe, left, and scap net, right, used for gathering soft clams. Photograph by author.

result of the propeller digging, they felt betrayed. Animosity existed between the two groups for a while (Interview, Jimmy White, 16 May 1986).

Soft clams sold for two to five dollars a bushel during World War II, five to six dollars a bushel immediately following the war, and eight dollars a bushel in the early 1950s. In the 1940s, the women who worked in the shanties were paid a dollar a gallon for shucking clams.

Soft clams became much scarcer in Raritan Bay after the 1940s. The eelgrass blight in the mid-1930s seems to have been largely responsible. Apparently the eelgrass had absorbed the energy from waves generated by northwesterly storms. By the time the waves broke on the flats, they were relatively small and thus did not adversely affect the clams. Since then, storm waves have washed out the juvenile soft clams and cast them ashore, where they died. These waves also shift sands in intertidal and shallow zones, and adult clams cannot inhabit shifting sands. In 1961, the state of New Jersey closed its entire portion of Raritan Bay to soft clamming along with hard clamming because it was polluted, but few clams were available in any case. The bay has not been reopened for soft clamming since then.

The soft-clam fishery was the third and last of the molluscan fisheries in Raritan Bay closed by pollution. The loss meant more than

58. *Fishermen gathering soft clams in Navesink River using churning hoes and rakes, circa 1950. Courtesy of John Seminski.*

unemployment for fishermen and shuckers. It had an effect on the eating habits of the entire region, because the clam-based meals in kitchens along the New Jersey bayshore, shipments of shucked clams to New York City, and supplies of these clams for clam bakes, restaurants, and taverns were no longer available. Of the bay fisheries, soft clamming from Keyport to Atlantic Highlands was one of the least lucrative. Nevertheless, when it ended, many interviewees along the bayshore hoped it would return someday.

In 1974, soft clamming did return for the Highlands fishermen when the first depuration plant for soft clams in Raritan Bay opened in that town. Owned and operated by Bob Soleau, it functioned similar to the depuration plants for hard clams, using ultraviolet lights to kill bacteria.

During the late 1970s and early 1980s, two more depuration plants for soft clams opened in Highlands. The three plants processed the clams for about thirty fishermen who gathered them by churning in the Navesink River. In the late 1980s, however, the soft clams became scarce in the river, the fishermen had to quit, and the depuration plants closed.

Lobstering

From the late 1940s to the early 1960s, only about three boat crews were lobstering, because most lobstermen had switched to fishing for porgies.

After the porgy fishery ended in 1963, the number of lobster boats returned to about thirty. Initially, most of the boats were docked in Highlands, with the rest in Keyport and Belford. By the 1970s and 1980s, however, none were in Keyport, about twenty docked in Belford, and eight to ten were in Highlands.

The history of lobstering after the mid-1940s featured improvements in gear and an increase in the number of pots set by each boat crew. In 1946 Lloyd Cottrell, then a thirty-three-year-old fisherman of Highlands, introduced the Nova Scotia-style lobster boat to Raritan Bay when he needed a new boat to replace his leaking lapstrake skiff. He wanted to find one cheaper than those sold by the King boat yard in Highlands, where lobstermen had been purchasing them for $6,000 to $7,000 apiece. Cottrell visited several boat yards from Connecticut northward and found that the farther he went the cheaper they were. Finally, he located a yard in Nova Scotia that sold new boats for only $3,700. But the boats differed from New Jersey skiffs in that they had smooth sides, a small deck on their stern and along their entire port side, and a cabin in the bow. Cottrell ordered one fifty feet long and twelve feet wide.

At first, he found the people in Nova Scotia too reserved. He learned that they had never seen fireworks, so he bought $60 worth on a trip to South Carolina and brought them up there to show them. That broke the ice and people got along well with him after that. The Nova Scotians told him that they could not sell a finished boat to be used outside Canada, so when his boat was nearly completed Lloyd paid for it and had it towed to a yard in Machias Bay, Maine. He finished it off there himself, installed an engine in it, and motored it to Highlands (Interview, Lloyd Cottrell, 5 August 1989).

The Nova Scotia boat had three advantages over the skiff for lobstering. First, at least twenty-five pots could be stacked on its stern and port decks. To reset them on the grounds, fishermen only had to push the first one off; as the boat steamed ahead the others were pulled off by those in the water. On the skiff, it had been more difficult to stack and reset a line; to do it, the pots had to be placed on its recessed deck and then be lifted off individually. Second, the cabin gave lobstermen protection from sprays breaking over the boat when it ran into seas. Third, the boat normally lasted twenty to thirty years, compared with about ten years for a skiff. It had two controls, one inside and another immediately behind the cabin. Upon seeing the features of Cottrell's boat, the remaining lobstermen purchased Nova Scotia-style boats when their skiffs wore out. They purchased them from Maine, Virginia, and Florida, where this design had become popular. The boats were complete with diesel marine engines.

When lobstermen switched to this type of boat, they changed the

59. Lobsterman Bill Richardson in his boat cabin steering toward his next line of pots, circa 1950. Courtesy of Bill Richardson.

arrangement and handling of their pot lines. They tied only about twenty-five pots on each line and did not anchor them. Instead of putting each pot back overboard after it was lifted, they stacked an entire line on the boat's port and stern decks until the last pot was handled. Then they reset the pots, usually in a straight line with other lines, so that if some marking buoys were lost they could determine from the other buoys where to tow a grapnel to recover the unmarked lines. Often, fishermen used one or two of their pot lines as "try lines." They laid these out in various places to determine whether lobsters were more abundant in areas where they did not usually have their lines.

Before the mid-1940s, the pot lines and the twine used to knit pot funnels were made of hemp, which lasted only one season. Every year, the fishermen had to purchase new rope and twine, cut and tie the rope, and knit funnels. Since then, fishermen have used nylon rope and twine, which lasts several seasons, saving them money and much work.

Since the 1950s, lobstermen have been using fish frames (the skeletons of cleaned fish, mostly flounders) instead of bunkers for bait because they lasted longer in the pots. Freight trucks carrying fish from Belford to Fulton Market and Philadelphia carried the fish frames back to Belford one or two days a week. The frames were kept chilled en route and did not rot. Fishermen bought enough bait each time to last several days and stored it in walk-in refrigerators on docks beside their boats; the refrigerators were secondhand salvages from worn-out refrigerator trucks. In the 1980s, the bait cost ten dollars per hundred-pound box. Since lobstermen began using fish frames, they have not had to obtain bait when the pound nets were lifted. Thus they have been able to arrive at their pots at dawn each morning. They get out of bed as early as 2 A.M. in June, when the days are the longest, but later as the season progresses.

Besides lobsters, almost every pot trapped several rock crabs or Jonah crabs, and a few ling, cunner, eel pout, or blackfish. Fishermen removed the claws of the crabs and sold them. They got from 5 to 165 pounds (55 pounds in a bushel) of crab claws each day. In the 1950s and 1960s, fishermen were paid twenty to twenty-five cents a pound for them; the money helped pay for their fuel. On some days, each crew's pots caught a bushel or two of fish; they were sold daily to the fishermen's cooperative in Belford, or else used as bait.

In the early 1960s, lobstermen switched from using wooden plugs to using strong rubber bands to immobilize the lobster claws. In the 1970s, the bands cost three dollars a pound, and in the 1980s five dollars a pound. Fishermen put the bands on both claws of the lobsters with a special metal bander while they ran between lines; if they were busy then, they banded the claws back in port.

In the mid-1960s, lobstermen made an important change in the design of their pots: they switched the funnel leading into their kitchen from their end to their side. Bill Richardson of Keyport introduced the change after seeing the design in Maine. Lobstermen have estimated that pots of this design catch about 25 percent more lobsters than those with the end funnel.

Bill Richardson's name is thus added to the list of notables who introduced important new gear, processing plants, processing methods, or relay systems to the bay. Others include George Eldridge (hard clam rake), George Thompson (oyster float), George Snediker (pound net), Martin Lohsen (fyke net design), J. and J. W. Elsworth (oyster plant), J. Howard Smith and Gilbert Smith (bunker factory), Arnold Pedersen (winch), Willie Alexander (otter trawl and rocking chair dredge), Lloyd Cottrell (Nova Scotia style lobster boat), William Ryan (hard clam depuration plant), Bob Soleau (soft clam depuration plant), Bill Jenks (hard clam relay plan in New Jersey), and Chuck Steidle (hard clam relay plan in New York). Unfortunately, the names of others who introduced other gears were never recorded.

In the early 1970s, the hydraulic hoist became available for boats. The lobstermen placed them on the boat's starboard rail next to the

60. *Lobstermen taking pots off their boat and stacking them on dock at end of season. Note pot lines in fish boxes. Photograph by author.*

controls behind the cabin. Winding in pot lines with the hydraulic hoist was easier than using the simple winch.

Beginning in the mid-1970s, new lobster boats were constructed of fiberglass. Hulls made of this material do not leak or require much maintenance, and they are stronger and last even longer than those made of wood. Also in the mid-1970s, lobstermen switched from wire to mesh bags for holding bait in each pot. In the ocean, bait in the bags remains good for four days, in contrast to three days when the wire was used. The bags enabled lobster crews to use a four-day system: they increased the number of pots from 900 to 1,200 and lifted groups of 300 a day every fourth day. When using 1,200 pots, each lobsterman needed 1,800 feet of rope per line of 25 pots, and, with 48 lines of 25 pots each, this totaled 16 miles of rope. In the 1970s, when the lobsters were abundant, a daily catch using the four-day system was about 300 lobsters, or perhaps 360 pounds. "Doin' about a pound a pot" was considered good fishing (Interview, Albert Thompson, 2 August 1989). The highest reported catch of lobsters by a boat in one day was 1,600 pounds, and the largest lobster reported weighed 15½ pounds. Ten-pounders were caught occasionally then also, but in the 1980s, the largest lobsters caught weighed four pounds. Since they started using the four-day system, lobstermen have become more prosperous.

In the late 1970s, lobstermen installed Loran (long-range electronic navigation and location system) on their boats. Using Loran bearings, they could locate pot buoys in the ocean more quickly than by using the earlier system, which involved the use of a compass and watch. They could also determine precisely where to tow a grapnel for lines if their buoys were lost. The more progressive lobstermen kept a record of the locations of their pot lines using Loran and logged the number of lobsters caught by each to determine which locations produced the most lobsters.

In a typical year, lobstermen lost about 10 percent of their pots; the percentage over the years varied from 0 to 30. In the bay, nearly all losses were from vessel traffic, including tugboats, tankers, and freighters, which caught buoys and lines in their propellers when they navigated the channels. In the ocean, large vessels also ran over the buoys at times, and some pots were stolen by lobstermen who fished lobsters at the edge of the continental shelf. In addition, severe ocean storms forced covers off pots and rolled pots and lines into tangles. Lobstermen carried ten to fifteen extra covers and several buoys on their boats as replacements and kept a supply of pots on their docks to replace losses.

Bill Richardson, of Keyport, explained that in the 1960s he once saw two barges that were supposed to be heading for the designated Dredged Material Dumpsite, eight nautical miles east of Sea Bright, New Jersey, dump short of the site and deposit quantities of rubble on his pots and lines. He lost some of the pots because their lines broke when he tried to lift them. He reported the incident to the Coast Guard, which warned the barge captains not to do it again. The lobsterman regretted reporting it, though, because the barge captains retaliated and almost put him out of business temporarily by purposely towing their barges through his buoys and catching every one. He had to move his pots to a different ground (Interview, 21 May 1986).

Before the mid-1980s, fishermen ignored size regulations that had been imposed by state authorities earlier in the century and landed lobsters of all sizes—keepers above the legal minimum and shorts below it. From World War II to 1989, the legal minimum size for lobsters was a carapace length of three and one eighth inches. Many fishermen said that they would not make it economically if they did not sell the shorts. Most of the time, about 90 percent of the lobsters landed were shorts; a typical daily catch per boat was about fifty dozen. While lobstermen held keepers in a water well in the skiffs and in barrels in the Nova Scotia-style boats, shorts were tossed into a burlap bag. The demand for shorts was high: their meat was sweeter and tenderer than that of the keepers, and they were cheaper—they sold for about two dollars a dozen. It was also illegal to land female lobsters bearing eggs. Nearly all lobstermen tossed them back alive; one or two scraped off their eggs and landed them.

Wardens rarely apprehended fishermen with shorts because they did not enforce laws stringently. One fisherman recalled, "The 'heat' would be on for about three weeks a year and then we wouldn't see a warden for another year or two." If lobstermen did see a warden on the dock as they approached their port, they dropped the bag of shorts overboard.

A few fishermen's wives established businesses of cooking shorts caught by their husbands and other fishermen and selling their meat. They cooked them in bushel-size retorts in sheds in their yards and sold the meat to local restaurants, which served it in salads and lobster rolls, a popular delicacy.

In the 1970s the states of New York and New Jersey tried to enforce the size regulation on lobsters by having wardens wait at the docks to measure lobsters as the fishermen landed them. To circumvent the regulation, fishermen twisted off the tails and claws from shorts, tossed the carapaces overboard as they were caught, and landed them separately. No law covered this practice, and the relationship of tail or claw size to carapace length was unreliable. Thus the landing of shorts in this form continued for several years. Finally, a regulation was passed in the mid-1980s stating that lobsters had to be landed whole, and the landing of shorts ended, except for minor infractions.

The government also made it mandatory to have an escape opening, measuring one and three quarters by six inches, in the parlor of every pot to allow the shorts to escape. Thereafter, far fewer shorts were trapped in pots. Most crabs escaped also, and the by-catch income from landing their claws was lost.

In the late 1980s, the penalty for landing shorts was high. The fine for the first offense was $100 to $3,000; for the second it was $200 to $5,000. Most fines actually levied were $500 for the first violation. If a federal permit was involved (one was required if potting in the ocean beyond three miles from shore), fines ranged from $2,000 to $3,000, but could be as high as $25,000. The violator had to pay both the state and federal fines. With three convictions, the state of New Jersey put the lobsterman out of business by taking away his license; he lost other state licenses, too, such as those for hunting and freshwater fishing.

One fisherman accused of landing shorts in the 1980s described his experience with the courts:

> If we get fined and take it to court to challenge it, the first thing that happens is they set the time at 10 A.M. so that you lose your day. They'll try to make that in July or August when you are catching the most lobsters. You walk into court with your lawyer; now, you have to pay your lawyer a day's pay. They see you come in with a lawyer, and they'll say: "Your case

comes up week after next at 10 A.M." Then you go in that day
with your lawyer. Then something else comes up. They'll jerk
you around like that until it'll cost you three times what the fine
cost. It's cheaper to pay the fine in the first place, but then
you've got a rap on your record. All the guys said that I should
have fought it, but it was cheaper for me just to pay the fine.

At first fishermen resented the government's restrictions on the
landing of shorts and predicted their earnings would fall. In 1988,
however, a year or two after the landing of shorts ended, catches of
keepers rose somewhat from earlier years and fishermen reversed their
attitude and became enthusiastic about the ban on shorts (Interview,
John Seminski, 14 July 1989). Apparently, the ancient fishery axiom—if
you leave the little ones and allow them to grow, there will be more big
ones—was being proven true with lobsters.

In 1989, however, the federal government increased the minimum
length of lobsters from three and one eighth to three and three sixteenths
inches, and in 1990, to three and a quarter inches. This reduced the
lobstermen's catches back to what they had been two or three years
before (Interview, Walt DeGrote, 1 May 1991). To compensate, in 1990,
each lobster crew increased the number of pots they set from 1,200 to
between 1,400 and 1,600. They lifted 400 a day, and it took them about
five and a half hours to do it, in contrast to about four hours when they
had lifted 300 pots.

In 1990 and 1991, the twenty-eight lobster crews from the bay had
about 42,000 pots set, mostly in the ocean, but some in the bay. Compare
this total with the 4,000 pots set in the 1920s and 1930s. Currently, there
is little space remaining in the productive lobster ground for more pots.
As lobstermen have increased the number of pots, they have been setting
them out earlier each season to beat each other to the best grounds. Some
begin in February.

In the 1980s and early 1990s, fishermen used more wire pots and
predicted that soon all pots would be made of wire. These pots, being
lighter, are easier to handle, and they do not have to be dipped in tar.
Arnold Pedersen was the first to popularize the use of wire lobster pots in
the bay. He began using them in the early 1940s because he found the
wooden pots too heavy. Wire pots had been used earlier by others on a
small scale, but Pedersen made most of his pots of wire, leading others to
copy him because they were easier to handle.

The history of the lobster fishery illustrates how fishermen improved
gear to catch more lobsters and lighten their workloads, and how conservation agencies had to impose laws, prohibiting the landing of small

lobsters and berried females and increasing the size of lobsters caught, to conserve stocks.

Some fishermen, especially the younger ones, believe that the states should impose a limited entry system in the lobster fishery. The veterans do not favor this, however. Norman Sickles, a veteran lobster fisherman, explained his feelings:

> The old-timers never talked about limited entry as the young ones do. They think that's the way to go. But cream rises to the top. The good fishermen will make it; the others won't. If you chase everyone out of the ocean, you won't do one bit better. How are you going to chase someone out of the ocean if he pays his taxes and he's a citizen? If they made limited entry retroactive to fifteen years ago, I'd be the only one in the ocean. (Interview, 21 October 1986)

Veteran lobstermen had trouble with some young lobstermen, who followed them and put pots next to their pots. The veterans became annoyed when the newcomers laid their pot lines across theirs. Bill Richardson explained:

> I would come in with three hundred to four hundred pounds of lobsters, and a young fellow would come in with maybe fifty to seventy-five pounds. He saw where I was working, and the next time I went out there'd be two or three lines laying across mine. Not alongside, but right on top. Us veterans honored one another and rarely crossed one another's lines. Most of the young guys won't do it; I was young once and never did it. At times, I used to go way out to the Cholera Banks to get away from the young lobstermen. It takes three to three-and-a-half hours to get there, though. If there is any weather, it's a long battle back. (Interview, 5 October 1985)

From the 1960s through the 1980s, fishermen sold most of their lobsters to local buyers or to seafood restaurants and fish markets, both of which became numerous. In the 1980s, they paid fishermen around $2.50 a pound for them. Each day, some of the fishermen delivered lobsters themselves. (In the 1940s and 1950s, they had also delivered them to clambakes.) While fishermen were lifting pots, their wives often took orders for the lobsters by telephone and informed their husbands where to take them when they returned to port. One fisherman related that over a period of years he rusted out three automobiles delivering his lobsters, even though he held the lobsters in galvanized tubs and protected the car floors with canvas sheets. Local buyers sold some lobsters to nearby restaurants, but shipped most to more distant markets by truck. Lobsters with one or two claws missing could not be sold readily, except as "salad" lobsters (to be cooked and chopped as lobster salad) at lower prices.

Blue Crabbing

From the 1940s onward nearly all blue-crabbing boats were docked in Belford and landed their crabs there; the remaining crabbers, perhaps five in number, dredged in the bay and docked in Brooklyn. The crabs were picked up by trucks and carried to markets. In the 1940s, about twenty-five crab boats constituted the fishery, but from the 1950s through the 1980s, there were usually only about fifteen boats. In these latter decades, only about five boats actually dredged for crabs each day in poor seasons; in the best seasons, other types of boats, even offshore trawlers and lobster boats, joined the fleet, and as many as thirty boats dredged daily.

A controversy sprang up among fishermen every fall over when the crab season should begin. Some believed that a few of the crabbers began the season too early each year, before the crabs were dormant. One fisherman said this about an "early bird":

> He's the first one who screws it up. He wants to be the first one to go every year, but the water is too warm and the crabs are not settled down. Dredging stirs them up and chases them into the ocean. The season shouldn't be opened until the crabs are bedded down for good, say about the first of December.

The retort from the "early bird":

> When a body of crabs is disturbed in the fall, it resettles nearby, and the total number of crabs caught for the season is the same. I go early to earn money, but it doesn't do any harm.

When crabs were exceptionally abundant, the usual markets, including Fulton Market, became glutted, and fishermen could not sell all the crabs they could catch. Thus they dredged for crabs a few days, stopped for two or three days until the market "cleared out," then dredged for a few more days, and so on. In some years of high crab abundance in the 1950s and 1960s, the fishermen made arrangements with the crab pack-

61. Emptying blue crabs from a dredge in Raritan Bay, circa 1950. Courtesy of John Seminski.

ers in Crisfield, Maryland, to buy their crabs. The packers sent as many as four trucks a week to carry the catch back.

In the 1970s and 1980s, typical crab catches for each boat were ten to fourteen bushels a day, with highest catches ranging up to fifty bushels. Wholesalers bought both sexes of crabs, but preferred the less common males, which were larger and contained more meat, thus bringing higher prices.

In the 1980s, wholesalers trucked live crabs to various markets in New Jersey, New York, and Pennsylvania. Within two days after they were caught, nearly all the crabs were served steamed in restaurants, taverns, and homes.

Prices for the dredged blue crabs rose through the years. Their landed price had been as low as fifty cents to a dollar and a half a bushel during the 1930s. It was five dollars a bushel during most of the 1950s, seven to eight dollars a bushel during the late 1960s and early 1970s, and from seventeen to thirty dollars a bushel in the 1980s.

PART
FOUR

The Present and the Future

11

Current Status of the Bay: Water, Fish, Fisheries, and Ports

Physical Changes in the Bay

With the passage of time, Raritan Bay has changed physically. For one thing, the level of the world's oceans has been rising for the past three centuries and with them that of the bay; from 1900 to 1990 the bay's level rose about eleven inches. That made it slightly larger, and now areas of the flats on its south side, which were once intertidal and in the late 1800s about a mile wide during blowout tides, are never exposed. The other changes are a few navigation channels, which were dredged mostly around 1900, and several sand and gravel borrow pits dug in its eastern part in the 1960s and 1970s. Most pits increased the original bottom depth from ten to thirteen feet, to thirty to forty feet; one pit was about ninety feet deep.

Physical changes have also been made in the bay's tributary rivers and streams. Early construction of dams and other physical modifications in the Hackensack, Passaic, Raritan, and Matawan rivers reduced the stocks of alewives, shad, and other fish there and in Raritan Bay. In 1901 installation of a dam on the Navesink River, six miles by water from Red Bank and eleven miles from the river's mouth, led to the loss of its spawning population of striped bass by making their upstream spawning and nursery areas inaccessible.

Pollution of the Bay and Its Effects

Since the 1940s, a major change has taken place in the quality of Raritan Bay water and sediments. Previously, most people around the bay derived a living by farming, fishing, and shell fishing, and the bay was relatively clean. The bottom of the bay was usually visible through at least six feet of water. Since then, industrialization and the human population in the surrounding area and in its vast drainage basins have burgeoned, and the bay has become contaminated with huge quantities of industrial wastes and treated and untreated sewage. In the 1970s, the copper concentration in the bay's water was sixty-five parts per billion (Waldhauer, Matte, and Tucker 1978), the highest ever reported for any estuary in the world; the concentrations of six heavy metals in sediments were highly elevated over natural sediments and was as high as a thousand parts per million, especially in muddy areas (Pearce 1979). The metals originated from factories and small businesses discharging their wastes into sewerage lines or directly into the rivers, domestic pipes (mainly copper and lead), non-point runoff and agriculture, and some natural sources.

During the 1940s, 1950s, and early 1960s, oil spills were so common in the bay and nearby waters that extensive oil slicks were present on the bay nearly every day. The bay and shoreline sediments became contaminated with petroleum hydrocarbons at concentrations from twenty-six to nearly four thousand parts per billion (Stanford and Young 1988).

The bay also had high concentrations of PCBs (polychlorinated biphenyls). At least several tons of PCBs were discharged into the Hudson River from two General Electric capacitor-manufacturing plants on the Hudson River from 1930 to 1977 ("Environmental Impact Statement," 1981). Average PCB concentrations in bay sediments from these discharges were about four-tenths of a part per million, while those in bay suspended matter were six to seven parts per billion (Olson et al. 1984).

From the mid-1970s to the mid-1980s, the estimated annual pollutant loading to the Hudson-Raritan Estuary from all sources was 710,000 tons of suspended solids, 49,000 tons of oil and grease, 13,000 tons of petroleum hydrocarbons, 5,360 tons of trace metals, and sixteen tons of chlorinated hydrocarbons (Stanford and Young 1988).

In the 1980s, three-fourths of the population of the state of New York and a half the population of the state of New Jersey lived within the boundaries of the Hudson River/Raritan Bay drainage basin. Fifteen million inhabitants of the greater New York City area contributed many tons of treated and, after heavy rainstorms, untreated sewage to the

Hudson River and Raritan Bay. The daily freshwater input from New York City sewers and sewage treatment plants was about equal to the low-flow volume of the Hudson River. The nitrates and phosphates from sewerage plants and farmland produced dense blooms of algae causing eutrophication in the bay. In the spring and summer, its water was often so turbid that a white-and-black Secchi disc measuring about twelve inches in diameter could be seen only two feet or less from the water surface during the blooms. The blooms did not persist, however, because the algae used up nearly all the available nutrients and then crashed. The water was relatively clear for a week or so, and then another bloom, stimulated by added nutrients, began to grow and within perhaps a month peaked again.

Besides algae, silt from land runoff also contributed to turbidity. Silt and clay ran into streams and then into the bay, especially on its southern side.

The quantity of fish present in Raritan Bay depends partly upon the success they have in spawning, surviving, and growing as eggs and juveniles in the Hudson and Raritan rivers (alewives, shad, striped bass, and sturgeon) and Raritan Bay (bluefish, bunkers, porgies, weakfish, and winter flounder). The physical changes and pollution have reduced the spawning areas available, and eggs and larvae are exposed to polluted waters. Fish that have extended residence times as juveniles, such as the striped bass, are the most susceptible (Esser 1982). Pollution of the Hudson River was partially responsible for the loss of thirty-five miles in upstream movement of shad (Walburg and Nichols 1967). The eggs of winter flounder are laid on the bottom and are susceptible to toxic wastes that accumulate in sediments; these wastes might also affect larvae and older stages (Azarovitz 1982).

Pollution also affects adult fish in the New York Bight. Erosion of the fins of fishes was more prevalent in polluted than nonpolluted areas (Ziskowski and Murchelano 1975). The effects of blooms and silt on fish health are unknown.

Some of the fish in the waters near Raritan Bay accumulated PCBs in their flesh at concentrations above federal guidelines. For this reason, in 1976 the New York State Department of Environmental Conservation issued a ban on the sale of striped bass and eels from the Hudson River, Upper New York Bay, Newark Bay, tidal portions of the Passaic and Hackensack rivers, Arthur Kill, and Kill Van Kull. In 1982 New Jersey authorities issued an advisory on eels, large bluefish (six pounds or twenty-four inches and above), striped bass, white catfish, and white perch. It warned people not to consume more than one meal per week of these fish, and recommended that pregnant women, nursing mothers, women of childbearing age, and young children should not eat them. The bans continue. Some types of pollutants, such as oil, tainted the flavor of fish and shellfish (Esser 1982).

Decline in Fish Abundance

Since the 1940s, the number of fish entering Raritan Bay has declined. Data for catches of food fishes in the bay are available for two years: 1910 and 1989. In 1910 the average catch for each pound net in the bay was 157,500 pounds of food fish, for a total catch of about 8 million pounds from the fifty pound nets in the bay. The fish netted an average of $6 a barrel (equal to about 2.5 cents a pound), or $210,000 (*Red Bank Register,* 8 March 1911). In 1989 the average catch per pound net was only 30 percent as large: 48,450 pounds of food fish per net, for a total of 484,500 pounds from the bay's ten pound nets. The average bunker catch per pound net was 89,000 pounds, for a total of 890,000 pounds.

Biologists believe that the decline of food fish in the bay since World War II is the result of heavy fishing on the continental shelf off the East Coast of the United States, because the effectiveness of fishermen in catching fish there increased sharply. Vast improvements in fishing vessel design and size, electronics, and gear increased the fishing power of individual vessels. The technologies also made ocean fishing much easier and safer for fishermen (Smolowitz and Serchuk 1988).

In 1976 the Magnuson Fishery and Conservation Act was mandated to control the huge fleet of foreign fishing vessels off the coasts of the United States. Combined with the effort of U.S. fishing vessels, the fleets had reduced the quantity of food fish in the northwest Atlantic by 50 percent from 1963 through 1974, and large declines were evident before that. But between 1976 and 1989, the number of U.S. fishing vessels has increased from 17,000 to 38,000, while the overall tonnage of the fleet has quadrupled. The fleet is now larger than the foreign fleets were in the 1960s and early 1970s. Currently, food fish stocks are depressed and continue to decline, mortality rates from fishing are at record highs, and the catch per boat has declined. For example, in 1987 the average daily catch per vessel of all marketable species combined was only 5,500 pounds. By comparison, from 1935 to 1960, when annual groundfish effort (measured in total days fished) was about a third of the present level and gear capability was much lower, the average daily catch of haddock alone was 12,000 pounds (Smolowitz and Serchuk 1988). In contrast to food fish, the abundances of dogfish and skates have not declined and may have increased.

Although they are not affected by trawling on the continental shelf, eels have also become much scarcer in Raritan Bay in recent years. In 1991 the two remaining eel pot fishermen had good catches in the spring, but later catches were so poor that one fisherman switched to potting blue crabs, and although the other one continued potting, he did not earn enough money doing it.

The reason bunkers became much scarcer in the northeastern United States was also heavy fishing. Besides the spotter planes and larger boats from Belford and other East Coast sites, seining boats in southern waters began taking smaller bunkers than they had in the past, especially in the large nursery areas of Chesapeake Bay (Ahrenholtz, Nelson, and Epperly 1987). In 1991 the pound nets and two purse seine boats in Raritan Bay were catching relatively small quantities of bunkers. During the usually good fishing months of July and August, the purse seiners had to go outside the bay along the coast south to and beyond Shark River looking for schools.

In 1991, hard clams were relatively abundant in the bay, soft clams were scarce, and lobsters were abundant in the ocean. Some oysters were growing on bottoms off Keyport.

Another sign of decline in fish and shellfish relates to the number of commercial boats in Raritan Bay. If the ocean trawlers that tied up in Belford are excluded, the number of other boats declined from about one hundred in 1980 to forty-four in 1991. The largest drop was in soft-clam boats in Highlands; those declined in numbers from thirty to zero. Bunker seine boats fell from seven to two, eel boats from sixteen to two, gill-net boats from four to one, and pound-net boats from six to four. The only boats whose numbers remained constant were lobster boats; there were about twenty-eight.

Vessel Traffic and Its Effects

Vessel traffic in the bay has become heavy. It includes container ships, dredgers, and barges laden with sludge, acid waste, and petroleum products (Bennett 1984) as well as sport fishing, pleasure, and military boats. In the early 1980s and probably to the present time, the various transportation endeavors in these and close-by waters provided about thirty-five thousand jobs in the Raritan Bay–Port Newark area (Pearce 1984). Frequently, sport and commercial fishermen have to abandon fishing and move their boats out of the way of passing vessels.

Occasionally, sport-fishing and pleasure craft run into pound nets at night and do considerable damage to the nets and poles. Commercial fishermen have a legal right to install pound nets in specified locations, their positions are marked on navigation charts, and there are lights on them at night so boats can avoid them. But the boats are gone when pound-boat crews find the damage, and they cannot collect any compensation.

After World War II, sport fishermen and pleasure boats on the bay began to lift commercial fishermen's pots and take eels and lobsters from them. To prevent such thefts, commercial fishermen have had to set their pots without buoys and drag for their lines with grapnels.

Status of Fishing Ports

Currently, all the harbors—Great Kills, Prince's Bay, Perth Amboy, Keyport, Leonardo, and Highlands—are crowded with sport-fishing and other pleasure boats during the warmer months. The exception is Compton's Creek, Belford, that has only commercial boats. However, twenty of those are draggers, and ranging from forty-eight to eighty feet long, they are much larger than boats there in the past. They trawl for fish in the ocean. This port has been entirely utilitarian and has had an unattractive appearance. Two of the principal fishing businesses there operate from trailer bodies, and lobstermen use freezers salvaged from worn-out trucks alongside their docks to store their bait. In addition, the short roads to the docks and the parking lots are rutted and usually lined with rotting nets, rusting dredges, and piles of broken fish boxes; unattractive swamp grass grows along unused edges and in corners.

Real estate on the bayshore has become increasingly valuable for housing and business. As a result of construction of condominiums, some marinas and public docks used previously for sport fishing have been lost, making access to the bay increasingly difficult. One example was Shoals Dock in Great Kills Harbor, once a popular public facility where several head boats moored and took on fishermen. In the early 1980s, it was purchased by a condominium owner and the head boats had to move to less desirable locations. Since the late 1950s, more than twelve small ramps for launching boats have been lost to land fillings, housing development, commercial building, and construction of bulkheads in the bay vicinity (Barrett 1985).

Further real estate developments are being planned. In the 1980s, a real estate developer purchased the property belonging to the former Seacoast Products Fish Factory on the west side of Compton's Creek, Belford, and, in the 1990s, plans to construct a housing-recreational development on the site. Named Spy House Harbor, it is projected to consist of about two hundred upscale townhouses, several shops, and an adjacent thousand-slip marina in the bay. Since the bay is shallow where the marina will be built and is unprotected from northerly winds, its construction will necessitate the digging of a large basin and the placement of a stone breakwater around it. This will eliminate a stretch of bay bottom used for centuries as a nursery area for juvenile fish and a feeding area for waterfowl. It will also interrupt current flow and fish movements along this section of the bay's south shore. The developer plans as well to construct an eighteen-hole golf course on the land adjoining the east side of Compton's Creek. The character of the port will be changed from one associated exclusively with commercial fishing, and the bay will produce slightly fewer juvenile fish and support slightly fewer waterfowl. In 1991 construction had not begun because the economy was in a recession.

The town of Keansburg has been trying to entice a developer to purchase an amusement center and construct a condominium-marina complex, which will similarly impinge on the habitat of the bay. One plan was to construct a $300 million complex of about 1,000 residences, shops, and restaurants, and a 850-slip marina, to be called Point Atlantic. Construction of the marina would require digging a large basin and placing a stone seawall in the bay, again affecting the bay's habitat and wildlife. The Spy House Harbor and Point Atlantic projects are comparable to many upscale housing-recreational projects that have been and are being constructed around the world. Each year natural habitats, seemingly too small to be important, are destroyed to improve human life, but as the destruction accrues, its negative effect on wildlife grows and becomes substantial.

In Highlands, intense competition has existed between fishing interests (eeling, head boating, and lobstering) and housing, restaurants, and bars for space along the waterfront. Recently, the town tried to resolve the conflicts by zoning the waterfront for commercial fisheries, but its decree has been ignored and ensuing development has been construction of restaurants and docks for their patrons. For the proper atmosphere to lure patrons, the restaurants encourage recreational boats to use their docks, but they bar commercial fishing boats, including head boats, which are less attractive. The result has been that commercial fishermen have little space remaining for docking and offloading. New residents of Highlands also complain about the early morning activities of fishermen (Caruso 1982).

In the 1980s and early 1990s, commercial fishermen and head-boat operators were threatened by higher taxes on their waterfront properties. Substantially higher taxes would make it difficult for them to survive, and they would have to sell out to housing and restaurant developments. High property taxes may force some lobster pounds in Highlands to consolidate or disappear.

62. William "Pop" Pedro, 104, explaining how, as a preteenager, he culled seed
oysters for a tonger in the Arthur Kill in the 1890s. Photograph by author.

Status of the Fishermen and Fisheries

By 1991 commercial fishing in Raritan Bay has declined sharply from the
past. As a result, the commercial fishermen now comprise a tiny minority,
both on the bay at least during the warmer months when compared with
the numbers of sport fishermen and as residents in bayshore towns.

Nearly all the people living around the bayshore now work in
business and service industries, and many have only come to the area
within the past twenty-five years. Most work locally, but others work in
New York City or its environs. In addition, the new residents include
many sport fishermen who compete for fish with the commercial fishermen. The effect on the commercial fishermen is felt mainly on a personal

level. The commercial fishermen are rarely recognized as such except around the waterfronts of Belford and Highlands; nonfishermen rarely ask them common questions of the past, such as how many fish they are catching, what fish prices are, and what the condition of their boat is; and few outsiders care whether they retire. In earlier periods, the local people hoped that old-timers could keep going; a fisherman's retirement or death was a severe loss to the community.

Around their docks and in their living rooms, commercial fishermen still lament about New Jersey and New York barring them from digging clams. One World War II veteran, who had been a sail dredger during most of the 1930s and enjoyed it, complained about the hard-clam beds being closed in the 1960s and 1970s. He spent four years of his life in Europe fighting to defend his country. Then, he came home, and only a few years afterward the clam beds were closed. He believed it was not just. Many others believe that the clams remain safe to eat. A few will eat raw clams from anywhere in this bay, believing that if the water is polluted the clams will not live. William Pedro, a 104-year-old man from Sandy Ground, Staten Island, became angry when he recalled the oyster beds being closed some sixty years earlier: "Those oysters were not polluted. They picked up that disease in the market in New York City. They should never have closed the bay" (Interview, 6 February 1986).

Fishermen have resented most of the recent laws, believing that they keep down their catches and earnings. Bud Thompson of Port Monmouth fretted about them: "One time, you could do anything you wanted to do in the bay. The Lord put all those fish and crabs out there for everybody to get. Now, they are trying to make a big thing out of it. Pretty soon, you won't be able to do nothin'. Do the crabs know the laws? How about the clams? We can't be kept from them if we are to make a livin'" (Interview, 7 January 1988).

12

On the Water:
Trips with Present-Day
Bay Fishermen

During the 1980s and early 1990s, I made trips on seven types of fishing boats, all but two operating from Compton's Creek, Belford, to observe the current fisheries firsthand. They were engaged in pound-net fishing, purse seining, eel potting, sport fishing, hard clamming, lobstering, and crab dredging. The fishery operators I did not observe were the only gill-netting boat, the few charter boats, and the many small fiberglass sport fishing boats.

The commercial fishermen of Belford comprise a somewhat closed society and are not very open to strangers. They are generally low spirited and bitter about the long hours they work and the low incomes they earn. While they were friendly toward one another, they rarely joshed or engaged in horseplay.

Most of the skippers and crewmen live within several miles of Compton's Creek, Belford. They go to bed around 10 P.M. after an evening of watching television, even though they rise at perhaps 4 A.M. every day; some need more sleep than others, however, and take a two-hour nap in the afternoons. They arrive at the docks in the early morning darkness in pickup trucks and automobiles and park near their boats. Some arrive about half an hour before their boats are to depart, to stop at the lighted dock of the fishermens' cooperative and socialize. They are joined by two or three crewmen who live on the boats or in sheds on the creek. In summer, these two or three bathe in the creek around 3 A.M. before anyone arrives.

These men are all the sons of fishermen and they are continuing a tradition they feel is important. They have some confidence that the work will provide them with a livelihood because commercial fishing in the area has endured for such a long period. However, several possibilities make them feel uneasy: New Jersey officials might raise license fees; wardens might catch them in an illegal act such as landing an undersized lobster; legislators might shut down another fishery; the prices of their catch could drop; fish, clams, or lobsters could become scarcer; their gear could break down; and development of Spy House Harbor could threaten to take over some of their docks. To a man, they feel that the state should protect the docks from outside development so that fishing can continue.

The wives of the skippers usually handle their paperwork. They order new parts and gear for the boats and vehicles, sell their lobsters, receive and cash checks from buyers, pay license fees, and make out income tax forms.

While on the water fishing, the fishermen seem to prefer that simple world to the hustle-bustle, information-packed environment they experience on shore. It is similar to the quiet, slow-paced life ashore the older men had experienced when they were young in the 1920s and 1930s, and it is a time to forget worries and to concentrate on making their catches.

A common characteristic of the commercial fisheries is that the fish, lobsters, and crabs are all too scarce for good fishing, and, to make adequate catches for a day's pay, the boat skippers are drawing consistently on their memories to recall what their fishermen teachers had taught them when they broke into this work as teenagers many years before. The ability of these men to make their catches is impressive; amateurs trying with the same gear would catch much less than they do.

A Trip on a Pound Boat

On 12 August 1986 I made a trip on a pound boat owned by Otto Schnoor, eighty-one years old. Otto had been a pound-net fisherman in the bay every year since he was a teenager. He was the crew's boss, but his grandson, Tommy, operated the boat and would take over as boss when Otto retired a year later. Otto and the crewmen were all wearing typical fishermen's outfits: nearly black button-down shirts and pants, rubber knee boots, and caps. We left their dock in Compton's Creek at 5:30 A.M., towing a fourteen-foot bateau, and headed toward their pound net installed near Sandy Hook. Otto's crew consisted of four men, including his grandson and himself. I chatted with one, a cheerful crewman named Frank, who was about sixty-two years old. He had begun fishing when he got out of the army at the end of World War II. He had worked on purse-seine and pound-net boats in the bay and draggers in the ocean ever since, but had not done any shellfishing. Frank did not know what prices Otto received for his fish. "Those guys handle all that," he said. During the winter, Frank trapped muskrats in a few rivers of northern New Jersey. The fourth crewman, Jim, in his mid-twenties, had joined the crew this season.

As we came within about fifty yards of the first pound net to be lifted, five cormorants that had been sitting on the pound's poles and occasionally diving into the pound for an easy meal of fish flew off low over the water toward the south. It was 6:10 A.M. When we arrived, Frank hopped into the bateau, went around to all sixteen poles of the pocket, and untied the draw-ropes fastened to them. When he finished, he returned to the pound boat, which the other three were pulling alongside the mouth of the pocket. The four crewmen then began to pull up the side of the pocket to concentrate the fish inside. As they drew it up tightly, a mass of wriggling fish, mostly bunkers, came into view. Then Tommy started the winch engine for brailing. Frank pushed the brail net into the mass and Tommy hauled it out with the winch and it swung over the open hold of the boat. Frank released the draw rope, and the fish fell about five feet into the boat. It took only seven minutes to transfer all the fish, a total of about ten barrels (two hundred pounds in a barrel in the 1980s), mostly bunkers but some weakfish and bluefish. The crew spent about twenty more minutes mending holes in the pocket. Bluefish made these holes with their teeth when they swam rapidly into the net trying to escape from the pocket. Then Frank got back into the bateau and went back to each of the poles. This time, he hauled on the ropes to pull down the bottom of the pocket until the net was stretched; then he fastened them using two half hitches. They were done here.

Next, the crew headed for the second pound net to be lifted off Belford. Otto sipped some coffee during the passage, and at 7:22 A.M. we neared the net. Otto had a pained expression on his face as he pointed to a group of about seventy-five dead bunkers, about ten inches long, which had tried to swim through the net of the little heart and got their heads caught in it. Otto said, "No matter what size mesh we use, we cannot avoid gilling fish of some size."

The crew repeated all the operations here, except this net did not need any mending. The net had only two barrels of bunkers and a loggerhead turtle weighing about 150 pounds; it was breathing loudly. For many years, pound netters retained and sold these turtles, but in recent years they have become so scarce they are classified as an endangered species. It is unlawful to kill them. Jim took an axe and shaved about twelve large barnacles off the turtle's back; then he and Frank lifted it overboard. They had everything done in twenty minutes.

Before we left, two sport-fishing boats approached us to buy some fish. One fisherman paid five dollars for a bushel of bunkers to mince for bluefish bait. The second bought two weakfish weighing about eight pounds apiece. Otto collected eight dollars for each one. Otto said that in the 1980s, relations between pound netters and sport fishermen were good, because pound nets caught few fluke, the principal species caught by sport fishermen, and most of the bunkers the nets catch are sold to sport fishermen for bait.

While heading back to Compton's Creek, the crew picked out the food fish from the pile of bunkers and put them in wire bushel baskets. Otto told me that when he was a young man, the crew he was with used to take extra-large loads of food fish directly to Fulton Market for sale. Occasionally, he stayed up late at night and then had to get up early to go on the boat. He was so tired on the way back from New York City that he would get on the roof of the pilothouse where the mouth of the exhaust pipe was, lie down next to it, and could go to sleep despite the loud noise coming from it.

On this day, they caught twelve barrels of bunkers, 250 pounds of weakfish, eight bluefish weighing about 50 pounds altogether, and a few alewives. At 8:15 A.M., we arrived at the dock. The weakfish and bluefish were weighed immediately and put in boxes with ice. Frank, Tommy, and Jim shoveled the bunkers into barrels, which Otto hoisted onto the dock with a winch. The crew then went to their rented field about a mile from the creek and spent the remainder of the morning mending alternates for the nets in the bay.

The boxed and iced food fish would be sold at the cooperative's fish market or shipped to markets by truck. The cooperative sold the bunkers to sport-fishing shops.

A Trip on a Bunker-Seining Boat

On 21 July 1990 I made a trip on the *Belatrix*, one of two boats licensed to catch bunkers with purse seines in the New Jersey waters of Raritan Bay. The *Belatrix* was sixty-five feet long and seventeen feet wide, was painted gray all over, and was powered by a 671 General Motors diesel engine. It was built in 1958 in Morehead City, North Carolina, for catching shrimp. Its owner and captain, Cris Anthropolis, purchased her in 1965 for use as a purse seiner. He made her deck larger by shortening the cabin, and built a lookout stand near the top of the mast. The

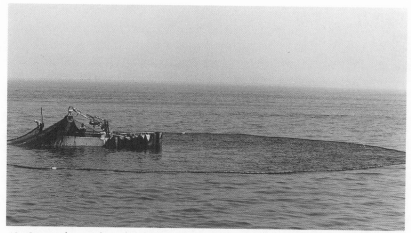

63. *Crew of purse boat hauling in seine around school of bunkers in Raritan Bay. Photograph by author.*

Belatrix towed an aluminum boat, thirty-eight feet long, carrying the purse seine. The seine was one thousand feet long and twenty-five feet deep, a sufficient size to surround any school of bunkers and to reach the bay bottom. The remaining crew consisted of Cris's brother, sixty-eight-year-old Ernie Anthropolis, "Mopsy" Harding and Ted Kenzia, both about fifty, and two other men, both college students earning summer money. Cris was five feet ten inches tall, sixty-four years old, and blind in one eye; his dark olive skin contrasted with his white hair. He had been

64. *Crew of purse boat draws seine tighter around school of bunkers in Raritan Bay. Photograph by author.*

65. *Crew on purse boat has tied one side of seine to side of seine boat and is drawing up seine tightly in preparation for brailing the bunkers aboard the seine boat. Photograph by author.*

fishing on the bay since he was a teenager, purse seining, gill netting, and otter trawling for porgies.

At 5:15 A.M., we motored out of Compton's Creek and headed toward Sandy Hook Bay. The air temperature was about eighty degrees, the sky was clear, and the wind blew about five knots from the south, scarcely rippling the water. Cris and members of the crew told me about purse seining. The bunker schools, which they call "pods" or "bunches," or, if small, "hubs," nearly always remain below the water surface where fishermen cannot see them. Cris keeps the *Belatrix* moving at a speed of about two knots hoping to spot a school on the surface; it can be detected by the bunkers "whipping" the surface water. They usually see one or two schools a day, but sometimes they do not see any. The weather is important: since schools tend to rise more frequently on a hot day following a warm, humid night, especially if there is a southerly breeze. They rarely rise during a cool northerly wind. Thus, if the wind has blown from the north during the night, the crew does not anticipate having any luck. Bunkers do not rise during and several hours following a thunderstorm or when many boats are motoring in the area. If the bunkers are to rise, they usually do it after the sun is up a way and has warmed the water. I asked if it were possible to catch bunkers with an

66. Brailing bunkers from purse seine onto the seine boat. Photograph by author.

otter trawl. The answer was no, because the schools are widely dispersed. Besides a purse seine, the only other type of net that would be effective is a paired seine towed by two boats, because it covers a wide area and fishes high in the water column. The crew rarely caught any fish other than bunkers; at most, three or four bluefish were caught with a school of bunkers. Catches of bunkers usually range from fifty to two hundred barrels (two hundred pounds per barrel, about three bushels) in one set of the seine.

In recent years, a New Jersey regulation has stipulated that bunker boats cannot set their seines within three-tenths of a mile of the shore; purse seining is illegal in the waters of New York's Richmond County (Staten Island). The *Belatrix*'s crew believed that these regulations substantially restrict their fishing because, it seems to them, that most schools of bunkers are inshore.

The crew fish five days a week; they do not fish on Saturday or Sunday because they cannot sell bunkers on those days. Of the five days they fish, Tuesday, Wednesday, and Thursday are the most productive; Friday is the worst because noise from the many pleasure boats on the bay keeps the schools down. Ernie said that the job is monotonous when they did not see fish because they just ride around for hours, waiting for a school to rise. During the day, Cris called to personnel at the fishermen's cooperative about once every hour to tell them how many bunkers they

67. *Brail net used to transfer bunkers from purse seine to seine boat.*
Photograph by author.

had and to find out how many they could sell that day. (These conversa-
tions are monitored in the homes of a number of retired fishermen who
have ship-to-shore telephone receivers in Belford and Highlands. I was
amused whenever I visited fishermen's homes and found that the fishermen and their wives knew just what the *Belatrix* had caught that day.)

We arrived in Sandy Hook Bay about 5:45 A.M. and began searching. While Cris was steering, he was constantly on the lookout for a
school; the remaining members of the crew looked occasionally from the
deck and the lookout stand on the mast. They had not seen anything after
the *Belatrix* had crisscrossed the entire bay about three times by 8 A.M.,
so Cris headed the *Belatrix* westward to see whether schools might be
rising there. We motored slowly as far west as Point Comfort, off
Keansburg, but did not see any schools, so we circled back toward Sandy
Hook Bay. Cris said that he always looks in the Raritan Bay channel
immediately after a tanker passes through if he is near it because bunker
schools often rise in their wakes. During the day, Cris told me about three
men who had taught him the tricks of purse seining for bunkers when he
was a novice nearly fifty years ago. I felt that he was trying to recall how
they might locate a school when the bunkers were as scarce as they are

68. *Crew of seine boat rest on return trip to Compton's Creek, Belford, after catching limit of bunkers, as set by fishermen's cooperative. Photograph by author.*

now, but with all his experience on top of their teaching he was probably more skilled at it than they ever were.

We reached Sandy Hook Bay again about 10 A.M. Almost immediately, the crew spotted a group of about twelve sea gulls resting on the water about three-fourths of a mile north of the breakwater at Atlantic Highlands. The site was also opposite Henry Hudson Spring on Mount Mitchell, where Henry Hudson had filled his water containers. At 10:16 A.M., Mopsy pointed to the gulls and yelled, "There they are!" He had spotted a school surfacing amongst the gulls. Quickly, Cris and four of the crew donned their oilskins, and at 10:19 A.M. they were in the purse boat and had cast off. Only Ted and I remained on the *Belatrix*. They eased the purse boat slowly up to the school so as not to drive it down and went around it in ninety seconds, the seine sliding off behind them. They had to go quickly around a school because, if bluefish were in it, they would scatter the bunkers and many would elude the seine. The crew's next job was to close the bottom of the seine lying on the bottom. By teasing the lead line along the bottom and then pulling it up into their purse boat, they had trapped the bunkers in the seine. For the next hour, the crew, using the large hydraulic power block on the purse boat and their own muscle power, shortened up the seine, closing the bunkers into

69. *"Mopsy" Harding and Ernie Anthropolis on seine boat rest on return trip to Compton's Creek, Belford, after seining bunkers. Photograph by author.*

a tight mass. At 11:25 A.M. Ted ran the *Belatrix* alongside the far side of the seine's cork line. Then the boat crew boarded the *Belatrix* and tied one side of the cork line to about fifteen lines hanging along its rail. Finally part of the crew returned to the purse boat and tied a wire line from a winch on the *Belatrix* to the opposite side of the cork line; they drew it up to concentrate the bunkers even more.

At 11:50 A.M. the crew began brailing from the seine with its bull net; it scooped about three-fourths of a barrel of bunkers each dip. Each crewman had a specific job: one pushed the bull net into the bunkers on one side of the seine, two others held ropes attached to the bull net and pulled it through the bunkers, Ted held the purse line, and Cris operated the winch lifting the net. First, they brailed 12 barrels onto a lobster boat, the *Costa Lotta* from Highlands, which had tied alongside. Then they brailed about 140 barrels onto the *Belatrix*. In all, about 200 dips were made with the bull net. After each dip, the mass of bunkers dropped wriggling onto the deck, but they died in a few minutes. About every fifteen minutes during the brailing, the crew stopped briefly to shorten up the seine to concentrate the fish because the dip net began to come up with smaller loads. In this set, only bunkers were caught. Cris said that he wished that people would desist from accusing him of seining food fish, because he rarely caught any with the bunkers.

At 12:50 P.M., the crew stopped brailing when the bunkers completely covered the deck in a layer about eighteen inches deep; they

70. At dock of fishermen's cooperative in Compton's Creek, Belford, the crew of seine boat is shoveling bunkers into barrels. The bunkers will be lifted onto waiting trucks. Photograph by author.

released the remainder from the seine because they did not have orders for more. At least 99 percent of the released bunkers swam away alive; gulls got the few dying floaters on the surface. Cris estimated that they released about 150 barrels and then lamented, "Fishing is feast or famine. Today we caught twice what we could sell; some days we don't get any." Cris did not record the quantity of bunkers he sold to the *Costa Lotta*. He said, "The captain'll tell me how many he got and pay me. I trust his count."

On the way back to Belford, Ernie told me that they sell the bunkers for $14 a barrel. Thus this catch grossed about $2,030; 15 percent of the value of those landed in Belford will be paid to the fisherman's cooperative. Ernie said that he and the other crewmen earn about $500 a week. They do not receive any benefits, such as vacation or retirement pay or medical insurance from the job. The *Belatrix* does carry compensation insurance to cover medical expenses if a crewman is injured. Ernie said that he was glad that his three nephews had gone to college rather than go into fishing; they now have jobs paying $40,000 to $50,000 a year. He said: "This fishing is for someone with a strong back and a weak mind."

At 1:30 P.M. we arrived back at the fishermen's cooperative dock in Compton's Creek to dispose of the bunkers. The air temperature there was about ninety degrees. To keep the bunkers from rotting, a dock worker dumped a large tub of crushed ice from a payloader onto the deck of the *Belatrix* and the crew spread it over the bunkers to cool them. A few minutes later, a truck carrying about one hundred empty blue plastic barrels backed onto the dock. Its driver threw some onto the deck of the *Belatrix*, and the crew began to shovel them full of bunkers. Using a windlass on the dock, Cris hoisted them up to the truck. The majority of the bunkers would be taken to New York City and sold as bait to sport fishermen trying for bluefish. The remainder were to be trucked to Virginia and North Carolina, where they would be sold as bait to blue crab fishermen.

A Trip on An Eel-Potting Boat

On 22 September 1986 I went on a trip from Compton's Creek, Belford, with eel potter, Ed Raposa. Ed lifted eel pots every weekday morning, as a sideline to his regular shore job as a newspaperman. His boat, twenty feet long and seven feet wide, had a flat bottom and was powered by a seventy-horsepower outboard motor. Controls for the motor were attached to a housing about five feet from the bow. On the starboard rail beside the wheel, Ed had attached a hydraulic winch to wind in his pot lines. He had seventy-five pots dispersed among four lines in the bay. When I arrived at his dock about 6 A.M., he was taking two basketfuls of frozen horseshoe crabs out of his freezer, which he had salvaged for twenty dollars from a worn-out delivery truck. Ed had cut the crabs in half before freezing them. He had paid twenty-five cents for each female crab and twenty-five cents for each pair of male crabs. Females were worth more because their eggs attract the eels, and pots baited with horseshoe crabs caught more eels than if baited with soft clams, a bait fishermen had to use when crabs were unavailable.

We left the dock about 6:30 A.M., passed through the creek and out into the bay toward Raritan Reach East Channel, where his pots were lying. The wind was light, the bay was calm; the weather would not interfere with his lifting. Ed said he had hired various mates in the past but gave it up: "If a man is good, he wants to go into the business for himself; if he is no good, he will remain with you." During most of the summer, Ed had caught about two hundred pounds of eels a day, but recently catches had fallen to less than one hundred pounds.

We arrived at the first line at 7 A.M. Ed tossed over his grapnel and towed it until he felt his pot line. He retrieved it with his hydraulic hoist and took in each pot. He dumped the eels from them into a galvanized wash tub, stuffed half a horseshoe crab into its kitchen compartment as bait, and set them on deck. After the fifteenth and last one had been baited, he strung out the line again in the same place. The pots had five, one, zero, two, one, eight, four, one, zero, zero, three, one, zero, two, and seventeen eels, respectively. Of the forty-six eels, eleven were too small for sale. The pots also contained a few small black sea bass, undersized lobsters, and rock crabs; Ed tossed them all overboard alive. Ed had dumped the eels into a tub because he wanted to see how many eels each line had. After lifting each line, he dumped the eels into a live car on deck. The eels did not have to be kept in water; they will live at least a couple of days in air if kept cool.

I asked him about two sayings about eels. One: "The first thunderstorm of the spring wakes up the frogs [spring peepers] and the frogs wake up the eels." He said that is not true here as the eels begin to pot before the frogs sing. Two: "Eels always pot better during a thunderstorm." Ed said that is not true either.

During the summer, Ed left the pots in one area of the channel because the eels move up and down in it. He and the other fishermen found that they get more eels whenever the U.S. Army Corps of Engineers dredges mud from the channels. Eels seem to concentrate around the roiled water, perhaps seeking worms and small crustaceans stirred up by the dredging.

During June, black mud snails deposit so many egg cases on his pots that the wire openings become almost completely sealed. Ed takes the pots ashore, replaces them in the bay with spares, lets them dry, then brushes off the hardened, brittle egg cases and dips the pots in tar. Then they are ready for use again.

We left his last line and arrived back at his dock in Belford at around 10 A.M. with only about seventy pounds of eels. Ed hooked the live car to a line on a pulley attached to a piling, lifted the car out of his boat and into the water, and then tied it near his dock where it floated nearly submerged. He was finished for the day.

A Trip on a Head Boat

On 6 October 1987 I took a trip on the head boat *Sea Pigeon III,* whose port was the Perth Amboy Municipal Marina. Its owner and captain was Marty Haines, about forty-two years old. He had taken fishermen on this and other head boats for about twenty years and had worked with his father running one since he was a teenager. The boat could carry 101 fishermen and had 81 vertical holders for rods spaced along its rails.

Marty now had two crewmen, both in their twenties, but in the summer he had a third man. Their job was to supply fishermen with bait, land and fillet fish, collect fares, operate pools, and clean up. The fare was twenty-two dollars a head, half-price for seniors. Nearly all fishermen who came had their own poles, but Marty had about twelve available for rent at three dollars apiece.

I arrived at 6:45 A.M. and boarded with thirty-seven fishermen (twenty-nine seniors and eight younger men), each of whom had a lunch, a rod and reel, and a bucket for the fish. The attitude they displayed was much different from commercial fishermen. In contrast to the serious, frequently bitter, attitudes of their counterparts in the bay, the men looked forward to a good time and acted like a closely knit, happy family having a frolic. They wanted to catch some fish, but a large catch was not necessary.

The boat left the dock at 7:00 A.M. and headed eastward into the bay. It first crossed by Ward Point and then went over Round Shoal, both prime oystering and hard-clamming beds in years gone by, and headed for the main bay channel and an area south of Annadale, Staten Island. Every winter for at least a century, fishermen have dredged blue crabs from the channel; for perhaps as long, sport fishermen such as these aboard the *Sea Pigeon III* have caught fluke there in the summer.

October 6 was the one hundred twenty-first consecutive day that the *Sea Pigeon III* had gone out fishing. En route, Marty said that he ran the boat all year, but February was a slack time. Since June, he had been fishing in the channel and would fish there until mid-October, when he expected the fluke to leave. After that, he would fish in the ocean, first for blackfish and later for ling. Many of his regular clientele would quit when he left the bay because often the water became too rough for them in the ocean, but others went year-round; he had one regular who went out one or two days a week all year. In March and April, he fished for winter flounders in the bay.

Marty always evaluated the weather as he headed out on the bay and went where he thought conditions would be best for catching the most fish. The more fish caught, the more fishermen he would attract for future trips.

Marty said there were always some protected areas in the bay where he could get good fishing. In strong northwesterly winds, he favored a protected stretch off the southeast side of Staten Island from Great Kills Harbor to the Verrazano-Narrows Bridge. During strong easterly winds, he fished along the sloping sand bank bordering on mud bottom off the west coast of Sandy Hook. This is the same bank that fishermen who sail-dredged hard clams had avoided, because the teeth of their rakes would bend if dragged across the hard bottom.

At about 7:30 A.M. we had reached the middle of the channel. Marty stopped the boat's engine opposite a rock pile marked M 20 on U.S.

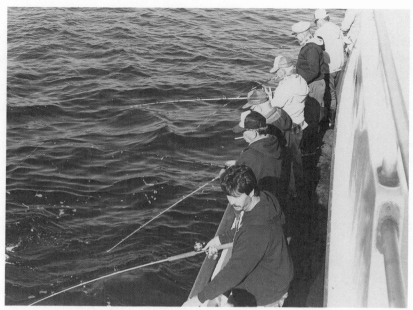

71. *Sport fishermen along rail of head boat,* Sea Pigeon III, *trying to catch fluke,* 6 October 1987. *Photograph by author.*

Department of Commerce navigation charts. The water was forty-five feet deep. The boat would then be blown slowly to the edge of the channel where the water was only twenty-five feet deep.

Most fishermen had tied a cloth on a hook beneath the rail for wiping fish slime from their hands and had placed their bucket under the seat behind them. They put out their baited hooks and sinkers. Three or four fishermen hooked fluke almost immediately.

After about fifteen minutes, the boat had blown to the channel edge, which Marty could determine by viewing his depth recorder. He gave the boat's horn a blast to signal the fishermen to reel in so he could return to the middle of the channel. Each succeeding time he did so during the day, he moved a couple of boat lengths up the channel to new bottom and, he hoped, more fish. During the day, Marty spent his time viewing the boat's depth recorder, looking down at the rails to determine how many fish were being caught, moving the boat, and engaging in banter on his radio with the captains of other head boats.

Around 8:00 A.M., Ed Raposa, the eeler from Belford, came out near us to lift his line of eel pots lying in the channel opposite a buoy. Marty said that he knew the locations of the various lines of eel pots and tried to avoid them so his fishermen would not hook them.

The fishermen used three-ounce sinkers and had two and a half feet

72. Sport fisherman holding one of fifteen fluke he caught on day trip aboard head boat, Sea Pigeon III, 6 October 1987. Photograph by author.

of line between the sinker and hook. They put two or three pieces of bait on a hook; a common bait was a strip of squid or the white belly of a fluke together with two shiners; each bait was about three and a half inches long. The bait usually remained intact when a fluke was caught, but fishermen had to add one or two pieces after landing about every third one. Usually, about three fishermen with bent rods were reeling in fish at any time and the fish came in steadily all day. Once, a fluke bit two baits and was reeled up by two fishermen standing side by side.

The fishermen could not keep small fluke. New Jersey has a

thirteen-inch minimum-length law for them; New York has a fourteen-inch law. In New Jersey, the fine for possession was twenty dollars per undersized fluke plus a twenty-dollar court cost. In New York, the fisherman and the captain were each fined twenty-five dollars per fluke. When head boats fished on the New Jersey side of the bay in the morning, the crew filleted all the fluke before moving to the New York side in the afternoon, so it would not have any aboard measuring between thirteen and fourteen inches long. One day in the previous week, New York wardens had boarded the *Sea Pigeon III* to measure every fluke and caught a man with one undersized. Fishermen were careful to obey the size laws and early in the summer had to release many fluke because the were undersize.

Unfortunately, the fishermen had to tear out the esophagus to remove hooks from perhaps one of every six undersized fluke because they had swallowed them. The fluke would die soon after being released. I imagined that at least their flesh would fertilize the water and also be useful as food for mud snails, bacteria, and molds as they rotted.

Occasionally, fishermen were surprised on these trips. For example, the day before, a fisherman caught and released a sturgeon four feet long and weighing twenty-five pounds. It was only the third sturgeon a fishermen on the *Sea Pigeon III* had ever caught.

All day, the two crewmen cleaned fluke for the fishermen, who paid them about twenty-five cents per fish for the service. They put the fillets in plastic bags. Marty said that fishermen used to clean their own fish, but in recent years they would not take fish home if the crew did not do it.

When Marty first began to fish for ling in the winter, he could not get many fishermen to go on the trips. He explained how he increased his clientele:

> Since the 1970s, fishermen have been taking ling home and eating them. However, before that they would not eat them, and I did not have many fishermen aboard on ling trips. So I asked my wife to fry about five pounds of ling fillets in bread crumbs. I brought them aboard, warmed them up, and passed them out to the fishermen. They are tasty and sweet. The fishermen loved them and asked what they were. After that, more fishermen brought ling home and more regular fishermen came on ling trips.

The fishermen engaged in friendly conversation and banter almost constantly:

—-Don't worry, if you fall in, I'll throw you the anchor.

—I told my wife that I was going fishing, not catching.

—See what I tell you Joe, hook 'em through the lip, not their throat, and you won't have to struggle to get them off.

—Even a fish would stay out of trouble if it kept his mouth shut.

—Don't fight with me fish, and I'll let you off the hook.

—That bucket isn't wide enough for my fish.

—That fish lost four pounds on the way up.

—I call this the Polish boat. See all the poles?

The fishermen believed that the bay's water was cleaner than it used to be when three copper plants and the National Lead plant, all since closed, use to dump wastes into the bay. Large oil slicks, leaks from oil tankers, were also common on the bay in the 1950s and 1960s, but these had mostly disappeared. The city of New Brunswick once dumped raw sewage into the Raritan River but does not anymore. The fishermen credited government action for the cleanups.

Marty said that 1963 was the last big porgy year. Before that, the head-boat catch was mostly porgies, rather than fluke. The crewmen used to open surf clams and cut them into little pieces as bait for the fishermen. There were so many porgies in the bay that the crew had to cut bait constantly to keep them supplied.

Marty used to sell beer, but he stopped because the fishermen sometimes became too raucous. In addition, if a fisherman bought beer aboard and had a traffic accident on the way home, Marty would now be liable. In recent years, if a fisherman brings a large quantity of beer to the dock, Marty does not let him on board.

Marty seemed to feel that all fishermen were brothers under the skin, so to speak, and hoped they all did well. However, sport fishermen often resent the commercial fishermen with their more efficient gear. One often hears such comments as: "All I have is a rod and reel and they have those big nets," and "It isn't fair that they can take so many." I asked Marty how he felt about the occasional Belford fishing boats that trawled for fluke illegally at night. He answered, "We have to live with the commercial people; they have to live with us."

I asked him what effect the dredged channels have had on the distribution of fluke. "They have concentrated them; before they were dug, the fluke were spread out more."

What did he think of the plan to fill in the dredge holes with contaminated dredge spoil and cap them over? "For one thing, these are excellent fishing areas; fluke lie along the banks. At times, I have seen thirty fluke at once being reeled in on this boat. For another, we do not want to see all those contaminants put here, and so we are against the plan."

Another concern he had was retaining his boat berth at Perth Amboy. He has tried to keep a large clientele of fishermen, and favors seniors with half fares, so he will have ample support if the city tries to make him relinquish the berth.

At 3 P.M., Marty sounded his boat horn three times, a signal to reel up for the last time. Each fisherman had caught about 15 fluke. Multiplied by thirty-seven fishermen, the total catch was about 555 fluke and 2 bluefish. The winner of a two-dollar-pool for the largest fluke received thirty dollars.

We docked at 3:45 P.M. The fishermen filed off the boat contentedly with their rods and reels, buckets, empty lunch bags, and five to seven pounds of fish fillets apiece. Six pounds of fluke fillets would cost about forty dollars in a market. The head-boat trip was a bargain!

A Trip on a Hard-Clam Raking Boat

On 15 July 1991 I took a trip on a hard clam boat, sailing from Brooks Marina in Sea Bright with owner Luke Jenks, twenty-two years old. He was one of the thirty or so "southern" men who dig clams in southeastern Raritan Bay and relay them on their leased sites in Barnegat Bay. He first dug clams in Shark River, New Jersey, with his father when he was five years old, and told me of being there again when he was eleven and making one hundred dollars in one day. Luke had two older brothers who were also clam fishermen. He loved working on the water and said he missed it when he was a construction worker the previous two years.

Luke lives in Point Pleasant and drives to Sea Bright every morning. He arrives at Brooks marina at 5:30 A.M. and returns to the marina around noon. He loads his catch into his pickup, has it sealed by a New Jersey conservation officer, leaves the marina by 1 P.M., and arrives at Swan Point, Barnegat Bay, at 2 P.M., where the seal is removed by the conservation officer. He then loads the clams in his second boat, runs out to one of his three leased half-acre plots to plant them, returns to shore by 2:45 P.M., and is home by 3:30 P.M., twelve hours after rising from bed. This summer, Luke had been raking two thousand to three thousand littlenecks a day from Raritan Bay, with much smaller numbers of cherrystones and chowders. He raked the clams off his leased sites on

Saturdays to sell and harvested about ten thousand in two to three hours. He found it more profitable to sell the clams to a wholesaler than to sell smaller quantities, such as a bushel here and there, to restaurants.

Luke's boat is a twenty-two-foot cedar garvey painted gray. While raking it is mandatory for him to put over each side a board about two feet long with his name and clam license number painted on it. The outboard engine is a 1989 leftover Luke purchased at a discount. The rake he uses is twenty-six inches wide, fitted with twenty-four three-inch teeth. The handle of the rake has four telescoping sections—it fits within the boat when collapsed.

We left Brooks Marina at 5:25 A.M. and headed north to Raritan Bay. The wind was blowing about ten knots out of the north. Luke anticipated a good catch of clams because the wind would blow his boat along as he raked. He got two or three times more clams on windy days than on still days. It was a beautiful summer day. The sky was almost cloudless and the air temperature was about 75° F.

He located his raking area by using shore ranges. He lined up the tip of Sandy Hook with the middle of the Verrazano Bridge in the north and the tip of the breakwater at Atlantic Highlands with one of the houses on the side of Mount Mitchell in the west. We arrived at the area at 5:55 A.M. The water was twenty feet deep at low tide; it increased to twenty-five feet at high tide. Luke's first job was to pull out the four sleeves of his rake handle to about forty-five feet and secure them by tightening hose clamps with a screwdriver. This took five minutes. The end of the handle had a foot-wide grip that he held while raking. On the handle, about a foot below the grip, he had secured an orange float; it prevented the handle from sinking deeply into the water when he laid it behind him every time he raised the rake. At 5:58 he began raking, jerking the rake through the muddy bottom, a sediment he preferred to work in. He said that raking in sand was as difficult as raking through a concrete sidewalk would be. During the day, he consistently raked for about three minutes and then hauled his rake up; it took thirty seconds to bring a rake to the surface. This was the hardest part of the work because the rake was always full of clams and mud. Within a minute, he shook out the mud, removed the algae, dumped the clams into a basket, and returned the rake to the bottom.

Luke continued raking without a rest break until the end of the morning, when he had to quit. The only breaks he took were to adjust the length of his handle; periodically, he lengthened it by eight to ten inches as the tide rose. He said that this slight lengthening meant the difference between catching poorly and catching well. He could feel whether the rake was catching clams well or not. The sound of the clams collecting in the rake rattled through the handle. Luke termed it, "money music," a pleasant sound to him.

During the day, Luke drifted across the clam bed, about a mile, three times; the drifts lasted from fifty-seven minutes to two hours and two minutes each. During the longest drift, he lifted the rake twenty-eight times to empty it. It took him from thirty-six to fifty-two minutes to fill each of his bushel baskets. I counted 111 littlenecks, 15 cherrystones, and 9 chowders in one of the rakefuls he brought up; it was a little fuller than average and had about a peck of clams.

Luke's catch was partially determined by the season, the tide, and, as noted, the wind. The clams are deeper in the sediments in the winter and also during the hottest part of the summer, so catches are lower then. On an incoming tide, the clams seemed to rise closer to the sediment surface, perhaps to feed on the water richer in food, and more are caught. The clams are also deeper during strong winds and resultant rough water, apparently to maintain themselves in the bottom.

As the time passed, Luke began to tire, and after getting three poor grabs in a row around 9:30 A.M., he said, "A few bad grabs like these and I don't feel like raking any more."

There were about thirty clam boats on the bed. They were spread over a one-and-a-half-mile-square area. Their numbers had been increasing because jobs in construction were diminishing in Monmouth County. Three of the boats had a woman along with the raker; her job was to cull the littlenecks, cherrystones, and chowders into separate containers. It saved the raker from doing it, allowing him time to catch more clams. One of the boats had two rakers aboard. The boat had barely moved when winds were light, and so they had rigged up a sail of plywood panels, measuring about six feet high and twelve feet wide. On still days, some rakers put up Sailfish sails to propel their boats.

Luke quit at 10:25 A.M. after about four and a half hours of raking. He was too tired to continue although he had the time to rake about another half an hour. He had had his fingers wrapped tightly on the handle much of the time since he started, and as he opened them slowly they pained him.

He then began "counting off"—putting the littlenecks into one basket, the cherrystones and chowders into another, then putting the filled baskets into bags approved by the state with his name and license number stamped in black on them. He would plant the littlenecks separately from the others on his leases at Swan Point. Luke finished with the counting at 11:25 A.M. His catch was 2,600 littlenecks (three and a half bushels) and two bushels of cherrystones and chowders mixed. There were also sixty-five seed, about an inch long, which he threw over. The state minimum size limit for the clams was one and a half inches, established about twenty years ago; before that, there was no minimum size. Luke sold the littlenecks for thirteen cents apiece, cherrystones for eight cents apiece, and chowders for six cents apiece, and thus with no losses from breakage, crab predation, and perhaps pilferage the catch would sell for about $350; with an anticipated 80 percent recovery he anticipated, they would sell for $280. Luke paid $1,000 a year to rent his slip at Brooks Marina and $600 a year to rent his slip at Swan Point. Besides gas to pay for, there was depreciation of his two boats, two outboard motors, his truck, and his rake. A state clamming license was fifty dollars, and a license for relaying clams, thirty dollars.

During 1991, the hard-clam rakers in Raritan Bay were doing well financially. Their major concern was whether the clams would remain abundant. Though the clams covered a relatively large area in southeastern Raritan Bay and most were littlenecks, large clam seed was not plentiful in the bed. Though small clam seed was plentiful, it was susceptible to predators.

A Trip on a Lobster Boat

On 14 October 1986, I went out on a Belford lobster boat whose crew had pots in the ocean about twelve miles southeast of Sandy Hook. The captain and owner of the boat was Norman Sickles, fifty-nine years old. He had fished for lobsters every year since he was sixteen, breaking in as a mate with his father. Norman was six feet three inches tall and had a wiry build. His face was ruddy from daily exposure to the sun and wind. When I had first approached him about going out, he was leery as he feared that I, being a government employee, would try to pass another law restricting lobstering further. After I assured him that I would cause no harm, he let me come. His mate was fifty-year-old Albert Thompson, who worked as a mate on Arthur Thorstensen's blue-crab boat during the winter and raked hard clams with Norman between seasons. He was from a large, old-time fishing family; his grandfather had opened oysters in Keyport before World War I, and his father, uncle, and cousin had done several types of fishing in the bay. Norman had hired a third man, George Fisler, in his early twenties, to help Albert fill bait bags and band claws. He was also from a large family of fishermen.

When I arrived at Norman's dock at 4:30 A.M., it was dark and Norman was there warming the engine of his boat and anxiously waiting for his crew. He was wearing a faded black shirt with long sleeves rolled up to his elbows, black pants, a pair of short boots, and a cap. Several minutes later, the headlights of two pickup trucks, one immediately behind the other, turned into Norman's property. Their beams bounced up and down as they headed toward his dock down the two-hundred-foot dirt road. Albert and George were the drivers. They opened Norman's refrigerator next to his dock, took out five boxes, each holding one hundred pounds of flounder frames, and put them on the boat along with a box of about three hundred empty bait bags.

We left the dock at 4:40 A.M. and headed down Compton's Creek, which was lined with boats on both sides. Three or four other lobster boats had their deck lights shining, engines running, their crews preparing to leave. One anguished voice was overheard in the darkness, saying, "I know you wanted me here earlier, Cap, and I'm sorry. My wife was supposed to get me up at three, but didn't; I'll have to get after her when I get home." We headed into the bay and, at first, went toward New York City, whose lights glowed pink and yellow above the black, irregular horizon; the sky was black everywhere else. The bay was calm and quiet; we could hear only the constant roar of our boat's engine. A beam of light from above the cabin illuminated the afterdeck, where Albert and George had begun filling the bait bags. They put three flounder frames in each bag. They emptied a box of flounder frames in thirteen minutes and filled about 250 bags in forty-five minutes.

Norman, who was steering, had aimed a searchlight on the water ahead to spot any floating logs or other objects that could damage his boat if he struck it. He told me that he did not like all the regulations connected with lobstering. In a serious tone, he said:

> There's no pencil-and-paper work in fishing; you take it as it comes. Lobsters're abundant today and they're gone tomorrow. That's the way it goes. That's one of the problems you have in fishing nowadays. You get new blood in the fishing business and they think that everything is cut and dried. The new guys figure: "If there aren't any lobsters, there's a reason why: either the fishermen are taking too many, or they're taking 'em too small." And they think everything is by formula. They figure: "If you cut down on the amount of small lobsters which the fishermen take, there'll be more big lobsters." But it don't work that way. It didn't work that way one hundred years ago and it won't work that way one hundred years from now. You can come up with all the management plans you want and you can burn up one hundred Apple computers compiling them, and when you get done, the Man upstairs decides how many lobsters there'll be! No formula will change that. If you stopped all the lobstermen from fishing there won't be any more lobsters!

Norman said that he was going to bring his pots ashore soon because catches had fallen and he anticipated much bad weather. One of his friends would keep going until Thanksgiving, but Norman believed that it would be too marginal. He said, "There is no set pattern to lobster abundance. This year, their numbers are tailing off in October. In other years, they have lasted through November. You can't set a clock by them."

Gradually, we turned eastward toward the tip of Sandy Hook and the ocean. Norman complained:

> Commercial fishermen are not welcome in this bay and ocean; this is a recreational area. If you're a commercial fisherman, you're a bastard. It's like the guy who cut my trawl line yesterday. It was unnecessary. He hooked it with his anchor; the easiest thing to do was to cut the line. It's too much trouble to put a trip line on the anchor about two fathoms long. All he'd have to do is pull the trip line and release the anchor from my line. It's easier to tie a knife on a gaff, reach overboard, and cut. It's tough if two "sports" cut the same line and you have a group of pots in the middle which you have to grapnel up. If the pots go in a bunch, they're difficult to find.

We arrived at the first pots as it was getting light, at about 6 A.M., almost an hour and a half from the dock. Norman left the wheel and went to a position on the starboard side of the boat at the front of the afterdeck. There, he handled a second steering wheel, throttle and gear shift, and the hydraulic hoist. He reached out with a boat hook for a buoy, brought it aboard, and put the pot line over the hydraulic hoist to wind it in. When a pot came to the side of the boat, Norman pulled it onto the rail, took its door off and set it on the pot, took out the old bait bag and emptied the fish bones remaining in it overboard, and pushed the pot toward Albert to his right, while putting the empty bait bag into a fish box. Albert took out the keeper lobsters and fish in the pot and put them in shallow boxes in the middle of the boat, tossed its two or three short lobsters and crabs overboard, put a fresh bait bag in the pot, and reinserted the door. Norman and Albert did these steps quickly; only fifteen seconds passed from the time the door came off until it was reinstalled. Then Albert carried the pot to a three-foot-wide deck on the port side where all twenty-five were to be lined up; the deck was level with the rail and extended along its full length. As he finished doing that, another pot broke the surface and the two repeated the steps. George measured and applied rubber bands to the claws of the lobsters; Albert had thought that a few large shorts might be keepers, but, after measuring them, George tossed them overboard. He put the keepers in plastic tubs holding about two bushels. The pots had trapped a few female lobsters carrying eggs and the crew released them. The eggs were a dull orange. Norman said that the females would still be carrying eggs the

73. *Norman Sickles hauling a pot aboard; Albert Thompson waiting to remove its lobsters. Photograph by author.*

next spring a short time before they hatched, but they would appear brown.

As soon as the last pot of the line was baited and stacked, they were immediately reset. Albert pushed over the first pot; then each of the others was pulled off one at a time by the line preceding it as the boat pulled away. Within a few minutes, they found the buoy of the next line and started lifting again. The crew lifted a line of twenty-five pots every fourteen minutes, and it lifted three lines an hour. Norman said that lobstermen have difficulty lifting their pots in rough weather because it takes much longer to get from one line of pots to the next. The boat cannot be run as fast because waves pounding against it could open cracks between the planks in its hull.

Around 10:30 A.M., another Belford lobsterman, who had been lifting pots about a mile away, came over and said that his engine was hot—he had rigged up a new gear incorrectly. Did Norman have some fresh water? Norman gave him four gallons he had in glass jugs stored below his deck. The other lobsterman emptied them into his engine and departed for Belford.

At 12:30 P.M., after lifting twelve lines (300 pots), we left the lobster grounds with about 180 pounds of lobsters. The average numbers of lobsters and crabs in each pot on this day were 0.6 keepers, 2.8 shorts, and 0.2 crabs. On one of the better pot lines, the number of keepers in each of the twenty-five pots was 0, 0, 0, 1, 2, 1, 1, 1, 2, 1, 1, 1, 2, 0, 0, 1, 0, 0, 1, 0, 2, 0, 1, 1, and, 1. The keepers all weighed about a pound, and measured just above the minimum legal size.

On the way, the crew opened their lunch boxes and ate sandwiches (meat and cheese on hard rolls) with some coffee. Norman said that he wanted to hire a man to clean the barnacles and other growth off the pots when he brought them ashore, so that he and Albert could go raking hard clams in the lobster boat.

We arrived at the dock in Compton's Creek at 1:50 P.M. Albert backed his truck to the boat and put on a tub of lobsters, about one hundred pounds, to take to a local seafood restaurant, which paid them a little more than wholesalers did. After he left, Norman backed up his truck and put on the remaining eighty pounds of lobsters. He said that he had to "hustle off" because he wanted to sell these lobsters to the Shoal Harbor Lobster Company in Belford and then go home so that he and his wife could play golf during the remainder of the afternoon.

―――――――――

Postscript: Following the 1986 season, Norman retired and sold his boat, pots, and dock lease to Albert, who intended to use the boat for lobstering, hard clamming, and crabbing. When Art Thorstensen, on whose blue-crab dredging boat Albert had been a mate for about fifteen years retired in 1987, he wanted Albert to have his crab dredges: "This way, I'll know they'll be fishin'."

A Trip on a Crab-Dredging Boat

To make firsthand observations of crab dredging, I went on a boat called the *Lovely* on 10 December 1985. The boat had been designed for pound-net fishing and was thirty-six feet long and ten feet wide, with smooth sides and a cabin in the bow; it was powered by a 671 Gray engine. Being relatively narrow, it could tow only three rather than the more typical four crab dredges.

Walt Thompsen, then sixty-three years old, ran the boat. He was born in Norway and came to Belford with his parents and brother, Art, in the 1920s. After graduating from high school in 1939, he dredged for blue crabs in the bay every year for forty-six years. Art, who had dredged crabs for forty-five years, had retired a year before. Their father had been a crabber and had taught his two boys how to do it, but they also sought advice about it from three or four other veterans. Other fishermen said that Walt was the best spotter among the crabbers; that is, he could find the sometimes narrow edges where crabs bedded down in the bay by

74. *Art Thorstensen, Walt Thompsen's brother, on his boat relaying a message to another crab boat while dredging for blue crabs in Raritan Bay. Photograph by author.*

using the thirty or so ranges on the shore better than anyone else. Jigs Apel, a retired fisherman of Belford, said:

> I went crabbing with Walt Thompsen for a season when we were both in our twenties. He was by far the best crabber in the bay. The only one close to him was his brother, Art. When the season began, we went all over the bay, mapping out where the crabs were. We would run into a good bunch, but he wouldn't stay there. He kept going. Some of those bunches covered an area only as big as my house. I said to myself, "What's he doing?" I wanted to remain there so we could make a good day's pay! I found out, however, that he was cataloging all those spots in his mind. Later on, when a spot of ours played out or the wind and tide were a certain way, he knew just where to go, while the other crabbers lost a day or two spotting for crabs. We wound up the season with way more money than anyone else! (Interview, 15 July 1990)

Walt's mate was Hank Brink, a fifty-four-year-old six-footer. He cautioned me that I would hear much cursing and complaining from them during the trip. Obviously, crab dredging in the winter was stressful for these two older men. Besides crabbing, Hank potted lobsters and dug hard clams in the warmer months. He said, "I like all the fishing I've tried, even hard clamming when I am catching clams good." Hank had a reputation in Belford for having the courage to "tell off" New Jersey state officials at every public fishery meeting he attended. He stood up at those meetings and delivered a short but loud derogatory speech, always ending with the statement "You're nothin' but a bunch of bureaucrats." He believed that most hardships felt by the commercial fishermen are a result of mismanagement by those officials. After every meeting, state officials politely informed Hank that they were trying as hard as they could to assist commercial fishermen, but Hank persisted with his speeches.

When Walt and Hank got aboard the *Lovely,* they told one another the news they had heard at home during the previous evening and expressed their opinions about it. To protect themselves from the water and wind, they each wore rubber knee boots, rubber pants, a rubber coat with a hood, a black wool stocking cap, and rubber gloves.

We left their dock at 7:10 A.M. and went into the bay. The wind blew only about ten knots out of the northwest, making small waves on the bay; the air temperature was in the mid-twenties, and the sky was a bright and clear blue. We headed for Flynn's Knoll, a shoal off the tip of Sandy Hook, where Walt believed that many crabs were bedded in along its soft, muddy southern edge, about twenty-five feet wide; the depth there drops off sharply from thirteen to at least thirty feet. It was one of his favorite spots. The top of the flat, sandy shoal consists of patches of mussels. On the way, Walt had high hopes for the season, saying, "We might do good this year. If the price is up and we hit the crabs right, we can do good in a hurry!" Concentrated in two areas about a half mile to the west were thirteen other crab boats, the only others on the bay.

At 7:52 A.M., they put one dredge over to try the edge Walt had located by lining up a buoy (always in the same place every year) with a structure on shore, references he had used perhaps hundreds of times in the past. After a tow lasting ten minutes, they retrieved the dredge. It had only two blue crabs. Nevertheless, they put over all three dredges and made a regular twenty-minute tow. This time, they had only about half a bushel of blue crabs. After three more tows, the total catch was only two bushels, so Walt decided to leave and try Chapel Hill Channel, where most of the other boats were dredging. "I know that the crabs are thick along that edge," he said with a grin, "but I couldn't quite get the dredges on 'em because the wind and tide are wrong. I'll be back after 'em another day."

On the way to the channel, he called to another crab boat on his

75. *Elmer Layton, a fisherman of Highlands, in his home listening to blue-crab fishermen converse on the water. Photograph by author.*

radio and chatted briefly. Then he said, "You have to be careful what you say on the radio. There aren't many crabbers out here today; the others are home listening to us on their ship-to-shore radios. If I tell another boat that we are making a big catch, they'll all be out here tomorrow and give us competition. We stay out here and keep going even when the crabs are scarce, because we never know when a quantity will come in from the ocean and we like to get a few big catches ourselves before a big fleet lands on 'em and makes 'em scarce again."

The two fishermen also dipped into their lunches on the way. Walt ate some steaming beef stew from a thermos bottle and Hank had a thick hamburger sandwich. Both drank from quart-size thermoses of coffee. By now, the cold wind was making their noses drip, and they wiped them periodically.

They began dredging in Chapel Hill Channel and got more crabs per tow than at Flynn's Knoll. This area also had more "trash" than Flynn's Knoll had. Dredge hauls from both bottoms brought in some shells of hard clams and mussels, lady crabs, rock crabs, spider crabs, horseshoe crabs, and windowpane flounders (so-called because its body is so thin that light can be seen through it when fishermen hold it up to the sky). In the channel they also had ten to twenty soda and beer cans, and bottles and fishing line in almost every tow, proof that it was a good sport-fishing area in the summer. Whenever Hank shoveled over material after each tow and some floated in the *Lovely*'s trail, a group of eight to ten laughing gulls noisily checked it over. Occasionally, one found a rock crab or small winter flounder and flew off with it in its beak.

When the dredges had relatively few crabs at Flynn's Knoll, Hank picked them at a slow pace, and he continued picking slowly in the channel. Walt got angry at this and told him in a stern voice that he would have to hurry up, because he would not be finished picking by the time the next dredges were dumped. Hank did not reply, but he increased his pace and had them all picked in time. About half an hour later, Hank took the wheel briefly to relieve Walt. When Walt went to the stern to pump water out of the hold, Hank leaned toward me and whispered that he did not mind Walt's getting mad at him, because "he's old."

As the day wore on, the wind increased from the northwest and made the bay choppy. The crabbers had to remain alert and think about quitting for the day, because the dredges could swing as they were lifted out of the water suspended under the boat's boom. A large roll of the boat could bring a dredge crashing into a man's body and knock him dangerously backward onto the other rail.

During the day, Walt and Hank made ten full tows. Dredge tows were twenty to twenty-two minutes long. It took about three minutes to winch in each dredge, and after the third was dumped, it took them about four additional minutes to get the boat back on the range and push the dredges overboard. The total time to complete a tow was thirty-three to thirty-five minutes. The number of crabs in a dredge ranged from nine to forty-nine and averaged twenty-two. Widths of the females averaged six inches; the males averaged six and a half inches; none of the females carried eggs. Walt and Hank had their last dredge aboard and dumped at 3:18 P.M. The catch totaled fourteen bushels, and, at $25 a bushel, it would gross them $350.

On the way back to Belford, Walt said that crabbers and other types of fishermen have problems they never used to have, involving restrictions and pollution:

> You can't blame us for complaining about all the laws, because we've been in the business for many years, we know what we are doing and we are honest. Everything is so regulated that it is almost not worth the effort to go commercial fishing. Just last year, Richmond County prohibited us from dredging crabs in its waters. We always could before. We used to go over there, especially when the wind was blowing hard from the northwest; the water was calm while it was rough in New

Jersey. Now we can't go crabbing during northwesters and lose many more days of work.

We arrived at the dock at about 4 P.M. Several minutes later, a truck from a Belford fish wholesaler backed down to the *Lovely* to pick up the crabs. Meanwhile, another crabber, who had to remain in port that day to repair the fuel pump on his boat, came over to see how many crabs Walt and Hank had caught.

Epilogue

Protecting the Bay, the Ports, and the Fisheries

Several federal and state agencies and public interest groups attempt to protect the habitats of Raritan Bay and other coastal bays and estuaries in the northeastern United States from various types of development projects that could damage them. The agencies include the National Marine Fisheries Service (NMFS) of the National Oceanic and Atmospheric Administration (NOAA); U.S. Environmental Protection Agency (EPA); U.S. Fish and Wildlife Service, U.S. Army Corps of Engineers (COE); New York and New Jersey Departments of Environmental Protection/Conservation; the American Littoral Society; and the Natural Resources Protective Association of Staten Island. By protecting habitats, they are generally protecting commercial and sport fisheries.

Government Programs

The National Marine Fisheries Service's Habitat Conservation Branch (HCB), which has a component at the NMFS's Sandy Hook Laboratory, has the responsibility to review and comment on proposals for development that might affect the spawning, nursery, and feeding habitats of fish in Raritan Bay and other local waters. Usually, the HCB recommends that proposals that will modify shallow nursery areas be denied, or changed to minimize effects. It also recommends that maintenance dredging of channels be done only during noncritical periods when fish and shellfish are not spawning and juvenile fish are not using the nurseries.

A project developer must apply for a permit from the state of New York or New Jersey and from the COE. The COE then issues a public notice, which enables the public to comment on the project. Biologists of federal agencies such as the HCB, the Fish and Wildlife Service, and the Environmental Protection Agency also review the permit application. They estimate the impact it would have on the environment and fisheries and send in their recommendations whether to approve, modify, or deny the permit. The COE considers a long list of items in making a decision about whether the public interest would be served by approving the project. The list includes: conservation, economics, aesthetics, general environmental concerns, wetlands, cultural values, fish and wildlife values, flood hazards, flood plain values, land use, navigation, shoreline erosion, recreation, water supply, energy needs, safety, food production, and, in general, the needs and welfare of people. Usually the COE follows the recommendations of the biologists and denies permits that will result in substantial damage to habitats.

If a large project is involved, the COE may be required to prepare an environmental impact statement, which follows the guidelines of the National Environmental Policy Act. This statement evaluates the project in detail, weighing its benefits versus its impacts, and then the COE makes a decision about whether to allow the project to be implemented.

Another type of environmental protection program is NOAA's "mussel watch," established in 1984. Once a year, mussels from 150 sites nationwide are analyzed for contaminant loads. Mussels were selected for analysis because they are sessile and store contaminants from the water. The mussels are examined for abnormalities as well as for contaminants. Three sites where mussels are present in the Hudson/Raritan system—the Hudson River, upper Raritan Bay, and lower Raritan Bay—are sampled. Two additional sites along the northern New Jersey coast in the New York Bight apex, both influenced by the outflow from the Hudson/Raritan estuary, are also sampled. The program examines sediments and bottom fish, too. Results from 1986–1988 combined collections showed that the concentrations of some pesticides, mercury, and copper in mussels from the Hudson/Raritan Estuary were the highest in the northeastern United States (NOAA Technical Memorandum NOS OMA 49 1989). If the contaminant load in mussels were to increase, presumably an investigation would be undertaken to find the cause, and actions to halt further increases would follow.

In 1988 New York Harbor, including Raritan Bay, was designated as part of the EPA's National Estuary Program. The goal of the program is to establish and maintain healthy, productive ecosystems. Through management, research, and public involvement, the program attempts to analyze the effects of pollution and preserve and restore ecologically important habitats, if possible, and manage and balance the competing uses of the estuary to improve environmental quality.

The likelihood of reducing pollution generally in the bay seems remote. Installing pretreatment units in factories would prevent the discharges of most heavy metal and other toxicants into the bay. Few units have been built, however, and since pretreatment is somewhat costly, politicians might be fearful that new firms would not want to establish businesses in the drainage basins of the bay and instead go somewhere else where such overhead costs are lower. Thus some politicians might be biased against legislation to require the installation of pretreatment units. The heavy metals already in the bay would decline extremely slowly even if future discharges were halted, because most are bound onto sediment particles.

Controlling bacterial pollution and eutrophication would also be difficult. Since much of the drainage area is paved over, large amounts of rainwater cannot drain into the soil where it would be naturally filtered and its nutrients used by land vegetation. Instead, it runs off streets and other paved surfaces where it collects additional wastes, including fecal coliform bacteria mainly from nonhuman sources, and flows into sewerage lines. Sewerage plants cannot handle the combined volume of sewage and rainwater when rainfall exceeds about an inch in twenty-four hours, and some untreated, unchlorinated sewage passes directly into streams, rivers, and then Raritan Bay. Pollution from these nonpoint sources is a major contributor to high bacterial concentrations in bay water and shellfish. Technically, this pollution could be controlled, but the cost would be high. Large reservoirs to collect the rainwater would have to be constructed and the excess water held in them for treatment during dry periods when sewerage plants could handle it.

In recent years, the amount of phosphate, one of the causes of eutrophication of the bay, has been reduced because less is used in soaps and detergents, but nitrates, another cause, remain highly elevated. To reduce nitrates substantially, sewerage plants would have to upgrade their treatment to the tertiary (treatment removes dissolved solids and nearly all metals and organics) from the secondary (treatment removes about 90 percent of solids, metals, and organics) level, a procedure that is too expensive now. Abundances of eelgrass, sea lettuce, and some species of microscopic algae would increase if eutrophication could be reduced.

In the 1980s some effects of government actions to control pollution in the bay were evident. For example, large oil slicks were seen rarely because after the early 1960s oil spillages decreased sharply. The water was a little clearer, too. On the other hand, plastic materials on shores, drifting, and on the bottom were widespread.

Protecting the Commercial Ports

Can the ports of Compton's Creek, Belford, and Highlands be saved for commercial fishing? Probably Compton's Creek can. Since Spy House Harbor will be constructed across a road from the fishing port, the two will contrast sharply in appearance unless the port is improved. In 1991 the fishermen's cooperative constructed an attractive building 165 feet long and 75 feet wide and removed its old, unattractive facility. If sheds over the trailers and freezers were constructed, the rutted roads and parking lots paved, and the discarded material and swamp grass removed, the port could take on the appearance of a New England fishing village and be compatible with the development. The commercial facilities in Highlands have been shrinking. Those that remain need tax relief or help from the state of New Jersey to survive.

Protecting the Fish Stocks and Fisheries

Fred Serchuk and Ron Smolowitz, fishery biologists with the Northeast Fisheries Center, National Marine Fisheries Service, at Woods Hole, Massachusetts, believe that fishing effort on the continental shelf off the East Coast of the United States should be sharply reduced to allow fish stocks to recover. In the future, they believe, finite supplies of fuel will require the reintroduction and expansion of more passive fishing techniques, such as hand lining. Such techniques are energy efficient and relatively nonpolluting. They feel that the greatest challenge management faces in the future is guiding and choosing appropriate technology to promote maximum resource utilization on a sustainable basis. Another means of controlling effort would be to limit the number of vessels in the fleet while permitting them to use modern gear (Serchuk and Smolowitz 1990).

Many sport fishermen also believe that the quantity of fish commercial fishermen take should be curtailed so that more fish would remain for them. In fact, the Sport Fishing Institute, founded in 1949, suggests that serious consideration should be given to having the sale of "wild stock" marine fish banned. Fish would be provided for the nation's needs by expanding the culture of them in farms. The Institute cited the example of beef. People once shot buffalo, deer, turkeys, and waterfowl to sell them as food. Later, the beef industry provided an alternate source of meat by farming cattle, and in the late 1800s and early 1900s the market hunting of the wild animals was banned. A statement by Norville Prosser, vice president of the institute, suggested that a commercial fishery could be curtailed or banned when an alternate source of employment was available for the fishermen (Bryant 1989).

The Institute's idea can not yet be carried out, however, because aquaculture cannot provide a sufficient supply of fish to meet the increasing demand for it in the United States as the beef industry did with meat. The space available to practice aquaculture is too limited. Moreover, fish so produced might be more expensive. Commercial fishermen are adamantly opposed to the idea because they wish to retain their independent working lives.

In 1991 state and federal agencies began to draft regulations to reduce the sizes of the catches of recreational and commercial fishermen, however. It appears as though fish populations are going to be subjected to the same conservation measures that game mammals and birds have been since the turn of the century (*New York Times,* 4 August 1991).

Federal, state, and university biologists and chemists could aid bay fisheries by conducting studies to determine the environmental factors that control abundances of commercial and related species, especially the young stages of those that use the bay as a nursery. Besides fish, these include hard clams, soft clams, lobsters, blue crabs, and various worms. Eelgrass and sea lettuce also need study. If biologists could show that specific pollutants or some type of construction were harming any of these species, perhaps their effects could be lessened with wise management and more animals and plants would survive. The knowledge required for implementing such management has been lacking in the past.

The bay's commercial fisheries have always been laissez-faire, functioning with little government help. Fishermen, being independent people with disparate ideas, never could generate political power to help them slow the inroads of other interests using the bay and adversely affecting them. If, since the early 1900s, there had existed a public agency that had as one of its goals protection of fishermen's interests, it might have been able to postpone pollution of the oyster and clam beds and reduce some other negative impacts. The fisheries remaining could benefit from such protection and support, while retaining independence for the fishermen. For example, the fishermen of Belford need help to improve the appearance of their port and to guarantee that docking sites for all their boats and landing sites for their fish will be maintained.

Commercial fishermen feel suffocated by a combination of declining numbers of fish, shrinking docking sites, and increasing governmental restrictions. But as long as sufficient numbers of fish and shellfish are available to take, many of these fishermen will be able to earn a living on Raritan Bay, pursuing their long tradition. The bay will also continue as a popular sport-fishing area. To ensure this, we must take the steps to take better care of Raritan Bay, its fish and shellfish, and its fisheries, if only so that they will provide for us.

References Cited

Ahrenholz, D. H., W. R. Nelson, and S. P. Epperly. 1987. Population and fishery characteristics of Atlantic menhaden, *Brevoortia tyrannus*. *Fish. Bull.*, U. S. 85(3):569–600.

Akerly, S. 1843. Agriculture of Richmond County. *In: Trans. N.Y. State Agric. Soc.* 1842. Vol. 2. Albany, N.Y. 188–214.

An atlas of the biological resources of the Hudson Estuary. 1977. Yonkers, N.Y.: Prepared by the Estuarine Study Group/The Boyce Thompson Institute for Plant Research, Inc.

Azarovitz, T. R. 1982. Winter flounder *Pseudopleuronectes americanus*. *In:* Fish distribution, ed. M. D. Grosslein and T. R. Azarovitz. *MESA New York Bight Atlas Monograph* 15. Albany, N.Y.: New York Sea Grant Institute. 119–122.

Barrett, P. 1985. Fishing for fun and profit. *In:* Fish and bricks. Plans, processes and problems of the Lower Hudson and Raritan Estuary, ed. A. L. Pacheco. Proc. Walford Mem. Conv., Highlands, N.J.: Sandy Hook Laboratory. *Tech. Ser. Rep.* No. 85–05:87–91.

Bean, T. H. 1897. Notes upon New York fishes received at the New York aquarium, 1895 to 1897. *Second Annual Report of the Commissioners of Fisheries, Game and Forests of the State of New York.* New York and Albany: Wynkoop Hallenbeck Crawford Co., Printers. 207–251.

Beck, H. C. 1984. *Forgotten towns of southern New Jersey.* New Brunswick, N.J.: Rutgers University Press.

Bennett, D. W. 1984. The Raritan: a big bad bay in need of friends. *In:* Raritan Bay its multiple uses and abuses, ed. A. L. Pacheco. Highlands, N.J.: Sandy Hook Laboratory. *Tech. Ser. Rep.* 30:1–6.

Bigelow, H. B., and W. C. Schroeder. 1953. Fishes of the Gulf of Mexico. *Fish. Bull.*, U. S. 74(53):1–577.

Bokuneiwicz, H. 1988. A brief summary of the geology of Raritan Bay. *In:*

Hudson/Raritan Estuary: Issues, resources, status, and management. *Proc. of seminar held February 17, 1987.* Washington, D.C. 45–57.

Botton, M. L., and J. W. Ropes. 1987. Populations of horseshoe crabs, Limulus polyphemus, on the northwestern Atlantic continental shelf. *Fish. Bull.* 85(4):805–812.

Bryant, N. 1989. Guidelines for marine species. Outdoors column in *New York Times.* May 14, 1988.

Burns, T. S. 1982. Northern lobster Homarus americanus. *In:* Fish distribution. *MESA New York Bight Atlas Monograph 15.* Albany, N.Y.: New York Sea Grant Institute. 122–125.

Caruso, L. A. 1982. New Jersey's commercial fishing industry. *N.J. Dept. Environ. Protection., Div. Fish, Game, and Wildl., Mar. Fish. Admin., Bur. Mar. Fish., Tech. Series* 82–2:1–70.

DeKay, J. E. 1842. Fishes. Part 4. *Zoology of New York, or the New York fauna; comprising detailed descriptions of all the animals hitherto observed within the state of New York.* Albany, N.Y.: W. A. White and J. Fischer

Edwards, R. L., and A. S. Merrill. 1977. A reconstruction of the continental shelf areas of Eastern North America for the times 9,500 B.P. and 12,500 B.P. *Archaeology of Eastern North America.* 5:1–44.

Emmons, W. H. 1907. Weakfishing around Staten Island. *Field and Stream.* June: 141–143.

Environmental impact statement on the Hudson River PCB reclamation demonstration project. 1981. U.S.E.P.A., Region II, 26 Federal Plaza, New York. 1–198 and Appendices.

Esser, S. 1982. Long-term changes in some finfisheries of the Hudson-Raritan Estuary. *In: Ecological stress and the New York Bight: science and management,* ed. G. F. Meyer. Columbia, S.C.: Estuarine Research Federation. 299–314.

Fahay, M. 1978. Biological and fisheries data on American eel, Anguilla rostrata (LeSueur). Northeast Fisheries Center. National Marine Fisheries Service. Highlands, N.J.: Sandy Hook Laboratory. *Tech. Ser. Rept.* 17.

First Annual Report of the Commissioners of Fisheries, Game and Forests, New York, 1896. Albany, N.Y.: J. B. Lyon, printers.

Frye, J. 1978. *The men all singing.* Virginia Beach, Va.: The Downing Co.

Galtsoff, P. S. 1964. The American oyster Crassostrea virginica Gmelin. *Fish. Bull., U.S.* 64:480.

Goode, G. B. 1880. *A history of the menhaden.* Orange Judd Company, New York.

Goode, G. B., and A. H. Clarke. 1887. The menhaden fishery. Part 5. *In: The fisheries and fishery industries of the United States,* ed. G. B. Goode. Section V. *History and methods of the fisheries.* Washington, D.C.: U.S. Government Printing Office. 327–415.

Gordon, T. F. 1973. *Gazetteer of the state of New Jersey.* Polyanthos. Cottonport, La.

Guthorn, P. J. 1982. *The Sea Bright skiff and other shore boats.* Exton, Pa.: Schiffer Publishing Co.

Hall, A. 1894. Notes on the oyster industry of New Jersey. *Article 5—*

Extracted from the report of the U.S. Commission of Fish and Fisheries for 1892. Washington, D.C.: U.S. Government Printing Office. 463–528.

Ingersoll, E. 1881. The oyster-industry. *In: The history and present condition of the fishery industries,* ed. G. B. Goode. Washington, D.C.: U.S. Government Printing Office.

Ingersoll, E. 1887. The oyster, scallop, clam, mussel, and abalone industries. *In: The fisheries and fishery industry of the United States,* ed. G. B. Goode. Vol. 2. Washington, D.C.: U.S. Government Printing Office. 507–622.

Jeffries, H. P. 1962. Environmental characteristics of Raritan Bay, a polluted estuary. *Limnol. Oceanogr.* 7:21–31.

Joline, B. J. 1950. Tottenville in retrospect. Unpublished manuscript. Library, Richmondtown Restoration, Staten Island, N.Y.

Kalm, P. 1937. *Peter Kalm's travels in North America: the English version of 1770.* Vol. 1. New York: Dover Publications.

Ketchum, B. H. 1951. The flushing of tidal estuaries. *Sewage and Industrial Wastes.* 23:198–208.

Kobbe, G. 1982. *New Jersey coast and pines.* Reprint of 1889 edition. P.O. Box 352. New York.: Walker News, Inc.

Kraft, H. C. 1977. The paleo-Indian sites at Port Mobil, Staten Island. *Current perspectives in northeastern archaeology.* 17:1–19.

Kraft, H. C. 1987. *The Lenape.* Coll. of the New Jersey Historical Society Ser. Vol. 21.

Leavens, J. 1986. Up-island catboats. *The Dukes County Intelligencer.* Edgartown, Mass. 27(3): 99–123.

Leonard, T. H. 1923. From Indian trail to electric rail. *The Highlands* (N.J.) *Journal.*

Lockwood, S. 1883. The American oyster: its natural history·and the oyster industry of New Jersey. *Part of the Vth Ann. Rept. Bur. of Statistics of Labor and Industries of the State of New Jersey.* 219–350.

MacKenzie, C. L., Jr. 1970. Feeding rates of starfish, Asterias forbesi (Desor), at controlled water temperatures and during different seasons of the year. Fish. Bull., U.S. 86:67–72.

MacKenzie, C. L., Jr. 1984. A history of oystering in Raritan Bay, with environmental observations. *In: Raritan Bay its multiple uses and abuses,* ed. A. L. Pacheco. Highlands, N.J.: Sandy Hook Laboratory. *Tech. Ser. Rept.* 30:37–66.

Marine paints seventy two years. 1925. *Power boating.* December. 61.

Mather, F. 1887. New York and its fisheries. *In: The fisheries and fishery industries of the United States,* ed. G. B. Goode. Section 2. A geographical review of the fisheries industries and fishing communities for the year 1880. U.S. Comm. of Fish and Fisheries. Washington, D.C.: U.S. Government Printing Office. 341–377.

Mayo, R. K. 1982. Alewife *Alosa pseudoharengus. In: Fish distribution,* ed. M. D. Grosslein and T. R. Azarovitz. *MESA New York Bight Atlas Monograph* 15. Albany, N.Y.: New York Sea Grant Institute. 57–58.

McCay, B. J. 1981. Optimal foragers or political actors? Ecological analyses of a New Jersey fishery. *Amer. Ethnol.* 8(2):356–382.

————. 1984. The pirates of piscary: ethnohistory of illegal fishing in New Jersey. *Ethnohistory* 31(1):17–37.

McHugh, J. L 1990. Fishery management in the New York Bight: experience under the Magnuson Act. *Fish. Res.* 8:205–221.

Miller, A. P. 1971. Legend in the making: Yankee inventiveness. *In: The inventive Americans,* ed. R. L. Breeden. Washington, D.C.: The Nat. Geogr. Soc.

Morse, W. W. 1978. Biological and fisheries data on scup, Stenotomus chrysops (Linneaus). Northeast Fisheries Center, National Marine Fisheries Service, Highlands, N.J.: Sandy Hook Laboratory. *Tech. Series Rept.* No. 21. 49 pp.

Murawski, S. A., and A. L. Pacheco. 1977. Biological and fisheries data on Atlantic sturgeon, *Acipenser oxyrhynchus* (Mitchill). Northeast Fisheries Center. National Marine Fisheries Service. Highlands, N. J.: Sandy Hook Laboratory. *Tech. Ser. Rept.* No. 10.

Murphy, M. H. n.d. Unpublished manuscript in twenty-seven chapters, chronicling the life memories of the author. Manuscript in custody of Barbara Eigenrauch, Red Bank, N.J.

Olsen, C. R., I. L. Larsen, R. H. Brewster, N. H. Cutsell, R. F. Bopp, and H. J. Simpson. 1984. A geological assessment of sedimentation and distributions in the Hudson-Raritan Estuary. *NOAA Tech. Rep.* NOS OMS 2:1–101.

Pacheco, A. L., and L. Despres-Patanjo. 1982. American shad, *Alosa sapidissima. In: Fish distribution,* ed. M. D. Grosslein, and T. R. Azarovitz. *Mesa New York Bight Atlas Monograph* 15. Albany, N.Y.: New York Sea Grant Institute, 59–61.

Pearce, J. B. 1979. Raritan Bay—a highly polluted estuarine system. *ICES, Marine Environmental Quality Comm., C.M.* 1979/E: 45:1–16.

————. 1984. Concluding remarks. *In: Raritan Bay its multiple uses and abuses,* ed. A. L. Pacheco. Highlands, N.J.: Sandy Hook Laboratory. *Tech. Ser. Rept.* 30:91–94.

Pearson, J. C. 1972. *The fish and fisheries of Colonial America. A documentary history of fishery resources of the United States and Canada.* Part 3. The Middle Atlantic States. Washington, D.C.: U.S. Fish Wildl. Serv. 679–1099.

Pepper, A. 1971. *The glass gaffers of New Jersey and their creations from 1739 to the present.* New York: Charles Scribner's Sons.

Powell, H. 1975. Wolfe's Pond. Typescript in archives of Staten Island Institute of Arts and Sciences, St. George, Staten Island, N.Y.

————. 1976. Prince's Bay, Lemon Creek and the oyster industry. Unpublished manuscript. Staten Island Institute of Arts and Sciences, St George, Staten Island, N.Y.

Powell, H., to C. L. MacKenzie, Jr. 3 December 1990. Staten Island Institute of Arts and Sciences, St. George, Staten Island, N.Y.

Rabl, S. S. 1947. *Boatbuilding in your own backyard.* Cambridge, Md.: Cornell Maritime Press.

Rathbun, R. 1887. The crab, lobster, crayfish, rock-lobster, shrimp, and prawn fisheries. Part 21. *In: The fisheries and fishery industries of the United States,* ed. G. B. Goode. Vol. 2. Washington, D.C.: Government Printing Office. 629–810.

Reintjes, J. W. 1982. Atlantic menhaden *Brevoortia tyrannus. In: Fish distribution,* ed. M. B. Grosslein and T. R. Azarovitz. *MESA New York Bight Atlas Monograph* 15. Albany, N.Y. New York Sea Grant Institute. 61–63.

Report of the shellfish commission. 1897. *Second annual report of the commissioners of fisheries, game and forests of the State of New York.* New York and Albany: Wynkoop Hollenbeck Crawford Co., Printers.

———. 1901. *Sixth annual report of the forest, fish and game commission of the State of New York.* Albany, N.Y.: J. B. Lyon, Printers.

Report of the superintendent of shellfisheries. 1905. *Ninth report of the forest, fish and game commission.* Albany, N.Y.: J. B. Lyon, Printers.

———. 1907. *Eleventh annual report of the forest, fish and game commission.* Albany, N.Y.: J. B. Lyon, Printers.

Report of the superintendent of marine fisheries. 1911. *Fifteenth annual report of the forest, fish and game commission.* Albany, N.Y.: J. B. Lyon, Printers.

Ritchie, W. A. 1969. *The archeology of New York State.* 2nd rev. ed. Garden City, N.Y.: Natural History Press.

Ronnberg, A. R., Jr. 1980. The coppering of 19th century American merchant sailing ships; some historical background with notes for modelmakers. *Nautical Research Journal.* 28(2):125–148.

Serchuk, F. M., and R. J. Smolowitz. 1990. Ensuring fisheries management dysfunction: the neglect of science and technology. *Fisheries* 15(2):4–7.

Sim, R. J. 1975. *Pages from the past of rural New Jersey.* Trenton, N.J.: New Jersey Agricultural society. 121 pp.

Smith, H. M. 1892. Economic and natural history notes on fishes of the northern coast of New Jersey. *Bull. U.S. Fish Comm.* 12:365–380.

———. 1894. The fyke nets and fyke-net fisheries of the United States, with notes on the fyke nets of other countries. *Bull. U.S. Fish Comm.* [for 1892] 12:299–355.

Smith, T. P., D. W. Lipton, and V. J. Norton. 1983. Quarterly report No. 3-Hudson/Raritan Estuary Project (HREP): Partitioning of national survey of recreational fishing statistics. Unpublished manuscript. College Park: University of Maryland Dept. of Agricultural and Resource Economics. 1–32.

Smith, W. G., and J. J. Norcross. 1968. The status of the scup (*Stenotomus chrysops*) in winter trawl fishery. *Ches. Sci.* 9(4):207–216.

Smolowitz, R. J., and F. M. Serchuk. 1988. Marine fisheries technology in the United States: status, trends and future directions. *In: Proceedings of Oceans '88: A partnership of marine interests.* The Institute of Electrical and Electronic Engineers. 975–979.

Squires, D. F. 1981. *The bight of the big apple.* The New York Sea Grant Institute of the State University of New York and Cornell University. Albany, N.Y.: NYSG-RS-81–00.

Stanford, H. M., and D. R. Young. 1988. Pollutant loadings to the New York Bight Apex. *Oceans '88 Proceedings.* Baltimore, Md. 2:745–751.

Stanzeski, A. 1981. Quahog shell tools. *Bull. Archeolog. Soc. New Jersey.* 110:15–18.

State of New York. Fisheries, game and forest law. 1896. *First annual report*

of the commissioners of fisheries, game and forests of the State of New York.
New York and Albany: Wynkoop Hallenbeck Crawford Co., Printers.

Stevenson, C. H. 1898. The shad fisheries of the Atlantic coast of the United
States. Report of the commissioner for the year ending June 30, 1898. Part 24.
U.S. Commission of Fish and Fisheries. Washington, D.C.: U.S. Government
Printing Office. 101–269.

Talbot, G. B. 1954. Factors associated with fluctuations in abundance of
Hudson River shad. *Fish. Bull.,* U.S. 56:373–413.

Townsend, C. H. 1896. 3.—The transplanting of eastern oysters to Willapa
Bay, Washington, with notes on the native oyster industry. U.S. Commission of
fish and Fisheries. Washington, D.C.: Government Printing Office. Part 21. 193–
202.

True, F. W. 1887. The pound-net fisheries of the Atlantic States. *In: The
Fisheries and Fishery Industry of the United States,* ed. G. B. Goode. Washington,
D.C.: U.S. Government Printing Office. 595–609.

U.S. Government Fishery Landings Statistics, published by the U.S. Government Printing Office. Washington, D.C. (On file at Sandy Hook Laboratory,
Northeast Fisheries Center, Highlands, N.J.)

Walburg, C. H., and P. R. Nichols. 1967. Biology and management of the
American shad and status of the fisheries, Atlantic coast of the United States,
1960. U.S. Dep. Int., Fish Wildl. Serv. *Spec. Sci. Rep.* 550:1–105.

Waldhauer, R., A. Matte, and R. E. Tucker. 1978. Lead and copper in the
waters of Raritan and Lower New York Bays. *Mar. Poll. Bull.* 9(2):38–42.

Walsh, M. 1982. *The rise of the Midwestern meat packing industry.* Lex-
ington: The University Press of Kentucky.

Wilk, S. J. 1977. Biological and fisheries data on bluefish *Pomatomus
saltatrix (Linneaus).* National Marine Fisheries Service. Highlands, N.J.: Sandy
Hook Laboratory. *Tech. Ser. Rep.* 11.

Wilk, S. J. 1979. Biological and fisheries data on weakfish, *Cynosion regalis*
(Black and Schneider). National Marine Fisheries Service. Highlands, N.J.: Sandy
Hook Laboratory. *Tech. Ser. Rep.* 21.

Wood, F. S. 1906. Shellfish culture in New York State. *Eleventh annual
report of the forest, fish and game commission.* Albany, N.Y.: Brandow Printing
Company.

Zeisel, W. 1988. *A history of recreational fishing on the Hudson River from
colonial times to 1920.* Final report to the Hudson River Foundation. Grant No.
025/85B/037. New York: The Institute for Research in History.

Ziskowski, J., and R. A. Murchelano. 1975. Fin erosion in winter flounder.
Mar. Poll. Bull. 6(2):26–29.

List of Interviews

All with author unless otherwise noted.

Adubato, Joe and Bea. Belford, N.J., 1 May 1987.
Anthropolis, Cris. Highlands, N.J., 27 March 1988, 21 July 1990.
Apel, Jigs. Belford, N.J., 11 March 1986, 21 October 1987, 5 November 1987, 19 September 1988, 18 April 1989, 21 August 1989, 1 March 1990, 12 July 1991.
Boyce, Jack. Belford, N.J., 1 November 1985.
Braun, Bill. Keansburg, N.J., 12 December 1986, 17 December 1986.
Cottrell, Lloyd. Highlands, N.J., 16 September 1988, 14 July 1989, 5 August 1989, 9 September 1989.
Cottrell, Stanley. Waretown, N.J., 26 March 1986, 12 May 1988.
Crosby, Leona. East Keansburg, N.J., 18 May 1987.
Cubbage, Mary G. Middletown, N.J., 4 February 1987.
Cunningham, Elvira. Tottenville, Staten Island, N.Y., 26 September 1989.
Decker, William. Rossville, Staten Island, N.Y., 15 December 1985.
Defonzo, Lou. Belford, N.J., 27 July 1991.
DeGrote, Walt. Port Monmouth, N.J., 4 August 1989, 14 August 1989, 7 January 1991, 1 May 1991.
Demlin, Mary. Keyport, N.J., 18 November 1985.
Egnatovich, Louie. East Keansburg, N.J., 14 February 1986, 27 February 1986, 20 March 1986, 14 April 1986, 8 March 1989, 9 March 1990, 7 August 1991.
Fisler, Ed, Jr. Belford, N.J., 28 January 1989.
Fisler, John. Belford, N.J., 3 November 1987, 4 December 1987, 15 January 1988, 22 August 1988, 20 October 1988.
Glass, Arthur Compton. Belford, N.J., July 24, 1977. Recorded by Kenneth Norton, New Monmouth, N.J.
Glass, Euretta Compton. Middletown, N.J., 16 July 1987.

Glismann, Pete. Prince's Bay, Staten Island, N.Y., 10 April 1986, 18 June 1987.
Hopkins, Stockton. Matawan, N.J., 19 November 1988.
Huylar, Wilbur. Keyport, N.J., 9 July 1986, 18 October 1986, 9 October 1987, 19 September 1988, 11 September 1989, 31 October 1990.
Irwin, Joe. Red Bank, N.J., 8 May 1987.
Jeandron, Jack and Angel. Keyport, N.J., 23 October 1987.
Jenks, Bill. Bricktown, N.J., 12 February 1991, 1 March 1991, 26 March 1991, 20 June 1991.
Johnson, Fred. Belford, N.J., 25 April 1986, 1 October 1989.
Kaplinger, Jim. Highlands, N.J., 1 November 1985, 21 October 1986, 26 April 1987.
Kaveleski, George. Leonardo, N.J., 15 October 1991.
Kendrick, Bill and Margaret. Highlands, N.J., 1 October 1985, 8 October 1985, 18 October 1985, 18 March 1986, 8 May 1986, 16 May 1986, 22 April 1987, 25 April 1987, 9 May 1987, 27 October 1987.
Kenzia, Ted. Belford, N.J., 23 March 1986.
Kohlenbusch, Cris. Highlands, N.J., 16 June 1986, 14 July 1986, 9 August 1988, 11 September 1989, 20 January 1990, 11 January 1991.
Layton, Elmer. Highlands, N.J., 15 December 1985, 18 April 1986, 22 April 1986, 16 May 1986, 24 April 1987.
Martin, Betty. Holmdel, N.J., 19 November 1987.
Matthews, Mrs. Chester. Keyport, N.J., 1 December 1987.
Moody, Harold. Rossville, N.J., 15 December 1985.
Morrell, Bill. Belford, N.J., 10 November 1987, 26 January 1988.
Morris, Anna. Prince's Bay, N.J., 18 June 1987.
Mount, Johnny. Highlands, N.J., 29 November 1988, 13 December 1988, 6 January 1989, 19 July 1989, 13 September 1989, 25 January 1990, 25 March 1991, 22 July 1991, 28 July, 1991.
Myers, Clara. Middletown, N.J., 26 September 1988.
Nelson, J. Richards. Madison, Ct., 10 March 1985.
Nelson, Lester. Middletown, N.J., 2 March 1990.
Norton, Ken. New Monmouth, N.J., 6 November 1985, 14 November 1985, 24 March 1986, 19 June 1987, 14 September 1987, 29 January 1988, 9 February 1988, 22 February 1988.
Parker, Mr. and Mrs. Irving. Highlands, N.J., 15 May 1986, 25 April 1987, 9 May 1987, 7 February 1988, 24 June 1988, 5 August 1988, 22 July 1989, 9 September 1989.
Pedersen, Arnold. Highlands, N.J., 14 December 1987, 17 November 1988, 13 July 1989, 20 July 1989.
Pedro, William ("Pop"). Rossville, Staten Island, N.Y., 15 December 1985, 6 February 1986.
Peseux, Mrs. Rudolph. Keyport, N.J., 17 November 1987.
Peterson, Elmer. Monmouth Beach, N.J., 1 March 1990.
Poling, Albert. Keyport, N.J., 19 November 1986.
Porter, George. Keyport, N.J., 29 September 1985.
Pulsch, Henry. Port Monmouth, N.J., 24 October 1985, 25 February 1988, 15 June 1988, 9 August 1988, 11 September 1989, 3 July 1991.

Richardson, Alfred. Belford, N.J., 5 May 1987.

Richardson, Bill. Keyport, N.J., 5 October 1985, 25 October 1985, 13 March 1986, 21 May 1986.

Richardson, Ray. Belford, N.J., 20 November 1986, 30 September 1987, 16 January 1989.

Rogers, Lester. Sea Bright, N.J., 16 October 1987, 29 October 1987, 13 May 1988.

Rosenberg, Pete. Highlands, N.J., 15 May 1986, 7 January 1988, 10 October 1988.

Sage, Harry. Leonardo, N.J., 9 September 1988.

Schnoor, Bill. Port Monmouth, N.J., 11 December 1985, 13 April 1987, 2 July 1987, 16 January 1991, 22 January 1991, 5 February 1991, 6 February 1991, 7 February 1991.

Schnoor, Charlie. Belford, N.J., 10 July 1977 (Recorded by Ken Norton, New Monmouth, N.J.).

Schnoor, Otto. Belford, N.J., 21 March 1986, 7 November 1987, 24 March 1988, 13 May 1988, 6 August 1988, 18 October 1988, 8 May 1989, 8 April 1991.

Schnoor, Ron. Keyport, N.J., 9 October 1987.

Seminski, John. Highlands, N.J., 19 April 1988, 22 April 1988, 28 April 1988, 10 May 1988, 2 June 1988, 14 June 1989, 14 July 1989, 7 June 1991.

Sickles, Norman. Belford, N.J., 11 October 1985, 14 October 1985, 21 October 1986, 13 June 1987, 15 October 1987.

Sonic, Al. Great Kills, Staten Island, N.Y., 16 April 1986, 21 October 1986.

Thompsen, Walt. Highlands, N.J., 6 January 1985, 26 February 1986, 3 April 1986, 1 April 1987, 8 October 1987, 25 April 1988, 2 October 1989, 10 April 1991.

Thompson, Albert. Port Monmouth, N.J., 2 August 1989.

Thompson, Bud and Marion. Port Monmouth, N.J., 14 December 1987, 17 December 1987, 6 January 1988, 7 January 1988, 24 October 1988, 11 March 1991.

Thompson, Dave. Belford, N.J., 18 March 1986, 19 May 1987.

Thorstensen, Art. Belford, N.J., 3 March 1988, 15 December 1989, 30 December 1989, 17 January 1990, 9 April 1991.

Timadowski, Dave. Shrewsbury, N.J., 7 January 1988, 2 October 1989.

Volk, John. Prince's Bay, N.Y., 10 April 1986, 20 December 1988, 23 January 1989, 2 February 1990, 12 February 1990, 23 March 1990, 31 October 1990, 29 April 1991.

Wallace, Johnny. Keyport, N.J., 29 September 1985, 15 October 1985, 20 October 1985, 8 December 1985, 8 October 1987, 19 October 1987, 5 November 1987, 11 November 1987, 2 December 1987, 10 February 1988, 25 June 1988, 12 July 1988, 18 July 1988, 17 November 1988, 31 January 1989, 10 September 1989.

Walle, Everett. Tottenville, Staten Island, N.Y., 12 May 1986, 9 December 1987, 16 July 1989, 9 September 1989.

Walling, James. Port Monmouth, N.J., 9 June 1987, 7 April 1988.

Walters, Ralph. Keyport, N.J., 5 August 1986.

Weigand, Mrs. Frank. Holmdel, N.J., 27 October 1987.
Werner, Elsie. Belford, N.J., 18 May 1987.
White, Jimmy. Highlands, N.J., 6 May 1986, 16 May 1986, 15 July 1989.
Wilson, Bob. Keyport, N.J., 24 February 1988.
Wittich, Margaret. Great Kills, Staten Island, N.Y., 8 February 1988, 20 July 1991.

Index

293